The Transformation of Scotland
The Economy Since 1700

T0322971

Contributors

Ewen A. Cameron is Senior Lecturer in Scottish History, University of Edinburgh.

T. M. Devine, FRSE, Hon MRIA, FBA, is Glucksman Research Professor of Irish and Scottish Studies and Director of the AHRB Research Centre for Irish and Scottish Studies (Aberdeen University; Queen's University, Belfast; Trinity College, Dublin).

C. H. Lee was formerly Professor of Historical Economics, University of Aberdeen.

David Newlands is Senior Lecturer in Economics in the School of Business and Economics at the University of Aberdeen.

G. C. Peden, FRSE, is Professor of History and Head of the Department of History, University of Stirling.

The Transformation of Scotland
The Economy Since 1700

Edited by T. M. Devine, C. H. Lee and G. C. Peden

Edinburgh University Press

© The Economic and Social History Society of Scotland, 2005

Transferred to Digital Print 2011

Edinburgh University Press Ltd
22 George Square, Edinburgh

Typeset in Ehrhardt by
Norman Tilley Graphics, Northampton,
and printed and bound in Great Britain by
CPI Antony Rowe, Chippenham and Eastbourne

A CIP record for this book is available from the British Library

ISBN 0 7486 1432 X (hardback)
ISBN 0 7486 1433 8 (paperback)

The right of the contributors
to be identified as authors of this work
has been asserted in accordance with
the Copyright, Designs and Patents Act 1988.

Contents

The Scottish Economy in Historical Context

G. C. Peden

This book is largely the conception of Clive Lee. It was far advanced when he suffered a disabling stroke in October 2003. The idea of an edited, thematic volume of commissioned essays on the economic history of Scotland was first discussed by the Council of the Economic and Social History Society of Scotland in 1998. It was noted that, after a burst of activity, mainly in the 1970s, the study of Scottish economic history had been relatively neglected, compared with social or political history.[1] The advances in scholarship and debate, which have characterised British economic history, have not been fully extended or translated to Scotland.[2] This situation cannot be remedied easily but this volume is intended both to help to fill a substantial gap in the literature and to encourage further research. An evaluation of the historical antecedents of the Scottish economy is timely, given the restoration of

---

1. R. H. Campbell's pioneering *Scotland since 1707* (Oxford: Basil Blackwell, 1965) was followed by S. G. E. Lythe and J. Butt, *An Economic History of Scotland, 1100–1939* (Glasgow: Blackie, 1975), A. Slaven, *The Development of the West of Scotland, 1750–1960* (London: Routledge and Kegan Paul, 1975) and Bruce Lenman, *An Economic History of Modern Scotland* (London: B. T. Batsford, 1977), covering the period 1660–1976. R. H. Campbell's *The Rise and Fall of Scottish Industry, 1707–1939* (Edinburgh: John Donald, 1980) provided a challenging interpretation that went largely unanswered. Richard Saville (ed.), *The Economic Development of Modern Scotland, 1950–1980* (Edinburgh: John Donald, 1985) explored the recent past. Edited volumes of essays on Scottish history since then have often included a chapter on the economy, but *Scottish Economic and Social History* has been much more a journal of social than of economic history. Christopher Whatley, *The Industrial Revolution in Scotland* (Cambridge: Cambridge University Press, 1997) is a useful survey of the state of scholarship at that date. Clive Lee, *Scotland and the United Kingdom: The Economy and the Union in the Twentieth Century* (Manchester: Manchester University Press) used historical analysis to explore the economic case for Scotland's continued union with the UK. T. M. Devine, *The Scottish Nation, 1700–2000* (London: Allen Lane/The Penguin Press, 1999) integrated political, social and cultural themes with economic change.
2. For the scope of these debates see Roderick Floud and Paul Johnson (eds), *The Cambridge Economic History of Britain*, 3 vols (Cambridge: Cambridge University Press, 2004).

a Scottish parliament in 1999 and opportunities associated with devolution.

While Scotland shares with the rest of the United Kingdom (UK) and north-western Europe a common experience of industrialisation and its consequences, there are issues, such as the distribution of income, which merit particular attention in Scotland's case. There are also contradictions in explanations of Scotland's economic performance that have to be addressed. In particular, Roy Campbell emphasised the competitive efficiency of low costs, mainly wages, in accounting for the rise of Scottish industry, whereas Bruce Lenman suggested that low wages generated poverty and insufficient consumer demand.[3] Any debate on this issue has to take account of the fact that Scotland was, and is, a small, open economy in which domestic demand has been, over time, a decreasing proportion of total demand for any given Scottish product, and it is worth asking how Scottish goods could have been made as competitive as they were in world markets before 1914 by means other than low wages. In this connection, attention has to be paid to labour productivity and transport costs.

This book takes the debates over the union of the English and Scottish parliaments in 1707 as its starting point. The first five chapters deal with the process of economic modernisation, in agriculture and services as well as industry. The next four deal with the dramatic change in Scotland's economic fortunes that occurred after the First World War. Prior to the war, Scottish heavy industry, the main vehicle of industrialisation in the nineteenth century, was expanding whereas from 1919 it entered into a prolonged phase of contraction and decline that was interrupted only briefly by the Second World War and associated rearmament and reconstruction. The twentieth-century experience differed from that of the two centuries that had preceded it in several key respects: in the emergence of government as a major determinant of economic decisions; in the increasingly problematic nature of international markets; and in the growth of external ownership and control of enterprises operating in Scotland. Scotland's experience, broadly speaking, has been similar to the experience of other early industrialising regions: northern England, Belgium or the Ruhr in Germany. All had relied heavily on coal and heavy industry, and all encountered difficulties when other sources of energy and other products came to the fore.

---

3. Campbell, *Rise and Fall*; Lenman, *Economic History*.

FACTORS IN ECONOMIC DEVELOPMENT

Nevertheless, much of Scotland's experience was shaped by its own geography and resources, and the ways in which these were exploited. The area of Scotland is slightly more than half of the area of England and Wales, but Scotland has always had a disproportionately smaller population: in 1700 the proportion was about 1:5; in 2000 it was below 1:10. Prior to industrialisation, the population that Scotland could sustain was largely dependent on what its agriculture and fisheries could support. Compared with England, much of Scotland comprises highland or upland areas with less fertile soil than lowland areas. In addition, Scotland's more northerly latitude and climate are generally less suitable than England's for growing wheat; hence Scotland's traditional dependence on oats, a hardier grain (and hence, too, Dr Johnson's dictionary definition of oats as 'a grain which in England is generally given to horses but which in Scotland supports the people'). The west of the country is better adapted to pastoral rather than arable farming. The east of the country north of the Forth is dry enough to be suitable for grain, but in the eighteenth century much had still to be done as regards removing glacial deposits of stone from otherwise fertile land, while some of the potentially most fertile land, in the carses of Stirling and Gowrie, was not drained until after 1750. Only the south-east of the country, from the Forth to the Tweed, enjoyed climate and soil comparable to England's. Scotland had some natural advantages: for example, fast-flowing rivers and streams were an advantage at an early stage of industrialisation, when most machinery relied upon water power.[4] It was, however, Scotland's deposits of coal and iron ore in the central belt that gave it a decisive advantage in industrialisation in the nineteenth century. In the last quarter of the twentieth century exploitation of North Sea oil had a considerable impact on adjacent coastal communities.

Natural resources are not, however, enough for economic development, and attention has to be paid to other factors of production. Labour is required to turn natural resources into commodities, and Scotland was able to secure increasing supplies of labour through natural increase or immigration. In the nineteenth century most immigrants came from Ireland; in the later twentieth century most came from England. The quality of labour reflected education and experience. On the whole the Scots were a literate people by contemporary standards, and industrialisation and trade required some literacy on the part of engineers and

4. John Shaw, *Water Power in Scotland, 1550–1879* (Edinburgh: John Donald, 1984).

clerks, even if little or none were required on the part of most factory workers or seamen.[5] Immigrants could also bring skills. For example, as Thomas Devine notes in Chapter 2, men with experience of English industry were sometimes appointed managers of early Scottish factories, while Irish immigrants included people with experience relevant to working in textile mills.

Labour, in turn, requires capital. In a purely agricultural society, fixed capital comprises not only equipment like farm buildings or ploughs, but also land that has been cultivated and drained. In the early stages of industrialisation, in the eighteenth century, the capital required was on a small scale, no more than hand looms that could be placed in weavers' cottages, plus stocks of flax or wool, which merchants provided. Larger capital investment was required as industrial processes came to depend more on machinery, and financial services had to be developed in consequence. As Clive Lee shows in Chapter 4, Scotland had already developed what was then an advanced banking structure by the middle of the eighteenth century. Capitalism also depends upon contracts being legally enforceable, and, as Devine notes in Chapter 1, the Scottish legal system was well developed in this respect before the Union of 1707.

The success of investment depends not only on finance but also on technology and enterprise. By technology is meant the adoption of improved methods, whether better ploughs or new industrial processes. Enterprise is the ability to organise production and trade in response to changes in markets. Improvements in technology and enterprise are largely responsible for the increased productivity of labour and capital that are characteristic of a modern economy. Technology and enterprise need not be native to an economy: indeed, they tend to migrate to where there are natural resources. Both Scotland and Belgium, with their rich coal reserves and proximity to England, benefited in the eighteenth and nineteenth centuries from the activities of English entrepreneurs. Both Scotland and Belgium had labour forces and native entrepreneurs that could take advantage of the technology then being transferred, in terms of acquisition of skills by the labour force and in terms of the establishment of native firms. What is less certain is whether Scottish experience of technology transfer in the late twentieth century, particularly with regard to the oil industry and electronics, has been as successful.[6]

5. Carlo Cipolla, *Literacy and Development in the West* (Harmondsworth: Penguin Books, 1969), esp. pp. 66–8, 71, 77, 89–90, 115.
6. See Sidney Pollard, *Peaceful Conquest: The Industrialization of Europe, 1760–1970* (Oxford: Oxford University Press, 1981), pp. 40–1, 87–93, 108–9 (for Belgium); Campbell, *Scotland since 1707*, pp. 63–7, 97–104; Peter Payne, 'The economy', in T. M. Devine and R. J. Finlay (eds),

Attention must be paid to the demand for goods and services as well as to factors determining their supply. Clearly the income of the community is one such factor, and total income increased with rapid population growth in the nineteenth century (see Chapter 5). Demand would have been even greater than it was had Scottish average incomes been as high as in England. Data are uncertain, but Scottish wages tended to be lower than in England. Lee discusses the multiplier effects of relatively low wages and a relative lack of middle-class occupations in Chapter 5. However, demand within Scotland is only part of total demand for Scottish goods and services. Trade with richer countries, such as England and its colonies, or France and the Netherlands in the eighteenth century, gave Scottish producers better markets. Demand also depended upon the relative prices of Scottish and other goods, and upon consumer's preferences, or taste. Initially Scottish goods, such as woollen and linen textiles, had to be sold cheap, because they were generally inferior to those of foreign competitors prior to the latter part of the eighteenth century. It was not until the nineteenth century that Scottish goods, such as woollen garments or whisky, could be sold at premium prices because markets had developed a taste for some distinctive Scottish goods.[7] The rise and fall of Scottish industry may be understood largely in terms of prices relative to those of competitors, and the ability, or otherwise, of Scottish producers to move up-market as simpler industrial processes spread to other, lower-wage, economies.

It is important to ask why Scotland seemed to be unable to take advantage of what has been called the Second Industrial Revolution, with the development of electrical power, the combustion engine and motor vehicles, organic chemistry and synthetics, and assembly-line production from the 1890s to the First World War.[8] Out of ten regions in Great Britain in 1921, Scotland had the second highest share of employment in shipbuilding, but had less than half of the average share in vehicles and electrical engineering.[9] Scotland did have a motor-vehicle industry in the early twentieth century, with Argyll, Arrol Johnston and Beardmore all making cars, but they did not achieve mass production

Scotland in the Twentieth Century (Edinburgh: Edinburgh University Press, 1996), pp. 13–45, at pp. 24–39.

7. See Clifford Gulvin, *The Scottish Hosiery and Knitwear Industry, 1680–1980* (Edinburgh: John Donald, 1984); John R. Hume and Michael Moss, *The Making of Scotch Whisky: A History of the Scotch Whisky Distillery Industry* (Edinburgh: Canongate, 2001).

8. David S. Landes, *The Unbound Prometheus: Technological Change and Industrial Development in Western Europe from 1750 to the Present* (Cambridge: Cambridge University Press, 1969), p. 235.

9. N. F. R. Crafts, *British Economic Growth during the Industrial Revolution* (Oxford: Clarendon Press, 1985), p. 171.

and by 1930 only Albion, which produced commercial vehicles, remained in the sector.

Changes in relative prices and the extent to which producers were exposed to competition were by no means confined to industry. Agriculture and rural Scotland also underwent great changes as improvements in transport created stronger linkages between regions and nations. As an example of how one Highland civil parish was transformed over time by transport developments one can take the case of Balquhidder, in what was once west Perthshire and what is now Stirling District. Balquhidder's climate and topography were always more favourable to pastoral than to arable farming, but so long as a lack of roads and bridges restricted access to wheeled transport, farmers, particularly in the drier eastern part of the parish, grew crops for human consumption as well as for animals. With improvements in communications in the eighteenth century, food could be brought in from areas more favourable for arable farming, and by the late twentieth century even hay was transported by truck from the Carse of Stirling. Meanwhile, the introduction first of the railway and then of motor vehicles had made tourism a more important source of income than agriculture, the tourists being drawn not only by scenery but also by the highly romanticised image created by Sir Walter Scott of Balquhidder's most famous cattle trader, Rob Roy MacGregor. While one hesitates to suggest that Scotland is Balqhhidder writ large, it is a remarkable fact that, after a considerable degree of de-industrialisation in the last third of the twentieth century, tourism was the largest single source of employment in Scotland by the year 2000.[10] The point to be made here, however, is that economic change is inevitable in a world in which relative prices are constantly changing with improvements in transport.

As Devine points out in Chapter 1, Scots had long traded with the Baltic before the development of an Atlantic economy created opportunities for ports on the Clyde. Scotland was well placed to take part in international trade. No part of the country is more than forty miles from salt water, giving readier access to shipping than was the case in most European countries, a not insubstantial advantage given that the cheapest forms of bulk transport are water-borne. International trade is related to, and reinforces, what economists call comparative advantage. Each country benefits from specialising in what its factors of production

---

10. For tourism see Alastair J. Durie, *Scotland for the Holidays: Tourism in Scotland, 1780–1939* (East Linton: Tuckwell Press, 2003), which deserves a sequel covering the period since 1939. For Balquhidder see James Stewart, *The Settlements of Western Perthshire: Land and Society North of the Highland Line, 1480–1851* (Edinburgh: Pentland Press, 1990).

– natural resources, labour, capital, technology and enterprise – enable it to produce best. In the process of industrialisation Scotland came to specialise in the production of textiles, coal, iron and steel, engineering products and shipbuilding. However, comparative advantage is not static, and once an economy has embarked upon a particular line of development it may find adaptation to changing market conditions difficult on account of what economic historians call path dependency. For example, once skills, capital and business organisation are developed for ships, it may not be easy to adapt to the production of motor vehicles. Moreover, adaptation from an economy based on a limited range of traditional export industries to one based on innovation and mass production proved to be particularly difficult for Scotland in the twentieth century.

OUTLINE OF THE BOOK

Devine starts his chapter on Scotland and the Act of Union from the perspective that the backwardness of pre-Union Scotland was until recently exaggerated, with the consequence that the impact of the Union appeared to be greater to historians than was the case.[11] The Union gave Scottish merchants greater, and secure, access to English markets, including the colonies, but the case of Ireland shows that an incorporating union may not be followed by economic development. Devine asks why Scotland was not converted into a colonial appendage of the English economy. He looks at how Scots took advantage of the opportunities offered by the Union, particularly in what he sees as the four critical decades after 1740.

Devine then analyses the process of industrialisation in Scotland in Chapter 2. He asks why there were unprecedented increases in rates of output in, first, textiles, then iron and steel, heavy engineering and shipbuilding. He highlights Scots' ability to take advantage of the development of a truly international economy, with nations specialising in what they could produce better or cheaper than other nations. He points out that the transformation that is called industrialisation affected

11. Indeed Saville has suggested that 1688 was perhaps a more significant date, in terms of preconditions for economic development, than 1707, although he does not deny the importance of the Union as regards access to markets. He argues that the overthrow of the old regime of James VII made possible a more deliberate effort on the part of leaders of society to modernise (Richard Saville, 'Scottish modernisation prior to the Industrial Revolution, 1688–1763', in T. M. Devine and J. R. Young (eds), *Eighteenth Century Scotland: New Perspectives* (East Linton: Tuckwell Press, 1999), pp. 6–23).

all economic activity, not least agriculture. Scottish agriculture had a symbiotic relationship with industry, as industrial workers provided new markets for food, and as industrial products in the form of agricultural implements and machinery allowed agriculture to share in a general increase in labour productivity. Higher labour productivity eventually produced a decline in rural employment, especially once Scottish agriculture encountered difficulties from the 1870s, when cheap imports of grain and refrigerated meat began to flood domestic markets. Nevertheless, modernisation was a better alternative to the systems of tenure that produced a potato monoculture and, in the 1840s, near famine in the crofting counties (and actual famine in Ireland).[12] The transformation of agriculture, Devine suggests in Chapter 3, was an essential element in the Scottish economic miracle.

Lee focuses in Chapter 4 on the establishment of Scotland's financial services, and their role in the growth of the Scottish economy, from the late seventeenth century to the eve of the First World War.[13] No simple model can be constructed of the relationship between Scottish capital and investment, certainly by the railway boom of the 1840s, which saw the integration of capital markets throughout the UK and beyond into a single system Moreover, Scottish financial institutions were often directed to investing overseas (with indirect effects on the Scottish economy in the form of cheaper imports of food and raw materials). Housing did not attract sufficient capital, but, as Lee points out, this was because most tenants were unable to pay rents for better accommodation. Scottish financial institutions became important actors in their own right, drawing in funds from outside Scotland as well as investing abroad, and generating white-collar employment.

Devine points out in Chapter 2 that the outcome of industrialisation in Scotland was flawed in two respects: a low standard of living, and wretched housing, of much of the population, and what proved after 1919 to be a vulnerable dependence on a limited range of export industries. Lee takes these points further in Chapter 5, where he raises the question of what is progress. He asks why the growth of prosperity

12. See T. M. Devine, *The Great Highland Famine: Hunger, Emigration and the Scottish Highlands in the Nineteenth Century* (Edinburgh: John Donald, 1988); P. Gray, *Famine, Land and Politics: British Government and Irish Society, 1843–1850* (Dublin: Irish Academic Press, 1999).
13. His intention was to follow up this chapter with another one dealing with financial services in the post-1914 period, but he was unable to do so following his illness. Certain Scottish financial institutions have been well served recently by authorised histories that cover the post-1914 period and put their work in economic context: Michael Moss, *Standard Life, 1825–2000* (Edinburgh: Mainstream Publishing, 2000); Richard Saville, *Bank of Scotland: A History, 1695–1995* (Edinburgh: Edinburgh University Press, 1996); and, slightly less recently, Charles W. Munn, *Clydesdale Bank: The First One Hundred and Fifty Years* (Glasgow: Collins, 1988).

over time has been so unequally shared between different groups or classes in Scottish society. He argues that the distribution of the benefits of progress is of crucial importance to the generation of sustained economic growth. There is ample evidence that much wealth in eighteenth-century Scotland was concentrated in the hands of a few landowners, as was normal in pre-industrial societies. Industrialisation enabled some fortunes to be made, but the rich, and even the moderately prosperous, were a small minority in society. Most Scots experienced low wages and irregular employment even after the new wealth had made Glasgow the second city of the Empire. Lee argues that the fundamental weakness in the Scottish economy was its inability to sustain all of its growing population in work, leading to a low-wage economy and considerable emigration.

Devine's accounts of industrialisation and agricultural change in Chapters 2 and 3 draw attention to sharpening regional differences as industries clustered in urban centres near, or with water-borne access to, coalfields, and as farmers specialised according to climatic and geological circumstances and market opportunities. David Newlands takes regional differences as his theme for the opening chapter of Part II of the book, covering the post-1914 period. He asks whether regional disparities have narrowed, as mainstream economic theory suggests should have happened in an integrated market. He also explores the extent to which public policy has had an impact on regional disparities. He concludes that, despite transport improvements and regional economic policy, Scotland is not just one economy but a fairly large number of regional economies of different sizes. These regional economies have had very different experiences in the twentieth century: most notably the decline of industrial Clydeside and the growing prosperity of the financial-services sector based in Edinburgh.

Ewen Cameron shows in Chapter 7 how the agriculture sector underwent considerable modernisation, becoming increasingly capital intensive and less labour intensive. Agriculture also benefited from various regimes of state subsidies, with a major change occurring when Britain joined the European Economic Community, with its Common Agricultural Policy, in 1973. By the end of the century environmental issues had began to have an impact on farming at a time when fewer people earned their livelihood from the land than ever before. Notwithstanding the link provided between the urban population and the countryside by commuting and tourism, Cameron considers that the urban population and the farming community were further apart in terms of shared interests by 2000 than they had been in mid-century.

In Chapter 8 Lee returns to the theme of Chapter 5: what is economic progress? How was generally high economic growth for most of the twentieth century reflected in the distribution of incomes and wealth? How did the distribution of spending power impact upon the economy? He shows that there were considerable variations in average incomes in different regions, reflecting different occupational structures. Scotland's average per capita income converged with that of the UK in the second half of the twentieth century, but the figure for Edinburgh in the mid-1990s was twice that of North Lanarkshire. Market forces were modified by the growth of state intervention and by progressive taxation from the 1940s to the 1970s, a period also marked by very low unemployment. Even after Margaret Thatcher's government sought to reverse the growth of the state, Scotland continued to benefit from substantial tax transfers from England.

Finally in Chapter 9 George Peden looks at state intervention from a different perspective: how did management of the UK economy, including macroeconomic policy as well as regional policy, affect Scotland? Macroeconomic policy was conducted from London by the Treasury and the Bank of England. UK microeconomic policy, including regional policy, was dealt with by the Board of Trade and its successor, the Department of Trade and Industry, but Scottish interests were represented in the Cabinet by the Secretary of State for Scotland and Scotland acquired its own agencies, such as the Highlands and Islands Development Board and the Scottish Development Agency. The development of the Scottish Office's capacity for economic planning from the 1960s led to Scotland being seen as an economic unit, notwithstanding the considerable regional differences identified by Newlands. Scottish economic planners played a major part in the transformation of the Scottish economy in the second half of the twentieth century.

Overall, the book shows that the Scottish economy has a mixed inheritance from the past, and that, while change is inevitable, universal progress is not. The problems that the restored Scottish parliament confronted in 1999 were deep seated partly because they were the consequence of three centuries of rapid economic transformation from an agricultural society to an industrial society, and then to an increasingly post-industrial society. However, the book also shows how Scots have embraced the opportunities offered by economic change and suggests that a similar attitude to change is the way forward to prosperity in future.

Part I
1700–1914

CHAPTER ONE

The Modern Economy: Scotland and the Act of Union

T. M. Devine

BEFORE THE UNION: SCOTLAND C.1700

Sustained investigation of the economy and society of early modern Scotland is a recent development of the last three decades or so. Earlier generations were content to focus almost exclusively on the developments of church and state in the period before the Union of 1707. Out of this neglect came the generation and widespread acceptance of an influential stereotype. It became a commonplace in the textbook literature until the 1960s that the Scottish experience was exceptional in relation both to England and other 'advanced' European economies. Scotland in c. 1700 was said to be different, not only in its poverty, the archaism of the social structures and timeless rigidity of the economic system, but also in its insecurity and instability, a direct result of weak central authority and the threat of baronial insurrection. In an article published in 1967 Hugh Trevor-Roper expressed the orthodoxy in succinct terms: '... at the end of the seventeenth century, Scotland was a by-word for irredeemable poverty, social backwardness [and] political faction'.[1]

Since then, however, a more complex and subtle evaluation of the national economic condition has emerged as a growing army of Scottish historical scholars has asked fresh questions and plundered the archives in the search for answers. The corpus of published work has therefore grown significantly, though, it has to be acknowledged, the recent historiography still lacks the sheer richness and density of that on English

---

1. H. R. Trevor-Roper, 'The Scottish Enlightenment', *Studies in Voltaire and the Eighteenth Century*, 28 (1967), p. 1636.

economic and social history. Key areas, such as demographic history, are constrained by the inadequacy of records. Not one Scottish parish register is suitable for family reconstitution while even extraction of baptism and burial totals poses serious problems. At the same time, rigorous statistical studies, of the kind which have forced reassessment of the nature and chronology of English industrialisation, are notable by their absence. Indeed the 'new' economic history in general has had little impact on the study of Scottish history. All that said, however, understanding of pre-Union Scotland has been much advanced by recent work. Some of the stereotypes of the past are no longer tenable.

In 1700 Scotland had an estimated population of little more than a million inhabitants or about one-fifth that of England. The distribution of these numbers reflected the natural endowment and topography of the country. Much of Scotland is dominated by mountain and moorland. Even today, after nearly 300 years of improvement and drainage, around two-thirds of the country is still only suitable for rough grazing. In the later seventeenth century, therefore, the main concentrations of population were in the more fertile areas of the lowlands of Aberdeen and Angus, the coastlands of the Forth and Tay, the Solway plain, the Merse of Berwickshire and the lower Clyde Valley. Nevertheless, compared to the nineteenth century, when massive migration decisively altered the national demographic profile in favour of the central Lowlands and the cities of Glasgow, Edinburgh and Dundee, Scottish population was much more widely dispersed in the early modern period. Perhaps as many as half the people lived north of the River Tay.

There were many Scotlands. The country, though small in size and population, was a veritable mosaic of regional societies. The familiar distinction between the Highlands and Lowlands concealed more subtle differences between the Hebrides on the one hand and the southern and eastern Highlands on the other. Galloway in the south-west retained strong particularist traditions while the Northern Isles had both a Norse legal system and traces of the Norse language well into the seventeenth century. Nevertheless, amid all this territorial complexity, some national generalisations are still tenable. Overwhelmingly Scotland was a rural-based society with only around 12 per cent of the population living in towns of over 2,000 in size. The raw produce of the land – skins, grain, wool and coal – were vital trading commodities, though linen and woollen manufactures were also increasingly important. Even in this early period, however, the significance of urban development should not be underestimated.

Between 1500 and 1600 the proportion of the nation's population living in the larger towns of 10,000 citizens and above nearly doubled, and did so again by 1700.[2] Edinburgh, the capital and biggest town, had a population of around 30,000 by the early eighteenth century. Aberdeen and Dundee had about 10,000 inhabitants each, while Glasgow had emerged as the second burgh in the land by the later seventeenth century, with a population reckoned at 15,000 and growing. Relative to Edinburgh and Glasgow, however, Aberdeen and Dundee were experiencing stagnation in the second half of the seventeenth century. Edinburgh's predominance in Scottish urban life was long-standing, but Glasgow's new pre-eminence reflected the growing importance of developing links to Ireland and the Atlantic economy, which were to prove so crucial to Scottish progress after c. 1740.[3] The vast majority of other Scottish burghs were little more than villages in this period. Few, apart from Inverness, Stirling, Dumfries and Renfrew, had more than 1,000 inhabitants each. Nevertheless, in some areas, most notably the coastlands of the River Forth, the sheer number and growth of small burghs created a regional urban network to rival any in western Europe in density.[4] Most urban areas, however, shared a similar insecurity over time because of the high level of their dependence upon the export of a limited range of primary products. This rendered Scottish towns in the early modern period especially vulnerable to sudden fluctuations in the patterns of both supply and demand.[5]

Against this background, much of the thrust of modern historiography has been to challenge the notion of the Scottish economy as peripheral, static and backward. Contrary to a great deal of received wisdom, Louis Cullen argued that Scotland's apparently 'remote' location off the far north-west coast of Europe was a positive advantage, affording easy access to Ireland, a land frontier with England and the possibilities for lucrative commercial connections to the east.[6] By the seventeenth century Scots merchants, pedlars and mercenary soldiers were to the fore in port towns across Scandinavia and the north German,

2. I. D. Whyte, 'Urbanisation in eighteenth century Scotland', in T. M. Devine and J. R. Young (eds), *Eighteenth Century Scotland: New Perspectives* (East Linton: Tuckwell Press, 1999), pp. 176–94.
3. T. M. Devine, 'Scotland', in Peter Clark (ed.), *The Cambridge Urban History of Britain* (Cambridge: Cambridge University Press, 2000), pp. 151–64.
4. M. Lynch, 'Urbanisation and urban networks in seventeenth century Scotland', *Scottish Economic and Social History*, 12 (1992), pp. 35–6.
5. M. Lynch, 'Continuity and change in urban society, 1500–1700', in R. A. Houston and I. D. Whyte (eds), *Scottish Society, 1500–1800* (Cambridge: Cambridge University Press, 1989), pp. 85–110.
6. L. M. Cullen, 'Scotland and Ireland, 1600–1800: their role in the evolution of British society', in Houston and Whyte (eds), *Scottish Society*, pp. 227–8.

Polish and Russian hinterlands.[7] These movements helped to consolidate commercial links with Europe's 'inland sea', the heart of economic development in the north of the continent, and so provide an impetus to urban development along Scotland's east coast. Equally, as the centre of economic gravity shifted south to the Amsterdam–London axis and thence towards the Atlantic world, Scotland was also strategically well placed.[8] New prospects opened up for the west-coast towns in supplying 'Scotland's first colony' in Ulster and, even before the Union of 1707, exploiting the new commercial opportunities in both America and the Caribbean:

> Scotland's good fortune was that its most advantageous port locations on the Clyde and its eastern on the Firth of Forth were both drawing on the same rich hinterland. Hence the growth of the Atlantic trades reinforced the existing wealth of the Lowlands rather than shifted its centre of gravity. The Lowlands, together with Edinburgh and Glasgow, constituted an effective and integrated economy in which talent and capital could be put to the best use and young men able to venture in the western world.[9]

In comparison, Ireland's Atlantic commercial expansion was constrained, not only by its colonial status but also because the hinterland of the country's western ports were relatively poorly developed.

Scotland's internal economy and society have also been the subject of more optimistic reappraisals which have collectively challenged the notion of national stasis and inertia. The older view of a land still riven by feud and strife has been conclusively refuted. Centralised justice took on a new meaning with the reconstituted High Court of Justiciary in 1672 and the creation of the circuit courts from 1708. The revolution of 1688–9 in Scotland was a remarkably bloodless affair while the infamous Massacre of Glencoe of 1692 is remembered in song and story partly because, by the new standards of the time, the incident was an entirely exceptional atrocity. Glencoe also illustrated the determination of the state to use its muscle against recalcitrant Highland clans. Not surprisingly, therefore, the militarism of clan society was also in decline.

7. T. C. Smout, N. C. Landsman and T. M. Devine, 'Scottish emigration in the seventeenth and eighteenth centuries', in N. Canny (ed.), *Europeans on the Move: Studies in European Migration, 1500–1800* (Oxford: Clarendon Press, 1994), pp. 90–5.
8. G. Jackson, 'Glasgow in transition, c. 1660–c. 1740', in T. M. Devine and G. Jackson (eds), *Glasgow*, vol. I: *Beginnings to 1830* (Manchester: Manchester University Press, 1995), pp. 63–105.
9. Cullen, 'Scotland and Ireland', in Houston and Whyte (eds), *Scottish Society*, p. 228.

The last major clan battle took place in 1688 and thereafter collective violence was confined to cattle raiding and protection rackets in some of the frontier lands of the Highlands.

At a more subtle level commercial forces were already opening up tensions within clanship. Markets were developing to the south for Highland goods – above all for cattle, which, alone of most Scottish products, did very well in the years after the Union of 1707 – but also for timber, fish and slate. The returns from these trades helped to sustain absenteeism and consumerism among the clan élites. Household accounts show a growing appetite for elegant furniture, fashionable clothing, pictures, books and musical instruments. The clan bards were alarmed at the trends and lamented the habits of chiefs who spent longer periods in Edinburgh or even in London and neglected their traditional patriarchal duties. There were already signs that profit was starting to take precedence over the ancient social responsibilities of the land-owners. The clans expected the ruling families to act as their protectors and guarantee secure possession of land in return for allegiance, military service, tribute and rental. But the evidence suggests that this social contract was already under acute pressure in some parts of Gaeldom even before the aftermath of the last Jacobite rebellion in 1745, which hastened the final demise of clan society.[10]

Throughout Scotland similar processes were at work to a greater or lesser extent. Landowners had come to regard their estates more as assets from which revenue and profit could be extracted and less as sources of military power and authority. The indicators of this historic transition in the priorities of the Scottish governing classes were very numerous. It can be seen for instance in their domestic architecture. The last fortified house in Scotland, Leslie Castle, was built in 1660. The emphasis was now more on comfort and aesthetic appeal rather than on defence. The tower house was giving way to the country house. There also was a much greater involvement in the wider economy with the aim of extracting better returns from the landed estate. North-eastern landowners were heavily engaged in the seaborne grain trade to Edinburgh and the Scandinavian countries. The great Border landlords were energetically expanding the numbers of sheep and cattle on their properties. Between 1500 and the early eighteenth century, around 170 new burghs of barony (authorised by the crown but created by lay and ecclesiastical land-owners) were founded by landowners with the majority established in

---

10. A. I. Macinnes, *Clanship, Commerce and the House of Stuart, 1603–1788* (East Linton: Tuckwell Press, 1996), pp. 159–209.

the decades immediately before the Union. Not all – or even the majority – were a success, but the commitment of the élite to small-town and village development is undeniable. There were also instances of large-scale investment in harbour and port development, such as that of the Duke of Hamilton at Bo'Ness, Sir Robert Cunninghame at Saltcoats and the Erskines of Mar at Alloa. Nor surprisingly, the new economic priorities of the élite filtered through into the public policies of parliament and privy council which they dominated. The records of these two bodies are full of references to attempts made to improve the national economy. These included Acts for the encouragement of colonial trade; domestic manufacturing; the foundation of the Bank of Scotland in 1695; the removal of the traditional monopoly rights of the royal burghs in 1672; and a series of statutes to facilitate agricultural improvement. Many of these initiatives were merely fine aspirations rather than real achievements. In a sense, however, this mattered little. What was more important was the confirmation that the Scottish governing classes were now on the side of material progress and lending their considerable political authority to the cause of national economic reform.[11]

Change and material progress can also be identified in the spheres of agriculture, international trade and domestic industry. The first of these was most crucial because of its dominant position in the economy as a whole. Judged over the century from the 1650s to the early 1740s, Scottish farms were remarkably successful in feeding the population in most years and, in some periods, producing export surpluses. Between 1660 and 1700 there were significant shortages only in 1674 and 1693–7. This last crisis has gone down in history as the 'Lean Years' when a series of consecutive harvest failures brought about famine conditions in some areas and effectively reduced the nation's population by death and emigration by an estimated 15 per cent.[12] For some writers, however, this disaster was an aberration, a break in the trend of increasingly stable food supplies, caused by freak weather conditions which also hit Scandinavia and France equally badly. For the following half-century there were difficult times, but not subsistence crises, only in 1709, 1724–5 and 1740–1. This record can be contrasted with the second half of the sixteenth century when Scotland suffered food shortages in some areas for around a third of the years between 1560 and 1600.[13]

11. T. M. Devine, 'The Union of 1707 and Scottish development', in T. M. Devine, *Exploring the Scottish Past: Themes in the History of Scottish Society* (East Linton: Tuckwell Press, 1995), pp. 37–53.
12. R. E. Tyson, 'Famine in Aberdeenshire, 1695–99: anatomy of a crisis', in D. Stevenson (ed.), *From Lairds to Louns* (Aberdeen: Aberdeen University Press, 1986), pp. 49–50.
13. I. D. Whyte, *Scotland before the Industrial Revolution* (Harlow: Longmans, 1995), p. 126.

Why this improvement occurred cannot yet be determined in precise terms. Some scholars argue that the decisive factor was more benign climatic conditions; others stress the demographic factor as pressure on food supply was reduced by the mortality crises of the 1640s and 1690s and the impact of large-scale emigration. In addition, however, there is also evidence of greater efficiency in the agricultural sector with a movement to enlarged single tenancies, longer written leases, an expansion of rural market centres, modest increases in grain yields in favoured areas and commutation of rentals in kind to money values.[14]

Parallel changes occurred in international trade. A shift was already apparent in Scotland's historic commercial connections with Europe towards England, Ireland and the Atlantic economy. In 1700 an estimated half of Scottish trade by value was already carried on with England in such key commodities as cattle, coal, salt, linen and grain.[15] Scotland's western ports in particular were now closely involved in commerce with the Scottish emigrant community in the north of Ireland. Recent research has also identified industrial expansion in coal, lead-mining and glass and paper manufacture.[16] As many as 106 large manufactories, mainly in the towns, were either proposed or established between 1587 and 1707 with almost 75 per cent of these recorded after 1660. But the real industrial triumph was in linen, a sector destined to become Scotland's main manufacturing industry for most of the eighteenth century. In 1599–1600, 18,000 ells of linen were sent to London. By 1700 the figure was around 650,000 ells. The old sixteenth-century raw material staples of skins and fish exports were now being replaced c. 1700 by linen, coal and live cattle.

What broader picture does all this reveal? First, the older orthodoxy of a static economic system no longer fits the facts. Second, the scale of development needs to be kept in perspective. In the critically important agricultural sector, subsistence activity was still dominant in many areas. The estate records of the time are full of references to the large numbers of small tenants, holding less than 20–30 acres, who rarely produced a surplus beyond that which was necessary for family consumption and landlord rents.[17] One estimate suggests that in the first few decades of

14. T. M. Devine, *The Transformation of Rural Scotland: Social Change and the Agrarian Economy, 1660–1815* (Edinburgh: John Donald, 1994), pp. 1–18; I. D. Whyte, *Agriculture and Society in Seventeenth Century Scotland* (Edinburgh: John Donald, 1979).
15. T. C. Smout, *Scottish Trade on the Eve of the Union, 1660–1707* (Edinburgh: Oliver and Boyd, 1963), pp. 194–236.
16. C. A. Whatley, *Scottish Society, 1707–1830* (Manchester: Manchester University Press, 2000), pp. 23–5.
17. Devine, *Transformation of Rural Scotland*, pp. 1–18.

the eighteenth century only a quarter of Scottish farmers were mainly producing for market.[18] The changes identified in the rural economy were real enough but they amounted to modest developments *within* the agrarian system rather than basic alterations to the system as a whole. Third, the foundations of some of the changes were hardly secure. The better times of the period 1660–90 were followed by a series of disasters in the following decade which had longer-term effects well into the first quarter of the eighteenth century: the savage demographic and financial consequences of the 'Lean Years'; war with France in 1689–97 and 1701–13; rampant economic nationalism across western Europe which inexorably squeezed Scottish markets, not least in England, where linen duties were raised significantly in 1698, thus contributing to a halving of Scottish exports to the south between 1698 and 1700 and 1704–6; and last, but by no means least, the serious financial losses associated with the failed expeditions to Darien on the isthmus of Panama.

Fourth, there is the issue of the comparison with England. The two countries certainly had some features in common and in that sense the 'exceptionalism' of Scotland has been exaggerated. These included *inter alia* the existence of an agrarian social structure mainly based on landlords leasing farms to tenants, a geographically mobile population and a governing class in each country increasingly committed to national economic advance. However, at the turn of the eighteenth century, the contrasts were perhaps much more apparent. Scotland was undeniably much poorer, a pattern not simply confirmed by the nation's vulnerability to famine but by wage data. The most recent investigations suggest that by the 1730s an English mason or carpenter had, on average, almost a 50 per cent (money wage) margin over their Scottish counterpart.[19] Little wonder that, later, Dr Johnson was to remark that the finest road a Scotsman ever saw led to England! Even in that later period, 1765–95, carpenters in Aberdeen and Edinburgh never reached more than 40–45 per cent of wages of London carpenters and nearly two-thirds of their wages in Exeter or Manchester.[20] Mortality figures point to a similar conclusion. Calculations of life expectancy at birth in 1755 give figures of 31 or 32 for Scotland against 36–7 for England.[21]

Again, while Scotland may not have been significantly out of line with other north-western European countries such as the Scandinavian states,

18.   R. A. Dodgshon, *Land and Society in Early Scotland* (Oxford: Clarendon Press, 1981), p. 244.
19.   A. J. S. Gibson and T. C. Smout, *Prices, Food and Wages in Scotland, 1550–1780* (Cambridge: Cambridge University press, 1995), p. 279.
20.   Ibid.
21.   Whyte, *Scotland before the Industrial Revolution*, p. 117.

the nation was manifestly less developed than most of England.[22] The industrial sector was both relatively small and suffering the joint impact of war and rising tariffs in the early eighteenth century while, at the same period, industry and commerce accounted for about a third of English national income.[23] There was also a marked difference in the perform-ance of agriculture, despite the advances described above in Scottish farming in the later seventeenth century. On Scottish east-coast estates (the area most favourable to arable farming) c. 1700–20, the seed-yield figures for oats were around 3 to 4.[24] On a sample of English estates the yields for the same crop were averaging 6.5 to 8.5, or double the Scottish equivalent.[25] Indeed current interpretations of the pattern of English wheat yields from probate inventories indicate major gains in the seven-teenth and early eighteenth centuries which exceeded those of the period after c. 1760.[26] In the Scottish case these timeframes would have to be reversed. Social indicators tell the same story. Access to some land, however minute, was still one of the defining characteristics of Scottish rural society until the second half of the eighteenth century. Small tenants, often renting land in multiple tenure, cottars, allocated a patch of land in return for seasonal work on larger farms, and tradesmen with tiny smallholdings made up the vast majority of the country population. It was a social order that had more in common with patterns in parts of continental Europe than the regions of commercial farming south of the border.[27]

THE AFTERMATH OF UNION, 1707–C. 1760

The parliamentary Union of 1707 between England and Scotland came about because of a complex mix of political, religious and economic factors, on which there is now a considerable historical literature. It is not the purpose of this section to rehearse the arguments concerning the origins of 1707, for which there are adequate sources elsewhere, but

22. C. A. Whatley, *The Industrial Revolution in Scotland* (Cambridge: Cambridge University Press, 1997), p. 17.
23. W. A. Cole, 'Factors in demand, 1700–80', in R. Floud and D. McCloskey (eds), *The Economic History of Britain since 1700*, vol. I: *1700–1860* (Cambridge: Cambridge University Press, 1981), p. 41.
24. Devine, *Transformation of Rural Scotland*, p. 55.
25. B. A. Holderness, 'Prices, productivity and output', in G. E. Mingay (ed.), *The Agrarian History of England and Wales*, vol. VI: *1750–1850* (Cambridge: Cambridge University Press, 1989), pp. 143–4.
26. M. J. Daunton, *Progress and Poverty* (Oxford: Oxford University Press, 1995), p. 31.
27. Devine, *Transformation of Rural Scotland*, pp. 1–14.

rather to probe the relationship between the Union and the Scottish economy in the first three decades or so of the new constitutional relationship.[28]

Above all else, 1707 was a constitutional watershed in Anglo-Scottish history, but it was also one with very significant economic implications. No less than fifteen of the twenty-five articles of Union were directly economic in character, the two of vital consequence being Articles IV and V. The former provided for free Scottish entry without payment of duty to both the English domestic and colonial markets, which at a stroke conceded Scottish involvement in the largest, richest and most rapidly growing free-trade area in the western world. The latter allowed all Scottish-owned merchant vessels to rank as ships of Great Britain from 1707, which afforded Scottish merchantmen the privileges of inclusion within the Navigation Acts and the armed protection of the Royal Navy. Another important Article, XV, created the so-called Equivalent by allocating to the Scots £398,085 10s. as compensation to the shareholders of the ill-fated Company of Scotland and for agreeing to assist in the repayment of England's national debt which was swollen by the massive financial demands of the War of the Spanish Succession.

In the context of the time all three clauses, together with further concessions to proprietors of salt and coal works and to grain exporters, promised considerable benefits when the Scottish economy suffered from rising tariffs throughout much of Europe, serious shipping losses from marauding enemy privateers to c. 1715 and financial difficulties following the Darien debacle. It is hardly surprising, therefore, that when the economy did develop rapidly in later decades some have seen that material success as resting ultimately on the legislative foundations of Union. This view, uncritically accepted, became the orthodoxy of the Victorian era and was hardly questioned in any significant way until fairly recent times.[29] It was consolidated and strengthened by three additional arguments. First, the Union was seen as forming the basis of a new political stability within the United Kingdom which was good for investment by reducing the threat of Anglo-Scottish conflict and providing enduring political and religious support for the revolutionary settlement of 1688–9. Second, the new unity of the two nations facilitated the easier flow of capital, ideas and techniques from a more progressive English economy to the north, there to combine fruitfully

28. C. A. Whatley, *'Bought and Sold for English Gold': Explaining the Union of 1707* (Dundee: Economic and Social History Society of Scotland, 1994), reviews the historiography.
29. Devine, 'Union of 1707 and Scottish development', in Devine, *Exploring the Scottish Past*, pp. 37–8.

with Scottish advantages of low-cost labour and mineral resources. Third, the Union brought the Scottish governing classes into frequent contact with a richer English society, heightened their awareness of Scottish inferiority and caused them to attempt to fashion a new Scotland through systematic improvement in the nation's material and cultural life.

However, at the time of the Union debates in 1706 not all commentators saw the rapprochement in such positive terms. Fears were expressed about the imminent threat of higher English taxation, the danger to already weakened Scottish industries by more technically advanced English manufactures and the possibility of the Scottish landed élite being seduced south by the political, social and patronage attractions of life in London. More recently, some scholars have also questioned the inevitability of Scottish progress within the Union. They point to the example of Ireland, where political integration with England doomed the country to the status of an economic satellite, a supplier of foods, raw materials and cheap labour for a more sophisticated industrialised society but with only limited chance of sustained manufacturing diversification. In this sense, Union might have been the prelude not to an economic miracle but the 'development of underdevelopment'.[30]

Systematic evaluation of these competing hypotheses in the short term to c. 1740 is not easy. Historical research on such key sectors as agriculture has only begun, output figures for Scotland's major industry of linen are available only after 1727 and coherent time series for overseas trade start from the 1740s. In addition, the end of tariffs on the Anglo-Scottish border makes it more difficult to plot the commercial trends between the two nations. Nevertheless, there are some pointers both in a positive and negative direction. Taxation did rise sharply, by all accounts showing approximately a fivefold increase overall between 1707 and the 1750s. The levying of duties on linen in 1711 and, most notoriously of all, on malt in 1725, plus new excise duties on candles and paper caused furious popular protest. After the War of the Spanish Succession ended in 1713, the tax burden in the UK as a whole shifted from the land tax to excise payments on a range of necessities such as beer, salt, linen, soap and malt. Smuggling soon became a way of life and the records of the Board of Customs are full of references to recurrent local disturbances which often resulted in attacks by the mob on the hated excise officials

---

30. T. M. Devine, 'The English connection and Irish–Scottish development in the Eighteenth Century', in T. M. Devine and D. Jackson (eds), *Ireland and Scotland, 1600–1850* (Edinburgh: John Donald, 1983), pp. 12–30.

and the plundering of customs warehouses.[31] In addition, English competition soon crushed the finer end of the woollen trade, which was already in difficulties before 1707. Other industries, such as brewing and paper-making were also badly hit, though no one can say how far this malaise was a result of the harsh winds of competition in the new common market or due to more fundamental problems dragging on from the years of crises in the 1690s. The pessimists were also confirmed in their predictions of an acceleration in the movement to London of many Scottish aristocratic and greater laird families. This absenteeism pre-dated 1707 but became more significant after the Union. Some interpreted the trend as a flight of wealth as aristocratic rentals were exported to the capital in order to sustain opulent lifestyles in English polite society.

But none of these were crippling blows. Modern estimates suggest only about 15–20 per cent of the increased tax burden actually left the country in the five decades after 1707, the rest was allocated to civil and military expenditure in Scotland itself.[32] The Malt Tax of 1725 unleashed a wave of popular anger with serious rioting in Stirling, Dundee, Ayr, Elgin, Paisley and, most violently of all, in Glasgow. But in order to help restore stability the government established the Board of Trustees for Manufactures and Fisheries with a mandate to improve the Scottish economy by allocating £6,000 per annum to the development of linen, wool and the fisheries. Historians agree that the impact was greatest in linen, where, despite the small sums involved, real progress was facilitated in the long run, especially in bleaching techniques. Again, landlord absenteeism may have forced up rentals but the insistent demand for more revenue was one key reason why the élites became more interested in the improvements of their estates, which, in the long run was a significant economic bonus. While some industries suffered, others such as linen, coarse woollen production, sea salt-making and coal-mining either maintained or increased production down to c. 1740.

After some early difficult years, some Scots merchants were also beginning to exploit the new free-trade opportunities. Grain and meal exports more than doubled between the periods 1707–12 and 1717–22 and, as commercialisation intensified, protests against meal exports became more violent in some parts of the Lowlands.[33] In large part this

31. Whatley, *Scottish Society, 1707–1830*, pp. 170–4.
32. R. A. Campbell, 'The Union and economic growth', in T. I. Rae (ed.), *The Union of 1707: The Impact on Scotland* (Glasgow: Blackie, 1974), p. 61.
33. Whatley, *Scottish Society, 1707–1830*, p. 53.

may have been due to the extension of export bounties on grain after the Union. The famous Levellers' Revolt in Galloway in 1724 started when small tenants in the south-west protested bitterly against the large-scale cattle enclosures which were being built to secure more benefit from English demands for stock. These popular disturbances were one important sign that the post-Union market was beginning to have an impact in some regions. Indeed, by the 1720s and 1730s the effect may have been more general. Recent research on the Lowland rural economy in these decades suggests that many of the estates studied were gearing their output of grain and cattle much more to the market. This is indicated by a widespread movement towards larger single tenancies and a general conversion of payment of rentals in kind to money values.[34]

In the long run one of the key advantages of the Union was that Scots merchants were able to trade legally with the English tobacco colonies of Virginia, Maryland and North Carolina. Even if the golden age of the Clyde tobacco trade lay some years in the future, there was already some evidence of dynamic enterprise by Glasgow merchants in the 1710s and 1720s. It was not so much that tobacco imports rose dramatically; that would have been difficult, because the general level of commercial activity in tobacco during these decades both in the colonies and Europe was fairly stagnant. Where the Scots excelled was in undercutting their English rivals by developing smuggling on a grand scale. Indeed, smuggling was by no means confined to the American trades but became the great growth industry in Scotland during the decades after 1707. This reflected not only a desire to make quick profits but also widespread popular opposition to the new customs and tax regime which had followed in the wake of the union. In the tobacco trade most of the systematic fraud involved conspiracies between merchants and customs officers persistently to under-weigh incoming cargoes. One estimate suggests that in the two decades after the Union Scottish merchants were probably paying duty on only a half to two-thirds of their colonial imports.[35] Needless to say, this gave them a significant competitive advantage over their rivals and, to the indignation of the merchants in Whitehaven, Liverpool and London involved in Atlantic commerce, the Scots went on to capture around 15 per cent of the legal trade in American tobacco to Britain by the early 1720s. This achievement was the foundation for even more spectacular success in the future.

34. Devine, *Transformation of Rural Scotland*, pp. 19–35.
35. T. M. Devine, 'The golden age of tobacco', in Devine and Jackson (eds), *Glasgow*, vol. I, pp. 142–3; R. C. Nash, 'The English and Scottish tobacco trades in the seventeenth and eighteenth centuries', *Economic History Review*, 2nd series, 35 (1995), pp. 354–72.

The new imperial context was also relevant in another sense. English colonies started to generate lucrative career opportunities for upper- and middle-class Scots. For centuries Scots had been a mobile people in Europe, as merchants, small traders, intellectuals, churchmen and soldiers. Current estimates suggest that anywhere between 90,000 to 115,000 Scots migrated to Ireland, Poland, Scandinavia, England and other countries in the first half of the seventeenth century alone.[36] The Union soon gave fresh and even more attractive opportunities. Even before 1707 the foundation of Scottish colonies in New Jersey and South Carolina illustrated the slow change in the axis of Scottish emigration from Europe to the Atlantic. The ill-fated Darien enterprise, the grand design to establish a Scots commercial emporium on the Isthmus of Panama, though it was a costly failure, also showed the new aspiration towards westwards migration. Several Scottish aristocrats were spec-tacularly successful in exploiting new career opportunities. Some 46 per cent of Scots soldier peers managed promotion to the general staff of the British army between 1701 and 1745, compared with just over 17 per cent from 1660 to 1706. At a lower level, one in four British regimental officers in the 1750s were Scots.[37] But it was far from easy for lesser mortals of Scottish birth to achieve success in the English capital in the fields of politics and civil administration before the 1760s, although an important exception to this generalisation was the growing Scottish merchant community in London, many of whom had close family and business connections with the tobacco aristocracy in Glasgow. Partly because openings were fewer and prospects less attractive in the south for the majority of Scots, many were more attracted abroad to the Empire, where their skills and educational background quickly enabled them to make their mark. In the 1690s the Company of Scotland Trading to Africa and the Indies which launched the Darien venture had signally failed to break the East India Company's (EIC) monopoly. But Scots began to infiltrate the Company's Directorate, and Scots banking families with continental associations, such as the Hopes and the Drummonds, were already prominent in its affairs by the 1730s. The first Scottish Director of the EIC, John Drummond of Quarrel, was appointed in 1722. Already by the 1750s, some time before Henry Dundas transformed the EIC into a veritable Scottish fiefdom, large

---

36. Smout, Landsman and Devine, 'Scottish emigration', in Canny (ed.), *Europeans on the Move*, pp. 77–90.
37. Linda Colley, *Britons: Forging the Nation, 1707–1837* (New Haven: Yale University Press, 1992), p. 132.

numbers of Scots were serving as army and civilian officers in Bengal and Madras.

Several conclusions emerge from this survey. Both the prophets of doom and the pro-Union propagandists were proven wrong. The nation's economy after Union was not in ruins; indeed there had been some modest recovery from the miseries of the 1690s and, though some activities were hit badly, others prospered. It is significant, for example, that the rural economy was much more able to cope with the bad harvests of 1739–41 than the harsher times of the 1690s. There is also the speculative counterfactual point to be considered. What would have been the consequence of English military invasion if union had not been achieved by consent or if the attempt of the Scots to gain entry to enlarged English markets had failed? Neither proposition suggests a particularly positive scenario. On the other hand, the predicted economic miracle was still an illusion by c. 1740. In the key agricultural sector yields (by English standards) were still low, the infield–outfield system prevailed outside the south-eastern counties and runrig cultivation was dominant. Recent work on living standards before c. 1750 shows them to be low, insecure and broadly static.[38] There were more clear lines of continuity back to the world of pre-Union Scotland and still little evidence of the transformations to come.

These judgements beg two questions: first, why had Scotland not been converted into a colonial appendage of the English economy by the 1740s and, second, what were the constraints on short-term structural change within the context of the Union? With ultimate political authority now vested in London and the Scots exposed to open competition in manufactures from the most advanced economy in Europe, the scenario did exist for a dependent relationship. But two factors might explain why Scotland did not rapidly sink to the economic status of a satellite. First, England sought union for reasons of political and military security and had no economic ambitions north of the border. After 1707, Westminster seems to have been mainly interested in ensuring order and stability in Scotland, and when that existed – as it did for most of the time – the London government was broadly indifferent to the Scottish situation. Significantly, between 1727 and 1745 only nine Acts of Parliament were devoted exclusively to Scotland, and seven of these were concerned with minor matters. In general, Westminster was apathetic and routine matters of government were normally delegated to the Scottish political 'manager' of the day, of whom the most powerful

---

38. Gibson and Smout, *Prices, Food and Wages in Scotland, 1550–1780.*

in the post-Union decades was Archibald Campbell, Earl of Islay and later third Duke of Argyll. Indeed, the primary strategy of securing political stability could itself be of economic benefit to Scotland. The Malt Tax riots of 1725 undoubtedly made London sit up. Westminster was so concerned that in 1727 it established the Board of Trustees for Manufactures and Fisheries, which was to be funded from some of the accruals of the hated malt tax. As has been suggested above, this was a deliberate attempt to placate the truculent Scots by setting up a public body charged to improve the linen, woollen and fishing industries.

Second, the nature of the Scottish trade connection with England preserved a degree of protection. While commercial links were growing in the later seventeenth century, more than half of Scottish trade by value in 1700 was still conducted with non-English markets. This can be contrasted with the position of Ireland, where, at the same date, between 75 and 80 per cent of the nation's external commerce was already carried on with England, the main market for Irish cattle, grain and wool and the principal source of supply of imported manufactured goods and essential raw materials.[39] The Scots were not yet as integrated into the English trade network as the Irish. If they had been, the threat of southern economic dominance would perhaps have been more real.

In relation to the second question, the absence of structural change is easier to explain. The famine years of the 1690s had hit hard. National population levels do not seem to have fully recovered until the 1750s and rent arrears which escalated in these crisis years were still being paid back on some estates three decades later. Also relevant was the condition of the English economy which stagnated for much of the 1720s and 1730s. It could not yet provide the powerful market motor for Scottish development which had been claimed by those who were pro-Union. Nor, despite the real advances before 1707, should the technical deficiencies in Scottish industry be forgotten, especially in the crucial sector of linen. Finally, the assumption that 1707 brought a final stability in Anglo-Scottish relations and so ushered in a new era of economic partnership can be seriously questioned. Popular opposition to the Union in the months leading up to the passing of the Act has been fully described in recent research.[40] Much of this was sustained for several years by the post-Union increases in taxation and the apparent absence of short-term material benefit. The successive Jacobite rebellions of 1708, 1715, 1719

---

39. L. M. Cullen, *Anglo-Irish Trade, 1600–1800* (Manchester: Manchester University Press, 1968), p. 97.
40. J. R. Young, 'The parliamentary incorporating Union of 1707', in Devine and Young (eds), *Eighteenth Century Scotland*, pp. 24–52.

and 1745/6 fed on this discontent and it also fuelled the grave crisis of public order in 1725 associated with the Malt Tax riots. For many years after 1707 the survival of the incorporating Union remained in considerable doubt.

THE LONGER-TERM PERSPECTIVE

Ultimately, however, the true test of the relationship between the Union and Scottish development would come in the longer term, and a survey of the decades after c. 1740 does suggest a clear beneficial effect in that period. Linen was Scotland's most important eighteenth-century industry and one which experienced dynamic growth between 1740 and 1780, with output of cloth stamped by the Board of Trustees for sale rising fourfold over that period. In addition, it was to play a key role in the early stages of Scottish industrialisation as the most important source of capital, labour and business skills for the manufacture of cottons, the 'leading sector' of the Industrial Revolution. Linen's success seemed to rest to a large extent on the common market created by the Union. In the 1760s, for instance, as much as two-thirds of stamped linen output was sold in the English home market or the American and Caribbean colonies.[41] But for the Union, this core manufacture would very likely have been confronted with an English tariff wall in competition with aggressive Dutch and German rivals. The Scots instead received protection within the Union and were also aided from 1742 by a series of bounties to encourage exports. These, rather than initiatives to improve efficiency, seem to have been the decisive influences on growth. Linen, therefore, was one case where the record shows the impact of Union to be clearly favourable in the long term.

To some extent it was a similar story with tobacco. The 'golden age' of the Glasgow tobacco trade dates from the 1740s and, astonishingly, by 1758 Scottish tobacco imports were greater than those of London and all the English outports combined. In 1771 the highest-ever volume of tobacco was landed, a staggering 47 million pounds. Glasgow had become the tobacco metropolis of western Europe, and in the west of Scotland the profits of the trade fed into a very wide range of industries, founded banks and financed agricultural improvement through merchant investment. The transatlantic trades played a key role in the

---

41. A. J. Durie, *The Scottish Linen Industry in the Eighteenth Century* (Edinburgh: John Donald, 1979), pp. 146–66.

development of the Glasgow area, the region that was to become the engine of Scottish industrialisation.

The legitimacy afforded by the Union was crucial to this dazzling story of commercial success. Scottish trade had been active in the tobacco colonies before 1707, though on a relatively small scale, and much of it clandestine in nature. Certainly no London government would have allowed the enormous illegal growth in Scottish tobacco imports outside the Union. Indeed, it was English protests against the boom in Scottish smuggling *within* the Union that led to the wholesale reorganisation of the customs service in 1723 and the formation of a more professional customs bureaucracy. This reflected the great political sensitivity of the issue, since it was widely recognised that much of the Scottish success was at the expense of English merchants. Smuggling before 1707 clearly had its limitations; the Union was therefore a necessary basis for the phenomenal Glaswegian performance in the American trades. Yet those successes were not inevitable. In the final analysis they were won by the Scottish merchant houses adopting more efficient business methods than many of their rivals. The big Glasgow firms were able to drive down their costs by a number of innovations in purchasing, marketing and shipping, which made them formidable competitors in American and European markets. So the Union did not *cause* growth in the Atlantic trades; it simply provided a context in which growth might or might not take place. Ultimately the decisive factor was the Scottish response.

This also conditioned the development of emigration within the Union. Before the end of the seventeenth century there was already Scottish settlement in America in New Jersey and the Carolinas. However, the Darien fiasco demonstrated unambiguously that Scotland did not possess the necessary military and naval resources to establish its own American empire. The Earl of Stair put the point cogently in the Union debates:

[W]e followed the example of other nations and formed a company to trade with the Indies. We built ships and planned a colony on the isthmus of Darien. What we lacked were not men or arms, or courage, but the one thing most needful: the friendly co-operation of England. The pitiful outcome of that enterprise is too sad a story to be told again. Suffice it to say that the English did not treat us as partners or friends or fellow-subjects of a British king but as pirates and enemy aliens. The union of crowns gave us no security; we were exposed to the hostile rivalry of

Spain; our colony was sacked; we suffered every cruelty an enemy can inflict.[42]

After 1707, however, several parts of British North America soon became surrogate Scottish colonies. By the time of the American War of Independence, around 15,000 Gaelic-speaking Highlanders had already settled in Georgia and the Carolinas, while over 60,000 Lowland emigrants were concentrated mainly in the Chesapeake, the Carolinas, New Jersey and Boston. As Linda Colley suggests:

> [E]ven the rawest frontiers of the empire attracted men of first-rate ability from the Celtic fringe because they were usually poorer than their English counterparts with fewer prospects on the British mainland. Having more to win and less to lose, Celtic adventurers were more willing to venture themselves in primitive conditions.[43]

Thus the Scots also became prominent in the East India Company (EIC) long before their position was further enhanced during the long reign of Henry Dundas as President of the EIC Board of Control after 1784. Unlike the patterns in the American colonies, where Scottish traders, clergymen and teachers were well established before 1707, the EIC had been able to prevent the involvement of Scots in India until after the Union. However, in the eighteenth century they penetrated the EIC in much larger numbers than the Irish and Welsh. Many were from landed backgrounds and, because the EIC strictly controlled the periods of service in India, Scottish writers, merchants and army officers often returned home with the accumulated profits of their Asian enterprise. They sometimes used their fortunes to invest in estate improvement, road building and village development. Scottish planters, physicians and traders who had prospered in the Caribbean were also deeply involved in this process of return migration.[44]

This diaspora itself was not caused by the Union, because the Scots had been mobile internationally long before 1707. What the Anglo-Scottish connection did, however, was to open up an unprecedented

---

42. D. Duncan (ed.), *History of the Union of Scotland and England by Sir John Clerk of Penicuik* (Edinburgh: Scottish History Society, 1993), p. 114.

43. Colley, *Britons: Forging the Nation*, p. 132.

44. I am grateful to Dr A. Mackillop, University of Aberdeen, and Dr D. Hamilton, formerly University of York, who are conducting important work on the East Indian and Caribbean connections respectively. See also T. M. Devine, *Scotland's Empire, 1700–1815* (London: Allen Lane, 2003).

range of new opportunities where success was not guaranteed but depended on skill, enterprise, drive, education and luck. But the overall result of these increasingly global emigrations was to the massive benefit of Scotland itself. The Scottish international network later helped to forge trade connections in America and Asia which supported markets for industries at home. It was common for some colonial adventurers who had made their fortune to return home and buy a landed estate as physical proof to all and sundry of their material success. Contemporary observers like John Ramsay from Stirlingshire and Thomas Somerville from Roxburghshire identified men returning from the East Indies as the prime influences on the active land market in these counties and, in several other parts of Scotland, tobacco and sugar money from the colonies helped to sustain agricultural advances and the financing of rural industries.[45]

All the evidence, therefore, suggests that, in the four decades after c. 1740, there was a critically important relationship between the protected common market created by the Union and Scottish economic expansion. But that vital connection was relatively short-lived. There is a compelling argument that perhaps by the 1780s and certainly by the early nineteenth century Scotland had achieved a competitive threshold that ensured the domestic economy was not quite as dependent on English and colonial demand. The economy, as will be shown in more detail in Chapter 2, was in the throes of an early and rapid process of industrialisation which facilitated much wider penetration of non-imperial markets. Much of the old Empire was lost in 1783 with the emergence of the United States of America as an independent state. But that momentous political revolution did not impede Scottish economic progress. On the contrary, trading relationships were quickly re-established, even in tobacco commerce, because the Scottish merchants were now able to compete more effectively in the provision of manufactured goods, business services and credit extension than their European counterparts. Further, between c. 1793 and 1815, while imperial markets in the Caribbean remained crucial to the burgeoning Scottish textile industries, new connections were also established with northern Europe, Latin America and the East Indies which did not depend on colonial protectionism.[46]

---

45. T. M. Devine, 'An eighteenth century business élite', *Scottish Historical Review*, 57 (1978), pp. 40–63; A. I. Macinnes, 'Landownership, land use and elite enterprise in Scottish Gaeldom', in T. M. Devine (ed.), *Scottish Élites* (Edinburgh: John Donald, 1994).
46. G. Jackson, 'New horizons in trade', in Devine and Jackson (eds), *Glasgow*, vol. I, pp. 214–39.

It is also important to note the dual causation of eighteenth-century Scottish economic development. The Union context was important, especially, as argued above, between c. 1740 and the 1780s. So too, however, was the indigenous response. The Irish experience is a telling reminder that close market association with England, the world's richest economy of the time, need not necessarily have led to sustained growth for the junior partner. That is why it is also necessary to consider those intrinsic native advantages which the Scots possessed and which enabled them to effectively exploit the opportunities brought by the Union. Some of these, such as the commitment of the landed élites to economic modernisation and the wealth of business experience gained from ancient trading connections with Europe, pre-dated 1707. Others, like the favourable geological endowment of abundant coal and iron-ore reserves, coupled with low labour costs, only became decisive at a later period. All of these factors and others were at least as crucial to the story of Scottish industrialisation as the English connection, and will be explored in more detail in the next chapter.

FURTHER READING

Campbell, R. H., 'The Anglo-Scottish Union of 1707: the economic consequences', *Economic History Review*, 2nd series, 16 (1963–4), pp. 468–77.
Devine, T. M., *Scotland's Empire, 1700–2000* (London: Allen Lane, 2003).
Devine, T. M., *The Tobacco Lords* (Edinburgh: Edinburgh Press, 1990).
Devine, T. M., 'The Union of 1707 and Scottish development', *Scottish Economic and Social History*, 5 (1985), pp. 23–40.
Devine, T. M., and Dickson, D. (eds), *Ireland and Scotland, 1600–1850: Parallels and Contrasts in Economic and Social Development* (Edinburgh: John Donald, 1983).
Durie, A. M., *The Scottish Linen Industry in the Eighteenth Century* (Edinburgh: John Donald, 1979).
Whatley, C. A., 'Economic causes and consequences of the Union of 1707', *Scottish Historical Review*, 68 (1989), pp. 150–81.
Whatley, C. A., *Scottish Society, 1707–1830* (Manchester: Manchester University Press, 2000).
Whyte, I. D., *Scotland before the Industrial Revolution* (Harlow: Longmans, 1995).

CHAPTER TWO

Industrialisation

T. M. Devine

TRANSFORMATION

As the previous chapter has shown, Scotland's economy was far from static before the middle decades of the eighteenth century. But there was a key difference between the limited, piecemeal and cosmetic changes of the early modern period and the scale of transformation during the one hundred years from the 1760s. A number of features distinguished this later period from any that had preceded it in Scottish history. One was the unprecedented increase in the rate of output of Scottish industry.[1] Between 1785 and 1835 exports rose ninefold, with manufactured goods becoming increasingly significant over time. The first stage of dramatic growth, c. 1760–c. 1830, was dominated by textile production. Linen output tripled in volume between 1773–7 and 1813–17 to an annual average of 26.6 million yards. By 1845 exports of linen cloth alone had climbed to 79 million yards in 1845. Growth was even more spectacular in cotton, though more difficult to measure because of the absence of reliable output figures. However, an indication of the scale of development was the number of cotton spinning mills, which stood at 39 in 1795 but had expanded to 110 in 1810 and 192 in 1839. Throughout the period c. 1760–c. 1830 cotton, linen, wool and silk production were the main motors of industrial advance with one informed contemporary estimate, by Sir John Sinclair, suggesting that by 1825 nearly 90 per cent of Scottish manufacturing was occupied in these four sectors. But it is equally important to stress that unprecedented growth in output was

1. C. A. Whatley, *The Industrial Revolution in Scotland* (Cambridge: Cambridge University Press, 1997), pp. 18–37.

also recorded in such industries as coal, paper, chemicals and distilling. Remarkably, by the census of 1851, Scotland, from a much narrower base a century before, had become apparently somewhat more industrialised than England. The national figure for employment in manufacturing was 40.9 per cent of the labour force but north of the border the proportion was 43.2 per cent.[2]

It is true to say, however, that before the 1830s iron production lagged some way behind the dynamic growth in textiles. Despite the early fame of the new Carron Iron Works, founded in 1759 and a great symbol of the new industrial age, no additional plant was created between 1798 and 1824 and existing firms were confronted by low levels of demand and recurrent financial difficulties. All this changed from the 1830s, at a time particularly between 1825–6 and 1832, when cotton was experiencing acute difficulties in overseas markets. Scotland soon became a key centre for the production of low-cost pig iron with output rocketing from c. 37,500 tons in 1830 to nearly 700,000 tons in 1849 and the Scottish share of British output rising from 5 to 25 per cent.

But this was merely the platform for even more spectacular advances in the second half of the nineteenth century. This was the era of triumphant advance across a range of heavy industries, in which Scotland developed global dominance in several sectors.[3] By 1913, Glasgow and its satellite towns in the surrounding region of intensive industrialisation produced one-half of British marine-engine horsepower, one-third of the railway locomotives and rolling stock, one-third of the shipping tonnage and about a fifth of the steel. On the eve of the First World War the Clyde not only built one-third of British output but almost a fifth of the world's tonnage, a record that was greater at the time by a considerable margin than all the German yards combined. At the heart of the heavy industrial complex with its world-wide markets was the huge range of engineering specialisms in engines, pumps, hydraulic equipment, railway rolling stock and a host of other products. Three of the four greatest firms building locomotives were in Glasgow; in 1903 they came together to form the North British Locomotive Works, 'the Titan of its trade', with a capacity to produce no fewer than 800 locomotives every year. This made the city the biggest locomotive-manufacturing centre in Europe, with engines being produced in large numbers for the Empire, South America and continental countries.

2. C. A. Lee, *British Regional Employment Statistics, 1841–1971* (Cambridge: Cambridge University Press, 1979).
3. T. M. Devine, *The Scottish Nation, 1700–2000* (Harmondsworth: Allen Lane/The Penguin Press, 1999), pp. 249–50.

In civil engineering, too, the west of Scotland was a famous centre of excellence symbolised by the career of Sir William Arroll (1839–1914), the building of the Forth Bridge, the Tay Bridge, Tower Bridge in London and numerous other projects in many parts of the world.

It is easy to lapse into superlatives when describing the global impact of Glasgow's heavy industries at this time. But two cautionary notes are necessary. First, Scottish industrial achievement was not confined to Glasgow and the west. Second, the heavy industries were not unique in achieving massive penetration of world markets in the decades after c. 1850. It is true that cotton-spinning, 'the leading sector' of the first Industrial Revolution, was in difficulty from the 1850s when the embroidered muslin trade dramatically collapsed. Although there were still 131 cotton mills operating in Scotland in 1868, the industry came under intense pressure from foreign competitors, who were protected in their domestic markets by tariffs, and from the impact of Lancashire producers at the finer end of the trade. By 1910, cotton-spinning had virtually collapsed, with only nine firms surviving, its demise accelerated by a failure to maintain earlier patterns of innovations, low levels of investment and a labour force which, owners asserted, was unwilling to accept the measures necessary to achieve higher productivity.[4] However, failure in cotton-spinning was more than compensated for by virtuoso performances in other textile sectors. When Coats of Paisley amalgamated with Patons in 1896, the world's biggest thread-making producer was created. Archibald Coats (1840–1912) became known as the Napoleon of the thread trade and his business was so profitable that eleven members of the family became millionaires. When faced with American tariffs, Coats invaded the USA and soon dominated the market in thread there. The firm eventually controlled no less than 80 per cent of the global thread-making capacity.[5]

Just as remarkable was the development of jute manufacture in the coarse-linen areas of Dundee and the surrounding districts. Jute was a fibre used in bagging and carpeting and was imported from Bengal in India. Dundee soon became 'Juteopolis', with the Cox Brothers' Camperdown Works in Lochee in the 1880s employing 14,000 (mainly women) workers, making it the biggest single jute complex in the world. Again, the product was sold throughout the globe with booming markets in the United States and the British colonies. Other Scottish towns and

---

4. W. W. Knox, *Hanging by a Thread: The Scottish Cotton Industry, c.1850–1914* (Preston: Carnegie, 1995).
5. P. L. Payne, *Growth and Contraction: Scottish Industry, c.1860–1990* (Dundee: Economic and Social History Society of Scotland, 1992), p. 37.

cities had their own textile specialisations: Kirkcaldy in floor coverings and linoleum; Galashiels, Hawick and Selkirk in the Borders, tartans, tweeds and high-quality knitted goods; Kilmarnock and Glasgow, carpets (in Glasgow, Templetons was the largest carpet manufacturer in Britain by 1914); and Darvel and Galston in Ayrshire, fine lace-curtain manufacture, which employed around 8,000 people just before the First World War. This range of activity ensured that textiles remained an integral part of the Scottish economy despite the malaise in cotton-spinning. Indeed, the numbers employed in thread- and lace-making in the 1910s in the west of Scotland fell little short of the labour force in both cotton-spinning and weaving in the 1870s.

Diversity was not confined to the textile sector. James 'Paraffin' Young (1811–83) pioneered the exploitation of the shale oil deposits of West Lothian through a series of inventions which led to the growth of a substantial industry producing 2 million tons of shale by the 1900s. Whisky distillation was, of course, a Scottish specialisation, with over 20 million gallons charged for duty in 1884. At Clydebank, the American Singer Company had developed the world's largest complex for the manufacture of sewing machines with a labour force that numbered over 10,000. Further evidence that heavy industry did not have a complete monopoly was the Barr and Stroud optical factory, the Acme wringer factory and the experiments in new ventures such as automobile and aircraft making on the vast 45-acre site of the engineering giant, William Beardmore and Co.

However, a narrowly based economic perspective, confined to a limited analysis of growth rates and industrial expansion, does not do justice to the magnitude of the transformation which had taken place. No part of the nation remained insulated from the multifarious impact of the new manufacturing dynamic: rural communities, the family, work, class relations, the status of women and children were just some of the facets of Scottish life which were enveloped in a sweeping and irreversible process of change. Lack of space means that only some of these areas can be scrutinised here and the reader is directed to social histories of the period for more detail.[6]

As already indicated, one inevitable corollary of past manufacturing growth was a relative decline in the number of Scots who worked in

6. See, *inter alia*, Devine, *Scottish Nation*; T. M. Devine and R. Mitchison (eds), *People and Society in Scotland*, vol. I: *1760–1830* (Edinburgh: John Donald, 1988); W. H. Fraser and R. J. Morris (eds), *People and Society in Scotland*, vol. II: *1830–1914* (Edinburgh: John Donald, 1991); T. C. Smout, *A Century of the Scottish People, 1830–1950* (London: Collins, 1986); W. W. Knox, *Industrial Nation. Work, Culture and Society in Scotland, 1800–Present* (Edinburgh: Edinburgh University Press, 1999).

agriculture and allied trades. Thus, in 1851, there was still marginally more men and women engaged in farming than in mining and textile work combined. Thereafter the pattern altered radically. The proportion of the population working in agriculture fell from 25 per cent in 1851 to 11 per cent in 1911. But, even more fundamentally, the voracious demands of the burgeoning urban and industrial areas for food, drink, raw materials and labour revolutionised agriculture and rural society throughout Scotland. The buoyant markets for kelp, fish, whisky, cattle and sheep commercialised Highland society, dissolved the traditional communal townships, encouraged the division of land into individual crofts and subordinated ancient landownership responsibilities to the new imperatives of profit. Similarly, customary relationships and connections between clan élites and followers swiftly disintegrated as the entire fabric of society was recast in response to the new rigour of landlord demands, ideological fashion and, above all, the overwhelming market pressures emanating from the south. In less than two generations Scottish Gaeldom was transformed from tribalism to capitalism.[7]

The scale and speed of the revolution was no less remarkable in the rural Lowlands. There too the explosion in grain and meat prices after c. 1780 as a result of urbanisation has been identified as the fundamental dynamic in rapid commercialisation. It was in the two or three decades after c. 1760 that a recognisable modern landscape of enclosed fields, trim farms and separated holdings started to take shape in the Scottish countryside. The single farm under one master became the norm as holdings were consolidated between 1760 and 1815. By 1830, most of those who worked in Lowland agriculture were landless men and women servants whose lives were often as much subject to the pressures of labour discipline and enhanced productivity as those who toiled in the workshops and factories of the larger towns. The market forces released by industrialism spanned the length and breadth of the land and brought a new social order into existence. Significantly, the population of all Lowland rural counties approached their peak levels by the census of 1831 and just less than a decade later in no county south of the Highland line was there a majority working in agriculture. Scotland was already set firmly on the path towards an industrial society and there had been a decisive and irreversible break with the past.[8]

7. T. M. Devine, *Clanship to Crofters' War* (Manchester: Manchester University Press, 1994), pp. 32–62; M. Gray, *The Highland Economy, 1750–1850* (Edinburgh: Oliver and Boyd, 1957); Eric Richards, *The Highland Clearances* (Edinburgh: Birlinn, 2000).
8. T. M. Devine, *The Transformation of Rural Scotland, 1660–1830* (Edinburgh: Edinburgh University Press, 1994), pp. 36–59.

Industrialisation also promoted radical changes in Scottish demography. National population, despite high levels of emigration, rose from 1.25 million in c. 1755 to 1.6 million in 1801, 2.89 million in 1851 and 4.76 million by 1911. Over the period 1851 to 1911 employment doubled from one to two million people in absolute numbers. The ethnic mix of Glasgow, Dundee, Edinburgh and several of the smaller towns in the central Lowlands altered dramatically with the mass immigration of Catholic and Protestant Irish (by the 1850s there was already a quarter of a million Irish-born in Scotland) and the more limited but still striking inward movement of Italians, Jews and Lithuanians. This set of demographic changes depended on the release of employments through the industrialisation process. At the same time, the economic revolution was far from painless. There were both winners and losers. Agricultural employment reached a peak in 1811 and thereafter went into steady decline. Between c. 1815 and c. 1860, the western Highlands suffered destitution and famine, in part because of competitive pressures coming from more favoured areas to the south, which soon crushed the growth points of textile, kelp and whisky manufacture in Gaeldom. Technological change also doomed such diverse groups as handloom weavers, country knitters in the north-east and salt producers along the River Forth. Economic change was uneven in its effects and volatile in its impact over time as Scottish industry became yoked to the global economy. Overall, however, the revolution created many more jobs than it destroyed.

Even more remarkable was the explosive rate of urbanisation in Scotland.[9] In fact, recent research in comparative urban development in Europe suggests that Scottish town and city growth was the fastest of any region on the continent between 1750 and 1850. In 1750, Scotland was seventh in a league table of 'urbanised societies', fourth by 1800 and second only to England and Wales in 1850. Yet as late as the 1830s, just over one-third of the Scottish population lived in towns of over 5,000 inhabitants. By 1911 this proportion had risen to nearly 60 per cent. This explosion of urban development was generated primarily by the expansion of the 'big four' cities, Glasgow, Edinburgh, Dundee and Aberdeen, where more than one in three Scots lived by the beginning of the twentieth century. Once again, Glasgow stood out in the colossal and continuous nature of its exuberant growth. An army of men and women

---

9. J. De Vries, *European Urbanisation, 1500–1800* (London: Methuen, 1984), pp. 122–3; T. M. Devine, 'Scotland', in Peter Clark (ed.), *The Cambridge Urban History of Britain*, vol. II: *1540–1840* (Cambridge: Cambridge University Press, 2000), pp. 151–64.

flooded into the city from the farms and small towns of the Lowlands, the Highlands and Ireland to satisfy the enormous appetite of the great staple industries for both skilled and unskilled labour. In the 1830s there were already over a quarter of a million Glaswegians. By 1871, the total had reached half a million, and just before 1914, partly as a result of boundary extensions, the magical figure of 1 million inhabitants was attained. Elsewhere, agricultural and market centres such as Lanark, Dumfries and Haddington continued to thrive, but the urban dynamic was in the final analysis primarily generated by the power of industry. Outside the 'big four', the most significant rates of growth were experienced by the Border textile towns, the iron, steel and mining centres of Lanarkshire (such as Coatbridge, Airdrie and Motherwell) and the Fife burghs. Throughout Scottish history the towns had been the adjuncts to an overwhelmingly rural economy. In the nineteenth century, however, they became the strategic presence, the dynamic centres of economic change. The food, drink and raw-material needs of the teeming cities transformed the social and economic structures of countless rural communities.[10]

Town and city growth, the offspring of industrialisation, also radically changed the location and distribution of people in Scotland. The concentration of people in the central Lowlands accelerated. The eastern region, centred on Edinburgh, grew from 785,814 to 1,400,675 between the 1830s and 1901, but the increase in the heartland of heavy industry in and around Glasgow was much more spectacular. The western zone expanded from 628,528 in the 1830s to nearly 2 million people by 1901. At that date the western counties had increased their share of national population to an astonishing 44 per cent. At the same time the overall share of the eastern Lowlands remained virtually static. Elsewhere the pattern was one of general haemorrhage. The population of the Highlands peaked in 1841 and then went into absolute decline. The far north reached its maximum population level in 1861, the Borders in 1881 and the north-east in 1911. The clear gainers were the counties where manufacturing or mining dominated. For instance, the population size of Fife, Angus, Renfrew and Stirling more than doubled; West Lothian trebled and Dumbarton increased fourfold. Remarkably, numbers in Lanarkshire rose by a huge 356 per cent. Rural depopulation is often associated with the Highlands, but it is clear that hardly any area of Scotland escaped the full impact of demographic transformation in this

10. R. J. Morris, 'Urbanisation and Scotland', in Fraser and Morris (eds), *People and Society*, pp. 73–102.

period. Special study of one decade, the 1860s, has revealed that the overwhelming majority of parishes in all parts of the country were losing people, especially in the south-west and in the east from Moray to Berwick. It was only the textile towns of the Border and parts of the central Lowlands which experienced significant levels of inward migration.[11]

At the heart of the economic and social revolution, as in other regions of European industrialisation, was the capacity of Scottish producers to make many more goods at lower costs per unit of output. At least three factors contributed to these radical gains in productivity at the macro-economic level. First, there was a quite unprecedented series of techno-logical innovations. The inventions in spinning technology associated with Arkwright, Hargreaves and Crompton delivered yarn that cost a small fraction of earlier techniques but at the same time was of far higher quality than anything that had gone before. The evolution of the steam engine, culminating in James Watt's introduction of the separate con-denser in 1765, was a critical advance. Previously energy was exploited through fire, animal power and the use of watermills and windmills. However, as Mokyr has argued, 'heat and work were not yet convertible into each other so that wood and fossil fuels could not be used to produce motion and watermills could not produce heat'.[12] The steam engine revolutionised the production of energy by breaking through this separation. It not only became over time the principal motive power in the textile industries (though in Scotland water power lasted much longer than in England as a major source) but the basis of a trans-portation revolution in railway development and marine propulsion. Of course, invention and innovation were not unique to the decades after c. 1760. What was distinctive about this era, however, was the extra-ordinary series of path-breaking advances which were mutually rein forcing and continuous.

Second, there was a marked increase in the regional and local con-centration of industry which gave considerable cost and comparative advantages. A classic example was the localisation of manufacturing in towns and cities and the withdrawal from villages and the countryside where much textile, iron-making and mining had earlier concentrated. As late as the 1830s, for instance, around two-thirds of Scotland's

---

11. M. Anderson and D. J. Morse, 'The people', in Fraser and Morris (eds), *People and Society*, pp. 8–45.
12. J. Mokyr, 'The new economic history and the industrial revolution', in J. Mokyr (ed.), *The British Industrial Revolution: An Economic Perspective* (Boulder: Westview, 1993), p. 21.

handloom weavers of cotton, linen and woollen cloth lived in country villages or small towns.[13] The water-powered cotton-spinning factories of the last quarter of the eighteenth century were more often to be found in rural settlements such at Catrine, New Lanark or Deanston than in the cities. Both coal-mining and pig-iron manufacture were also located in small towns and country villages. The continued presence of industry in a variety of forms in the countryside helps to explain why a majority of the Scottish people still lived outside large urban areas in 1830. Yet, in the long run, there were obvious advantages in industrial concentration in towns. Manufacturers were able to gain from 'external economies': firms saved the costs of providing accommodation and other facilities for their workers from their own resources; they were guaranteed access to a huge pool of labour, and transport costs between sources of supply, finishing trades and repair shops could be markedly reduced or virtually eliminated by the close proximity of complementary economic activities. These advantages built up a dynamic for urban expansion even before 1800. Thereafter, the new technology of steam propulsion and conspicuous progress in transport developments through the construction of canals and roads steadily intensified the forces making for urban concentration. In cotton-spinning, and eventually in other textile industries, steam power encouraged industrial settlements on the coalfields and removed the one major obstacle that had previously constricted the expansion of manufacturing in the larger towns. But urban concentration was part of a wider process which conferred similar cost benefits at a regional level. Thus, west-central Scotland became the undisputed heartland of Scottish heavy industry, while linen and jute were the specialisations of Dundee and smaller centres such as Forfar, Brechin, Dunfermline and Kirkaldy. By the later nineteenth century, the Border towns of Galashiels and Hawick dominated woollen cloth and hosiery production.

Third, though not yet subject to precise measurement, there must also have been substantial gains in labour productivity. Partly this was due to the new time and work discipline demands of factory working, though for much of the period considered here most jobs were still carried on outside the confines of the large workshop or the factory. Indeed, the drive towards greater control and more 'rational' organisation of labour was omnipresent as employers, especially in the first phase of industrialisation to c. 1830, launched a determined assault on customary practices,

---

13. N. Murray, *The Scottish Handloom Weavers, 1790–1850* (Edinburgh: John Donald, 1978), pp. 83–114.

irregular atttendance, trade unions, informal collective agreements to limit output and drunkenness.[14]

CAUSES, C. 1750–C. 1830

The origins of such an epochal transformation have long been the subject of debate among economic historians. One point is clear, as is confirmed by the example of Ireland and some European societies: the process was not inevitable. In the eighteenth century, Ireland had shared with Scotland a common experience of commercial expansion. Indeed, in two key areas, linen manufacture and the trade in agricultural exports of beef, pork and butter, the Irish were significantly ahead of the Scots. But the promise of long-term growth then faded in the early nineteenth century with de-industralisation in textiles and the rapid contraction of intensive manufacturing to Belfast and the Lagan valley.[15] To see the Scottish case as simply another regional variant of pan-European industrialisation is equally unsatisfactory. This hardly explains the early timing of the Scottish transformation relative to all other nations apart from England, nor the particular and distinctive advantages which placed Scotland among a handful of European regions that successfully achieved the transition to an industrial society. This and the following sections on causes will consider these influences.

Markets

In 1755 Scotland's population numbered some 1.25 million. By 1801 this had grown to 1.6 million, and to 2.6 million by 1841. The rise in Scottish population was relatively slow and modest by comparison with other nations, with an annual rate in the second half of the eighteenth century of around 0.6 per cent, just over half that of England, and significantly behind the Irish increase of 2.1 per cent from 1791 to 1821. The home market in Scotland was therefore relatively small and not expanding in numbers very rapidly in the later eighteenth century. Nevertheless, the purchasing power for more goods and services was certainly rising. Urban development opened up more demand for foodstuffs, drinks, construction materials and coal. In addition, the middle-class element in the town populations was rising in both absolute and proportionate

---

14. C. A. Whatley, *Scottish Society, 1707–1830* (Manchester: Manchester University Press, 2000), pp. 301–37.
15. T. M. Devine, 'The English connection and Irish-Scottish development', in T. M. Devine, *Exploring the Scottish Past* (East Linton: Tuckwell Press, 1995), pp. 54–73.

terms. Nenadic reckons that the middle classes made up 15 per cent of urban inhabitants in the 1750s but around 25 per cent by the 1830s.[16] These groups were demonstrating their collective identity in visible material terms by increasing expenditure on town houses, elegant furniture, fashionable clothing and numerous other items. At a different social level, agricultural wages, especially around the larger towns of the central Lowlands, were buoyant between 1770 and 1800. Farmers now had to compete more vigorously with manufacturers for labour precisely at a time when agricultural improvements were generating new demands for extra hands on an unprecedented scale. It is clear also that in many rural communities in the later eighteenth century family incomes were rising as many more women and children became involved in the labour market as spinners, bleachers, day labourers, factory workers and harvesters. The *Statistical Account* of the 1790s confirms that this new role for women in the labour market contributed significantly to increased working-class expenditure on coal, linen and cotton clothes, as well as on modest luxuries such as tea and sugar.[17]

Despite its dynamism, however, the Scottish domestic market was overshadowed by the force of external influences, which became ever more powerful over time. Between 1785 and 1836, exports rose ninefold and Scotland became a key player in the Atlantic economy, the fastest growing market place in the world in this period. Partly, the advantage came from the Union of 1707, which provided duty-free protected access to the English domestic and colonial markets. Before the American War of Independence, for instance, these two areas together took over 60 per cent of the official output of Scotland's vital linen manufacture.[18] But the Union connection became less crucial in the later eighteenth century. Scottish merchants were not content to rest behind the protective walls of mercantilist regulation. On the contrary, the disappearance of the major colonial market with the emergence of the independent United States in 1783 seems to have given them the impetus to expand on almost a global scale. During the first few decades of the nineteenth century, new Scottish trade links were established with South America, Asia and Australasia. At the end of the Napoleonic Wars in 1815, America and the Caribbean accounted for nearly 70 per cent of

16. S. Nenadic, 'The rise of the urban middle classes', in Devine and Mitchison (eds), *People and Society*, p. 115.
17. A. J. S. Gibson and T. C. Smout, *Prices, Food and Wages in Scotland, 1550–1780* (Cambridge: Cambridge University Press, 1995), pp. 337–64.
18. A. Durie, *The Scottish Linen Industry in the Eighteenth Century* (Edinburgh: John Donald, 1979), pp. 143–66.

the tonnage leaving the Clyde. Much of the rest was destined for the European continent.[19]

Natural Endowment

Success in the global market place was not inevitable but dependent ultimately on the Scottish commercial response. One favourable factor which conditioned this was geographical position and natural endowment. As argued in the previous chapter, not only did Scotland have a land frontier with England, the richest European economy of the eighteenth century, but it also had easy access by sea to Ireland in the west and Scandinavia and the Baltic in the east. This last connection had encouraged the migration of Scottish merchants, pedlars and soldiers in large numbers to Sweden, Norway and Poland in the sixteenth and seventeenth centuries. But when Ireland and the transatlantic economy became more influential in the later seventeenth and eighteenth centuries, Scottish traders found it relatively easy to transfer the focus of external commercial links from east to west. The rich hinterland of the central Lowlands through the ports of the Forth and Clyde afforded the Scottish merchant classes a window *both* to Europe and to the Americas. Therefore, when Glasgow exploited the new transatlantic opportunities before and after the Union, the city's merchants were able to draw on the capital, expertise and commercial traditions built up over centuries with northern Europe through the ports and the eastern end of this land corridor.

Indeed, the central Lowlands were almost fashioned by nature for industrialisation. By 1800 they contained by far the largest proportion of urban dwellers of any region, with fully 60 per cent of the total town and city population of Scotland living in Glasgow and Edinburgh alone. Market demand was therefore concentrated and buoyant. Moreover, several areas (and in particular Ayrshire, Lanarkshire and Fife) were rich in coal and ironstone, the most important minerals for early industrialisation, and had the additional bonus of close location to ports, sources of labour in the towns and water transport. The two great estuaries of the Forth and Clyde penetrated deep into the narrow waist of the Lowlands, a natural advantage which was then maximised by the building of three great canals, Monkland (1790), Forth and Clyde (1790) and Union (1822), all of them important for the carriage of coal and other goods low in value but heavy in bulk. With the construction of

19. G. Jackson, 'New horizons in trade', in T. M. Devine and G. Jackson (eds), *Glasgow*, vol. I: *Beginnings to 1830* (Manchester: Manchester University Press, 1995), pp. 214–39.

more roads and the continued expansion of the coastal trade, the central Lowlands acquired a first-class transportation network capable of large-scale exploitation of the very favourable geological advantages of the region. Some question the strategic importance of coal and iron in the first phase of industrialisation since they really came into their own as crucial assets only after 1830. However, steam power, and hence the extensive use of coal as a fuel, was already widely employed in both cotton- and linen-spinning by the early nineteenth century. While water power did continue to be used extensively in all sectors of the economy, steam gave a new and decisive competitive advantage to the export-orientated textile industries not only by allowing unbroken production in all weathers but also through relocation of the mills from the countryside to the cities with their abundant supplies of labour. The Belfast cotton industry did not possess such easy access to rich sources of coal in the neighbourhood of the city, failed to compete with Glasgow and Paisley in the age of steam and fell behind from the 1820s.

Capital

In the seventeenth century, Scotland was one of the poorest countries in western Europe, as is shown by its persistently high levels of emigration and the experience of devastating famines in the 1620s and 1690s. Yet, a few decades after this last disaster, the country was on the threshold of a rapid economic transformation which demanded increases in investment in commerce, agriculture, industry and urban infrastructure. This presents a paradox and a problem for the historian: how did such a traditionally poor society finance industrialisation? Four explanations might help to provide an answer.

First, the élite of the old society, the landed classes, mobilised resources on an impressive scale. Landowners were essential to the progress of agricultural improvement and invested large sums in enclosures, new farmhouses, roads and bridges. But many were also very active in financing industry, not least because so much of it was for a long period rural-based, and so manufacturing and mining could be regarded as an extension of and complementary to estate improvement.[20] Coal, lead and ironstone mining proved particularly attractive investment to the flower of the Scottish aristocracy, such as the Dukes of Hamilton, Sutherland and Buccleuch and the Earls of Eglinton, Wemyss and Leven. Road-building, canal construction and banking were other

---

20. R. H. Campbell, 'The landed classes', in Devine and Mitchison (eds), *People and Society*, pp. 91–108.

favoured ventures of the landed classes. The nobility formed the most influential group of directors of the three chartered banks, the Bank of Scotland, the Royal Bank and the British Linen Company, and several other landowners were partners in the expanding network of provincial banks. Old wealth therefore helped to finance the new economic order. But it is important to recognise also that landownership was the main channel through which new money from the Empire, the East Indies, government contracting and military service flowed back into Scotland, some of which percolated through into industrial investment.

Second, the impact of the American trades was a direct consequence of the imperial connection and was especially significant in the west central region, the heartland of the Industrial Revolution. Colonial merchants funded 18 manufactories in Glasgow and its environs between 1730 and 1750, and a further 21 in the years 1780 to 1795. More than half the city's tobacco merchants had shares in industrial ventures in the eighteenth century into linen, cotton, coal, sugar-boiling, glass-making and many other activities. The tobacco lords also founded the city's first three banks, the Ship Bank (1752), the Arms Bank (1752) and the Thistle Bank (1761). Taken together, these activities represented a substantial influx of capital from commerce to industry.[21]

Third, Scottish society mobilised capital more efficiently through the banking system. The nation's banking assets per head rose from £0.27 in 1744 to £7.46 in 1802. Some argue that Scottish bankers were more adept in using these sums to facilitate industrialisation than their more conservative counterparts in England. Certainly the banks were creative and innovative, notably in the development of the cash credit and also in increasing the small note issue.[22] All of this helped. Nevertheless, all the detailed case studies of the accounts of industrial and merchant firms suggest that, while banking finance was commonly employed, its significance was much less than the reploughing of profits, personal and bonded loans, trading credit and often vital support from family and friends.[23] Fourth, the new industries were built up by men of modest means who carefully reinvested as their businesses prospered. The most famous example of the breed was David Dale, who rose to become the greatest cotton magnate of his time in Scotland. He started as a weaver

---

21. T. M. Devine, 'The colonial trades and industrial development in Scotland, c. 1700–1815', *Economic History Review*, 2nd series, 29 (1976), pp. 1–13.
22. S. G. Checkland, *Scottish Banking: A History, 1695–1973* (Glasgow and London: Collins, 1975), pp. 245–80.
23. Whatley, *Industrial Revolution in Scotland*, pp. 54–5.

and then became a linen dealer and importer before founding the first of the great factory villages at New Lanark in 1786.

Technology and the English Connection

The early phase of Scottish industrialisation was based overwhelmingly on borrowed technology and expertise. Ideas and skills were freely imported from Holland, France and Ireland, but England was far and away the major source. 'Technology transfer' on a remarkable scale took place from south to north, reflecting Scotland's relative backwardness and also the strategy of English businessmen who were on the lookout for cheaper labour and low-rented factory sites.[24] The spinning revolution in cotton was entirely based on the seminal inventions of the Englishmen, Kay, Hargreaves, Arkwright and Crompton. Men with experience of English mill practice were often appointed the managers of the early factories. The best-known of them was Archibald Buchanan, who, after serving an apprenticeship at Cromford in Derbyshire, became the technical genius behind the rise of the great Scottish cotton empire of James Finlay and Co. Sulphuric-acid manufacture was pioneered at Prestonpans in 1749 by Roebuck and Garbett after their earlier venture in Birmingham. The first blast furnace and the coke process of smelting were both introduced from England, as was the coal-fired reverberating furnace, which was central to technical progress in the brewing, chemical, pottery and glass industries. Perhaps the most famous example of the penetration of English know-how came with the foundation in 1759 of Carron Company, Scotland's largest manufacturing plant of the day, based on the coke-smelting techniques pioneered at Coalbrookdale. The speed of Scotland's economic transformation also created technical bottlenecks and recurrent shortages of skilled labour which were often relieved by a steady trickle from England of experienced smelters, moulders, spinners and malleable ironworkers.

This is far from being a definitive list, but it is enough to demonstrate that Scottish economic progress would surely have been impeded without English technical expertise and skills and, to a lesser extent, those of other countries. But these new processes were assimilated swiftly, confirming that Scotland had the appropriate social, cultural and economic environment to achieve fast industrialisation. Like a precursor of Japan, having borrowed ideas from others on a grand scale, the country soon moved rapidly to the cutting edge of the new technology. A whole stream of key inventions started to emanate from Scotland,

24. Ibid., pp. 47–8.

including James Watt's refinement of the separate condenser for the steam engine (perhaps the fundamental technological breakthrough of the age), Neil Snodgrass's scutching machine, enabling wool to be processed effectively before being spun, Archibald Buchanan's construction of the first truly integrated cotton mill in Britain in 1807, where all the key processes were carried out by power within a single complex, Henry Bell's *Comet* of 1812, which pioneered steam propulsion for ships, J. B. Neilson's invention in 1829 of the 'hot-blast process', which helped to transform iron manufacture by radically reducing the costs of production, and a long series of pathbreaking discoveries in marine engine design.

It is dangerous, however, to focus too much on technology when considering those distinctive advantages which gave the Scots a competitive edge during the Industrial Revolution. Most tasks, both in agriculture and industry, continued to be done by hand; even in cotton, the most advanced manufacturing sector of all, two of the three core processes, weaving and finishing, remained mainly labour-intensive until the 1820s. The cost of labour was therefore critical as was the way in which working people reacted to the strange new manufacturing processes and environments. Undeniably, wages in certain trades were rising in the later eighteenth century. Nevertheless, most Scottish wages remained below those of England, and it was partly because of this attraction that English tycoons like Richard Arkwright were investing in Scottish factories in the 1780s. Arkwright boasted that the lower costs of production in Scotland would enable him to take a razor to the throat of Lancashire. Almost a century later, in the 1860s, when the first rigorous wage censuses became available, Scotland was still unequivocally a low-wage economy in most occupations compared to England.[25] The key test of national differences in this respect was the balance of migration. When good figures were first produced in the 1840s, around 67,000 Scots and English had migrated across the border. However, over three-quarters of this number were Scots, who were plainly much keener to move to the greater opportunities in the south than the English were to move north.

A second advantage for Scottish entrepreneurs was the mobility of labour. Historically the Scots were a migratory people. But in the eighteenth century internal migration became more common precisely at the time when industry needed to attract more workers.[26] Seasonal movement for harvest work from the southern and central Highlands for

---

25. R. H. Campbell, *The Rise and Fall of Scottish Industry, 1707–1939* (Edinburgh: John Donald, 1980), pp. 80–4.
26. M. Gray, *Scots on the Move* (Dundee: Economic and Social History Society of Scotland, 1990).

work in the Lowland harvests was more significant after c. 1750. In the same region the first clearances for sheep, the transfer of people from inland straths to the coastlands as the new crofting system was established, and the social strains coming from rampant commercialisation all led to more internal migration as well as promoting a large-scale exodus of people across the Atlantic after c. 1760. In the Lowlands agricultural improvement was radically altering the traditional social order and in the process drastically cutting back the large numbers who had always had a legal or customary right to land. The tenant class contracted further and cottar families with smallholdings possessing skills in spinning and weaving were steadily replaced by landless servants and labourers. Those who have little other than their labour power to sell are always more likely to be mobile than a land-holding peasantry who, in the last resort, can rely on their smallholdings as a source of subsistence. Lowland Scotland certainly had larger numbers of people detached from land holding by c. 1800 than ever before and the resulting rates of short-distance migration were often remarkable. One case study shows that two-thirds of the families listed for the village of Kippen in Stirlingshire in 1789 were no longer resident there in 1793. In the household of the Earl of Leven and Melville in Fife, 97 per cent of women servants and 90 per cent of men remained for only four years or less in the Earl's employment.[27] Certainly by comparison with many rural parishes in parts of France and Germany, where most lived and died in the parish of their birth, Scottish internal mobility was a decided bonus for manufacturers keen to hire more labour.

Nevertheless, acute difficulties remained. Skill shortages abounded in coal and ironstone-mining, pottery and glass-making, bleaching and nail-making and, as already noted, could often only be made good by relying on English workers to hand on their expertise to the natives.[28] More seriously, there was the major problem of recruiting labour to the new textile factories and large workshops. The mills crystallised the conflict between the culture of work in the old and new worlds. Full-time work, though not unknown, was unusual outside the towns, and the majority of people had little interest in labouring for much longer than their basic needs required. But factory employment was radically different. Costly machinery had to be employed on a continuous basis and that meant long hours, a disciplined workforce and more rigorous supervision of labour. By the early nineteenth century, in the cotton

27. R. A. Houston, 'Geographical mobility in Scotland, 1652–1811: the evidence of testimonials', *Journal of Historical Geography*, 11 (1985), pp. 379–94.
28. Whatley, *Industrial Revolution in Scotland*, p. 21.

mills night working was not unknown when trade was brisk. Workers normally laboured for six days a week, with Sundays off and usually only a few further days annually. It was hardly an environment likely to attract large numbers of male workers at a time, in the 1780s and 1790s, when work in agriculture and handloom weaving was paying better than ever before.

But this potential recruitment crisis in the early years of industrialisation was avoided. Scottish industry quickly developed a considerable dependence on women and children as sources of low-cost labour. By the 1820s they formed over 60 per cent of the total workforce in manufacturing industry and, in the cotton and flax mills, the proportion of women employed was significantly higher in Scotland than in the industrial areas of Lancashire.[29] Women were also vital as bearers in the collieries, in the preparation of flax, the manufacture of woollen stockings and in the bleachfields. Again, unlike the pattern in Yorkshire and Lancashire, the immigrant Irish started to stream into the mills as early as the 1790s as both skilled and unskilled labour. It was significant that when the powerful Glasgow Cotton Spinners Association emerged in the early nineteenth century the leadership was dominated by second-generation Irishmen whose families had earlier achieved a position in the industry in the late eighteenth century. In the early 1800s it was reckoned that around half the mill workforce in the city were either Irish-born or of Irish descent.[30] By that time, national population growth in Scotland was starting to accelerate and in the cities the swelling number of migrants was relieving any scarcities that had previously existed in the industrial labour market. But for a period in the 1780s and 1790s, only the recruitment to the mills of Irish immigrants, Scottish women and pauper children prevented a slowing down in the momentum of industrialisation.

Enterprise and Scottish Society
The proven advantages of favourable natural endowment and expanding markets would have been of little consequence if they had not been exploited effectively by enterprising merchants and manufacturers. In the Scottish case, overseas and especially imperial demand was particularly crucial to the key textile industries. It is best then to examine the quality of the business classes through their achievements in the international market place. The record is undeniably impressive.

29. P. Bolin-Hort, *Work, State and the Family* (Lund, Sweden: Lund University Press, 1989).
30. M. J. Mitchell, *The Irish in the West of Scotland, 1797–1848* (Edinburgh: John Donald, 1998), pp. 111–13.

The most striking feature is the radical geographical change in the axis of mercantile migration. By 1700 the long-established migration to Europe had dropped off and only the movement to Holland remained significant. Instead, by the later seventeenth century the Scots were starting to find new commercial opportunities across the Atlantic. In the British West Indies their role was at first less important than that of the Irish, but they soon caught up and surpassed them in numbers, especially in commerce and plantation ownership. They became particularly influential in Jamaica, which produced more sugar than all the other British islands combined by the 1770s and where in 1771–5 Scots accounted for 40 per cent of the inventories after death of above £1,000. Over the same period, the share of the Irish and Jews was only 10 per cent.[31] The impact was even more remarkable in North America. Clusters of Scottish merchants were to be found by the 1750s in Chesapeake, where the Glasgow tobacco interest was dominant, New Jersey, Boston, Philadelphia, northern New England and the Carolinas. A few decades later, there is considerable evidence of Scottish commercial activity in India and Asia. Even before the end of the East India Company's monopoly, Scottish adventurers had set up agency houses which were permitted on licence from the Company to carry on local trade. By the 1790s, the dozen or so most powerful houses in Bengal and Bombay were dominated by Scots merchants, and jealous rivals vociferously criticised them for their clannish instincts, which, they alleged, helped them to engross the business.[32]

The jewel in the crown of this developing global network was the tobacco trade between the Clyde and the colonies of Virginia, Maryland and North Carolina. Here the Glasgow merchant firms were formidable and aggressive competitors. The first strategy in the commercial war with London, Bristol, Liverpool and Whitehaven in the 1710s and 1720s, as seen in Chapter 2, was to develop smuggling and fraud to unprecedented levels. The outcry of the English outports and government alarm led to new legislation in 1723 and 1751 and a reform of the customs service, which meant that fraudulent practices soon went into rapid decline. Ironically, however, the 'golden age' of the tobacco trade started at this juncture, based on efficient business practices rather than clandestine smuggling. In 1758 Scottish tobacco imports were for the

31. L. M. Cullen, 'The Irish diaspora in the seventeenth and eighteenth centuries', in N. Canny (ed.), *Europeans on the Move* (Oxford: Clarendon Press, 1994), pp. 126–8.
32. T. C. Smout, N. C. Landsman and T. M. Devine, 'Scottish emigration in the seventeenth and eighteenth centuries', in Canny (ed.), *Europeans on the Move*, pp. 91–9; J. G. Parker, 'Scottish enterprise in India, 1750–1914', in R. A. Cage (ed.), *The Scots Abroad: Labour, Capital, Enterprise, 1750–1914* (London: Croom Helm, 1985), pp. 191–203.

first time greater than those of all the English outports combined. Throughout these decades the Glasgow houses were carving out a greater and greater share of British imports at the expense of their southern rivals. As late as 1738, they accounted for only 10 per cent of the British total. By 1765 this had reached 40 per cent.

To some extent this achievement was based on the shorter sea crossing, and hence lower freight costs, between the Clyde and the Chesapeake compared to the voyage time from southern ports. But geography was not the decisive factor because the Scots had no such advantage over London in relation to the European markets of France and Holland, where they sold most of their tobacco imports. Rather, the key influence was the effectiveness of the commercial methods of the Glasgow firms. The giant syndicates, such as John Glassford and Co., William Cunningham and Co. and Speirs, Bowman and Co., who together controlled almost half the trade, established chains of stores in the colonies run by Scots factors and clerks who bought up tobacco from the planters in advance of the arrival of the ships. This significantly reduced turnaround time in colonial ports and hence operating costs. This was an advantage which increased over time. The Glasgow houses moved from chartering ships to owning them. By 1775, 90 per cent of the Clyde tobacco fleet were 'company ships'. This allowed for better planning of shipping schedules and thus cut back the costly 'stay in the country' even more. It also helped to produce a pool of crack skippers who were absolutely familiar with the sea routes and whose skills further reduced passage time on the 7,000-mile return journey between Scotland and Chesapeake Bay. In 1762 the first dry dock in Scotland was opened in Port Glasgow with pumping machinery designed by James Watt to allow the speedier careening of the tobacco ships, especially vital because of their regular exposure to the teredo worm-infested waters of the Chesapeake. Ship design also improved. The move to provide the tobacco fleet with fore-and-aft sails, rather than square sails, enabled ships to sail closer to the wind, making it easier to navigate the shoal waters of the Chesapeake rivers where the stores were situated. Similarly, the carrying capacity of those vessels regularly engaged in the trade rose substantially over time. The average annual volume of tobacco carried per ship in the Clyde fleet increased from 219,800 lb between 1747 and 1751 to 530,000 lb in the years 1770 to 1775, indicating a notable gain in economies of scale.[33]

33. R. F. Dell, 'The operational record of the Clyde tobacco fleet, 1747–1775', *Scottish Economic and Social History*, 2 (1982), pp. 1–17; T. M. Devine, 'The golden age of tobacco', in Devine and Jackson (eds), *Glasgow*, vol. I, pp. 139–83.

This short case study of the tobacco business reveals some of the qualities of enterprise and business drive that existed in the eighteenth-century Scottish merchant community. There is no reason to believe that the tobacco trade was untypical, other than in terms of its size, as it accounted for over half of the value of Scottish exports in the early 1750s. As has been seen, Scottish merchants were also pushing aggressively into the Caribbean islands and the British trading enclaves in India. Some have seen this thrusting commercial spirit as the result of Calvinist ideology, which is said to have promoted the business ethic of hard work, thrift and the confident assurance which came from the awareness of membership of God's elect.[34] But equally the Scottish capacity to exploit opportunities in the British Empire may also be explained by the long tradition of merchant adventuring in Europe in the fifteenth, sixteenth and seventeenth centuries, which had broadened horizons, refined commercial techniques and reduced fear of foreign cultures. Long before the Reformation, the Scots had shown themselves to be aggressive and feared traders, pedlars and craftsmen with mercantile communities stretching from Dieppe, Rouen, La Rochelle and Bordeaux in France, to Bruges and Campveere in the Low Countries, Malmo in Sweden, Copenhagen in Denmark, and Danzig, Cracow and Warsaw in Poland. This far-flung commercial empire, which spanned much of western and north Europe before c. 1700, confounds any notion that the Scots suddenly discovered the spirit of enterprise in the eighteenth century as a consequence of Enlightenment and rationalism or under the stimulus of a Calvinist religious ideology.[35] A more convincing model, which better reflects the actual historical experience, would suggest that traditional entrepreneurial energies, which existed alongside the nation's relative poverty in the early modern period, could be turned to dynamic exploitation of the new market opportunities opening up at home and in the burgeoning Atlantic and Asian economies in the eighteenth century.

The linen, cotton, sugar and tobacco merchants of the era of industrialisation were part of the same cosmopolitan commercial breed who had plied Scottish trades in earlier times from the ports of France to the steppes of Russia but the context of their activities had now changed dramatically. First, the British state provided a new and rapidly expanding trading environment under the protection of tariff duties and the Royal Navy. The spectacular series of colonial acquisitions after the

34.   Campbell, *Rise and Fall of Scottish Industry*, p. 28.
35.   Smout, Landsman and Devine, ' Scottish emigration', in Canny (ed.), *Europeans on the Move*, pp. 77–90.

Seven Years War and during the 1790s in North America, the Caribbean and Asia created rich pickings for Scottish adventurers. Second, property rights were well protected in Scotland. For instance, legal and political privileges surrounding land gave estate owners an enviable power and security which was said by the contemporary commentator Sir John Sinclair to be unique among all the states of western Europe. Third, since the British landed classes dominated parliament and were also committed to economic reform, UK legislation began to be shaped in favour of the owners of private capital and property. There was an absence of confiscatory taxation, unlike the experience of some European states, such as France.[36] Indeed, after c. 1810, taxation policy moved even further away from levying taxes on income and towards the drawing of revenue from imposts on commodities. In addition, legislation in coal-mining in 1775 and 1799 and for handloom weaving in 1812 had the effect of weakening Scottish workers' attempts at combination while the removal of the old controls over bread prices and tradesmen's wages introduced the power of the free market both in food consumption and industrial relations. Fourth, and finally, eighteenth-century Scotland, like English society at the same time, gave social recognition and esteem to the business of successful money-making. As Adam Smith noted in his *Theory of Moral Sentiments*:

> To what purpose is all the toil and bustle of the world ... the
> pursuit of wealth, of power, and preeminence? Is it to supply the
> necessities of nature? The wages of the meanest labourer can
> supply them. ... What then is the cause of our aversion to his
> situation? ... Do the rich imagine that their stomach is better,
> or their sleep sounder in a palace than in a cottage? The contrary
> has so often been observed ... What are the advantages [then]
> by that great purpose of human life which we call bettering our
> condition? ... It is the vanity, not the ease of the pleasure, which
> interests us. But vanity is always founded upon our belief of our
> being the object of attention and approbation. The rich man
> glories in his riches, because he feels that they naturally draw
> upon him the attention of the world. ... Everybody is eager to
> look at him ... His actions are the objects of the public care.
> Scarce a word, scarce a gesture can fall from him that is altogether
> neglected. In a great assembly he is the person upon whom all
> direct their eyes. ... It is this, which ... renders greatness the

---

36. Mokyr, 'The new economic history', in Mokyr (ed.), *The British Industrial Revolution*, p. 44.

object of envy and compensates ... all that toil, all that anxiety, all those mortifications which must be undergone in the pursuit of it.[37]

In Britain, so Smith was suggesting, there were greater rewards through enhanced social status for successful enterprise in addition to simple material success. Wealthy industrialists, merchants, soldiers and professionals returning from the Empire were able to buy into land, found a family dynasty and in time gain the social acceptance of the great and good. Unlike more traditional European societies, money in Britain bought more than just comfort. Thus, the counties around Glasgow were ringed with the estates of tobacco lords and sugar princes, the parishes around Edinburgh with the rural retreats of the élite of the capital's legal aristocracy and, throughout the land, properties were bought up by returnees from the Caribbean, India and Asia eager to mark their successful careers abroad. It was a social system by which new wealth could be afforded the social recognition it craved. Whatever the influences, however, the internationally mobile Scottish merchant, opening up markets from the Americas to India and beyond, was to prove one of the country's greatest assets in the age of industrialisation.

CAUSES, C.1830–C.1880

There were some similarities between the causation process before 1830 and the origins of industrial change during the Victorian era. Most crucially of all, the economy continued to rely on overseas markets. Some 38 per cent of all Scottish coal production went abroad or coastwise in the 1910s, apart from that consumed by the export-orientated iron, steel and other industries. The giant North British Locomotive Company sent nearly half its engines to the British Empire in the years before the First World War, with India as the primary destination. The rise of Dundee jute was generated from the 1840s by the demand for bagging for international commodities as varied as East India coffee and Latin-American guano, as well as the enormous requirements for sandbags during the Crimean War, the American Civil War and the Franco-Prussian War. At the end of its first major phase of precocious growth in the 1840s, two-thirds of Scottish pig-iron was exported, a significantly higher proportion than the pattern elsewhere in

37. Quoted in ibid., pp. 37–8.

Britain. Even in the later 1860s, around one half of total production was still being sent overseas. The ships that poured out from the yards of Clydeside relied for orders on the condition of international trade, even if increasingly from the 1890s the needs of the Admiralty for naval vessels were becoming ever more significant. It was the same story elsewhere, from quality Border knitwear to malt and blended whiskies. As far as Scotland was concerned, the international market was king.[38]

It follows, therefore, that the global trade revolution of the second half of the nineteenth century was a strategic factor in Scottish industrial success. Its basis was a new and dynamic set of commercial relationships forged between Europe and the Americas, Asia and Australia based on the exchange of foods and raw materials for manufactured goods. Grain, meat, raw cotton, timber, wool and numerous other commodities went to Europe. In return the primary producers obtained ships, locomotives, bridges and railway lines, together with many other requirements for their developing infrastructure from the countries of the northern hemisphere. The whole system was facilitated and massively expanded by a revolution in transportation: the improvement in sailing ship design and speed; the ocean-going steamship from the later nineteenth century; refrigeration; the spread of transcontinental railway networks, which unlocked the productive potential of territories as far apart as the plains of India and the American prairies; and the opening of the Suez Canal in 1869, which considerably reduced the travelling time to India and beyond.

All this had dramatic consequences for Scottish industry. The effect was twofold. One the one hand, the earnings which accrued to the primary producers enabled them to purchase more capital goods. On the other, the vast investments in the global transport system opened up a voracious demand for ships, locomotives, railways, bridges and jute bagging. Scottish investors added to this momentum by themselves putting money into American, Australian and Asian railway stock, land and cattle companies, mining ventures, tea plantations and state bonds. Scottish-originated foreign investment rose from £60 million in 1870 to £500 million in 1914, a figure that was much higher per head of population than the average for the United Kingdom as a whole, though some of this may have derived from English investment in Scotland's finance houses.[39] This outflow from what, for the majority of the population, was a poor country had a circular impact on the development of

---

38. Devine, *Scottish Nation*, p. 254.
39. W. J. Jackson, *The Enterprising Scot* (Edinburgh: Edinburgh University Press, 1968).

the Scottish economy, as these investments then helped to fuel demand for Scotland's great industrial staples. As Bruce Lenman has put it: 'The wheat of the Canadian or American prairies, for example, had to be taken by rail to eastern ports, and in Canada the locomotive could well be made in Glasgow while both in Canada and in America the sacks holding the grain were quite likely to have been manufactured in Dundee. The ships which crossed the North Atlantic with the grain were often enough built and engineered on the Clyde.'[40] The world economic setting was therefore the essential precondition for economic success. What will now be considered are those crucial advantages which gave the Scots a cutting edge in this international market place.

A prime foundation was the rich economic heritage which had developed in the decades before 1830. Scotland's early industrialisation had given it a head start over virtually all European rivals – with the exception of the country's nearest neighbour, England. A number of key advantages were already in place which helped to provide a platform for the great achievements of Victorian times. They included a large and experienced business class; a political and social élite committed to national economic growth; a labour force which had already developed skills in engineering, mining and textiles and, crucially, had become accustomed to the more rigorous time and work disciplines of industrial capitalism; a sophisticated infrastructure of ports, roads and canals; and an international network of trading connections not only to Europe and North America but increasingly to the countries of the Empire in the southern hemisphere. Some specific connections between this varied inheritance and the halcyon days of Victorian industrial achievement are worth mentioning. The meteoric rise of Dundee jute was partly based on these relationships. Samples of jute were first sent from Bengal by the East India Company to leading textile centres in Britain in the hope that the cheapness of the coarse fibre might prove attractive to manu-facturers. Dundee was the first to solve the technical problem of the dryness and brittleness of the new fibre, not only because the city and the surrounding region specialised in coarser linens but because raw jute was softened by the process of 'batching', or the application of a mix of whale oil and water. Since the later eighteenth century Dundee had become a leading whaling centre in Scotland.[41]

An even closer link can be established in shipbuilding, which in the second half of the nineteenth century became the strategic heart of the

40. B. Lenman, *An Economic History of Modern Scotland* (London: B. T. Batsford, 1977), p. 193.
41. E. Gauldie (ed.), *The Dundee Textile Industry, 1790–1885* (Edinburgh: Scottish History Society, 1969), p. xvii.

west of Scotland's heavy industrial economy. In the early decades there was little competitive advantage in ship construction. In fact, the Clyde had limited traditional expertise in building modern ships and as late as 1835 it launched less than 5 per cent of total British tonnage. The central early advantage was the Clyde's pre-eminence in the development of steam engines for ships, which in turn depended on the range of engineering skills that had accumulated in the region during the first epoch of industrialisation. Steam engines were used in the pits to pump water and raise coals and in the cotton factories they were becoming increasingly common. The foundries and workshops of the region not only built but repaired the improved engines. As James Cleland remarked in the early 1830s: 'Glasgow ... has already large establishments for the manufacture of Steam-Engines and Machinery, and for making the Machinery employed in the process of Cotton-Spinning, Flax-Spinning and Wool-Spinning. In these works everything belonging to, or connect with, the Millwright or Engineer department of the manufacture is fabricated.'[42] It was perhaps almost inevitable that from these great congeries of skills in precision engineering would come an interest in the application of steam propulsion to ships. Henry Bell's historic launch of the steamboat *Comet* in 1812 and its successful voyage across the Clyde demonstrated that it could be done. By 1820, 60 per cent of all British steam tonnage was launched on the Clyde, even if all these vessels were small, had low boiler pressures and consumed huge amounts of coal. The foundation of later greatness depended upon an effective solution to these basic problems of high cost and low performance. It is acknowledged that an important catalyst here was the Napier family, headed by David and, later, by his cousin Robert, who pioneered key technical improvements at their Camlachie foundry and Lancefield yard.[43] The Napier firm became a kind of advanced school of marine engineering and construction. David Napier (1790–1869) was the first to combine engineering and shipbuilding in one firm, while many other foundries became active in the supply of boilers and engines for ships as well as their traditional market in the mines and mills. What is striking, however, is that virtually all these engineering ships were clustered in the cotton districts of Glasgow, such as Tradeston and Camlachie. The close connection between the textile industries of the

42. J. Cleland, *Enumeration of the Inhabitants of the City of Glasgow and County of Lanark* (Glasgow: John Smith and Son, 1832), p. 151.
43. A. Slaven, *The Development of the West of Scotland* (London: Routledge and Kegan Paul, 1975), p. 129.

first Industrial Revolution and later fame in shipbuilding in the west of Scotland was confirmed.

These were the foundations, but a number of basic influences then helped to accelerate the transformation of Scotland into a world economic power in the next few decades. A primary factor was a remarkable rate of strategic invention and innovation in metalworking and ship construction. In iron, the seminal advance was made by James Beaumont Neilson (1792–1865), the manager of Glasgow Gasworks, who had developed considerable expertise as a chemist and engineer. He revolutionised the iron industry through his hot-blast process. It resulted in great savings in material, costs and fuel and also in increased production per furnace. Neilson's invention was the basis of the exceptional growth of pig-iron manufacture in Scotland because it allowed the Scots ironmasters to undercut their English and Welsh rivals significantly. Between 1825 and 1840, Scottish output expanded 20 times to 504,000 tons. Growth was concentrated in Ayrshire and, to a much greater extent, in Lanarkshire, where the Bairds of Gartsherrie built the core of their great iron-producing empire in the Monklands area. In just 40 years from the 1830s this family developed a reputation as the world's leading pig-iron producer with, in 1870, 42 furnaces with a capacity of 300,000 tons per annum and a profit in that year alone of £3 million. Thomas Tancred, the commissioner appointed to report on the conditions in the mining districts, described the Monklands in graphic terms in 1841: '... the groups of blast furnaces on all sides might be imagined to be blazing volcanoes at most of which smelting is continued Sunday and weekdays, by day and night without intermission. By day a perpetual steam arises from the whole length of the canal where it receives waste water from the blast engines on both sides of it and railroads traversed by long trains of waggons drawn by locomotive engines intersect the country in all directions.'[44] Here, indeed, was the scarred industrial landscape of Victorian Scotland in its classic form.

In shipbuilding the rate of innovation was continuous from the 1830s. The Clyde achieved world-wide renown by its capacity to make radical and ingenious modes of propulsion and at the same time pioneer new materials of construction. There was a remarkable list of Clydeside firsts which kept the Scottish yards at the leading edge of the burgeoning global market for ships. These included the development of the screw propeller in place of the paddle, which increased speed, the compound marine engine which dramatically expanded power, and the use of new

44. Quoted in ibid., p. 119.

materials such as iron and then steel in ship construction. In the second half of the nineteenth century the fortunes of shipbuilding, iron and steel became very closely linked, primarily because the Clyde yards were so keen to pioneer new materials. In the 1840s almost all iron tonnage was launched on the Clyde, and between 1851 and 1870 accounted for over two-thirds of all British production. Steel-making was established in Scotland in the 1870s. Expansion had been constrained because Scottish iron ores were phosphoric and the main steel-making techniques, the Bessemer converter and the Siemens–Martin open-hearth process, relied on low-phosphoric ores. This problem was remedied by the Gilchrist—Thomas process of the 1880s. In the event, however, the Scottish industry developed by using the open-hearth process and imported ores. By 1885 there were already ten firms producing almost half of all British-made Siemens steel. The link between the open-hearth process and shipbuilding is deeply significant. Essentially, steel was the child of shipbuilding and the result of determination by the major yards to use metal plates of even greater strength, lightness and durability in order to maintain their leading position in world markets.

The economic achievements of Victorian Scotland were also built on local supplies of fuels and raw materials and low costs of labour. Coal reserves were abundant throughout the central belt and had helped to power the steam-driven textile mills of the early nineteenth century. However, with the vast expansion of iron-making, coal came into its own. In 1800 there were probably around 7,000–8,000 miners in the country. By 1870 this labour force had risen to nearly 47,000 men, working in over 400 pits. The Baird ironmasters accounted for their extraordinary success in large part on the fortuitous presence of rich seams of the invaluable splint coal in close proximity with reserves of blackband ironstone in Lanarkshire. From the later eighteenth century, access to coal and iron ore supplies had been much improved with the development of a network of roads and canals. From the 1820s, however, the railway added a revolutionary new dimension to the transport of heavy raw materials and finished products. It is significant that the earliest ventures, such as the Monkland and Kirkintilloch Railway (1824) and the Garnturk and Glasgow (1826), were promoted in order to maximise the exploitation of mineral deposits. Capital raised by Scottish railway companies was a mere £150,000 in 1830. By 1850 it stood at over £20 million and at nearly £47 million in 1870. Trunk lines were promoted linking Glasgow, Edinburgh, Paisley, Greenock and Ayr as early as the 1830s, followed by the creation of coastal routes to England. The railways had far-reaching effects on almost all aspects of Scottish life, but their impact on the heavy industrial economy was particularly profound. They were more reliable than canals, which were likely to freeze in winter. Like them, they could shift bulk goods at low cost but did so much more rapidly and with greater regularity. It was also technically much easier for industrial and mining plants to connect to an intricate network of railways by sidings and spur lines than to a system of canals. The mineral riches of particular localities were unlocked and industries with complementary specialisations could concentrate on an unprecedented scale. It was the railway more than any other factor that helps to explain the sheer density of industrial activity in parts of Glasgow, Ayrshire, West Lothian and Lanarkshire.

In spite of the marvels of the new technology, most industries still depended on human labour. Shipbuilding was to a significant extent a huge assembly activity in which skilled workers were much more crucial than machine tools. Coal-mining, despite significant Scottish advances in cutting machinery from the later nineteenth century, remained a 'pick and shovel' industry. In 1890 one estimate suggests that labour costs constituted around half the overall cost of finished steel and anything between one-third and two-thirds in shipbuilding. The engineering, tool-making, metalworking, furniture, woodworking and printing industries could function only on the basis of skilled labour. In 1911, seven out of every ten men and women in Glasgow found employment in a range of manufacturing activities. Those sectors where skilled male workers were dominant or significant accounted for almost a quarter of the entire Glasgow workforce, compared to only 10 per cent in 1841.[45]

Furthermore, Scottish labour worked for lower wages than the average in England, the country which was Scotland's main competitor for much of the Victorian period. Scholars are agreed that this gave Scottish industrialists a strategic cost advantage, even if the Anglo-Scottish gap narrowed somewhat in the later nineteenth century. Scottish wages were low in comparison to the average for the United Kingdom in iron and steel, shipbuilding, cotton and brewing, according to data for the 1880s.[46] In the crucial sectors of iron and steel and shipbuilding, the Scottish average was £70 per annum compared to £76 for the United Kingdom. In textiles there was an even more entrenched system of low pay, based on the widespread employment of female labour. By the 1880s two-thirds of the 100,000 workforce in textiles were women. The cottonmasters in the west had embarked on a strategy of

45. Devine, *Scottish Nation*, pp. 259–60.
46. Campbell, *Rise and Fall of Scottish Industry*, pp. 76–91.

hiring low-paid women operating self-acting mules rather than men, while in Dundee the employment of poorly paid female labour was the city's first line of defence against the growing threat of Indian competition. Any bottleneck in recruitment to the collieries was also eliminated in two stages. The first was the ending of collier serfdom by legislation in 1775 and 1799. These measures were not enacted in a spirit of philanthropic benevolence but rather to recruit more labour, destroy the collier trade unions or 'brotherhoods' and keep wage claims in check. The second was through the increase in Irish immigration, which helped to solve any problem of labour shortage in the long term as coal production grew rapidly after c. 1820. There is little doubt that the swelling coal and iron communities of Lanarkshire and Ayrshire depended heavily on the Irish as production levels escalated spectacularly. In 1861 in Coatbridge, fewer than half of the colliers and miners were Scots-born. The rest were Irish migrants.

It was not simply the cost and availability of labour that was of critical importance to these great staple industries. Also of relevance was the response of the workforce. By the early twentieth century, trade unionism was expanding and labour relations became more tense. This was symbolised by the foundation of the Scottish Trades Union Congress in 1897. But the later image of 'Red Clydeside' did not fit the west of Scotland at all in earlier decades. The Glasgow Cotton Spinners' Union had successfully resisted the introduction of self-acting spinning mules, but in the strike of 1837 and the aftermath it was effectively destroyed and never again represented a threat to innovation. There were stoppages among Clydeside engineering and shipyard workers in the 1860s and again in the 1880s and Dundee female jute workers did strike at regular intervals. However, William Knox has concluded that 'trade unionism was all but wiped out in the shipbuilding and mining industries' during the 1860s.[47] Union membership was low by the standards of England and Wales and there was a much stronger tradition of small, local unions with few members and little muscle. Demarcation disputes were common, especially in metals, shipbuilding and building, and this occupational sectionalism was aggravated by sectarian tensions between Irish Catholics and Protestant Scots workers. For these reasons Scottish labour seemed both cheap and docile. It was because of this perception that the American Singer Sewing Machine Company was primarily attracted to Clydebank in 1900, where its factory soon

47. W. Know, 'The political and workplace culture of the Scottish working class, 1832–1914', in Fraser and Morris (eds), *People and Society*, p. 147.

achieved the capability of turning out 13,000 sewing machines a week. In general, during the golden years of the Scottish economic miracle the employers held the whip hand. Some, like the Bairds and the Neilsons, were resolutely opposed to trade unions as an unmitigated evil and virtually all of them took a hard line in industrial disputes, sometimes pooling their strength in such alliances as the Shipbuilders' Employers Federation, the National Association of Master Builders and the East of Scotland Association of Engineers. Edward Young reported to the United States Congress in 1872 that the Clydeside workers 'must work for a mere pittance, to enable his employer to sell his goods abroad at low rates, or there will be no work for him to do, and he will be left to starve'. He added that the world-wide success of Clyde-built ships was to be explained in the final analysis by 'the abundance of skilled workmen and the low wages paid to them'.[48]

A FLAWED ECONOMIC REVOLUTION?

Some look back on the Victorian economy with nostalgia. The nine-teenth century was a time when the great Scottish industries were not only owned by Scots but sent their products to all corners of the globe. Scotland was truly a force to be reckoned with in the world economy and had achieved a position of manufacturing supremacy out of all proportion to the small size of its domestic population. All this is in sharp contrast to the pattern in the new millennium. Scottish owner-ship of much of manufacturing industry has virtually disappeared, the nation's prosperity seemingly depends on the fickle decisions of overseas investors and Scotland is often dismissed as a 'branch economy' controlled by external forces over which there is little indigenous political control. Yet the temptation to glorify the Victorian and Edwardian economy should be resisted. It was seriously flawed in two respects: first, its impact on the welfare and standard of life of the Scottish people and second, the emergence of structural economic weaknesses which had a potent effect on the nation's industrial crisis after the First World War.

A handful of families did make colossal fortunes from the profits of the export industries. Sir Charles Tenant of the chemical empire, William Baird, the ironmaster, Sir James and Peter Coats of the thread-making dynasty and William Weir, colliery owner and iron manufacturer,

48. *Labour in Europe and America* (Washington, DC, 1876).

were among the forty individuals in Britain reckoned to be worth £2 million or more between 1809 and 1914. In addition to these fabulously wealthy but exceptional tycoons, there were the solid ranks of the prosperous middle classes, which ranged in occupational status from highly paid professionals, such as lawyers and doctors, to small business-men and senior clerks. In his analysis of national income, published in 1867, the Victorian economist R. Dudley Baxter reckoned that the 267,300 people in this group in Scotland had an annual income of between £100 and £1,000 and represented nearly one-fifth of the total number of what he termed 'productive persons' in the country.[49] The impact of the spending of this middle class could be seen in the elegant suburbs that blossomed around the major cities in the nineteenth century, Broughty Ferry near Dundee, the graceful terraces of the West End of Glasgow and the substantial villas of Newington and Corstorphine in Edinburgh. The extraordinary increases in the outflow of capital from Scotland after 1870 was also in part a reflection of the increases in savings among the Scottish middle classes. For instance, in the two decades after 1870, Scottish investment in Australia grew ninefold. Most of this came through Scottish solicitors and chartered accountants raising funds on behalf of overseas clients from professional and business families at home. It was said that Edinburgh in the 1880s was 'honeycombed' with the agents of these companies who were the main channel for this substantial mobilisation of middle-class capital.[50] Middle incomes were on average fewer and lower than in London and the metropolitan area of the south, but in the early twentieth century were on a par with the major English industrial centres of Lancashire and Yorkshire.

The picture is, however, somewhat gloomier for the rest of the population. Scotland was a grossly unequal society in the heyday of its industrial success. Baxter's calculations for 1867 suggest that around 70 per cent of 'productive persons', or almost a million people in total, belonged to his two bottom categories of 'lower skilled' and 'unskilled' which consisted of male workers who earned on average below £50 per annum.[51] For many at this level, short-term unemployment was always a threat. Shipbuilding and other capital goods industries were subject to intense and savage fluctuation in 1884–7, 1894, 1903–5 and 1908. In this last year, unemployment among Clydeside skilled engineers rose to

49. Smout, *Century of the Scottish People*, pp. 109, 111.
50. E. Richards, 'Australia and the Scottish connection, 1788–1914', in Cage (ed.), *Scots Abroad*, p. 145.
51. Smout, *Century of the Scottish People*, pp. 109, 111.

nearly 20 per cent and among shipyard workers to almost a quarter. In the four cities there were large pools of seasonal and casual labour, reckoned in the early 1900s at around a quarter of the workforce, who were engaged in jobs such as portering, catering and street-selling and whose earnings were both paltry and unpredictable.

Previous discussion demonstrated that for most of the period between 1830 and 1914 Scottish industrial wage rates were lower than the English average. The Board of Trade estimated in 1912 that real wages (after taking into account living costs) were fully 10 per cent less in Scottish towns than in their counterparts in England. Living costs on the other hand were higher. For Glasgow, recent work by Richard Rodger has shown that the city's inhabitants paid on average over 5 per cent more for their food and rent (which accounted for four-fifths of the weekly working-class budget) than the population of Manchester, Leeds, Salford and Nottingham – and this against a background of low wages and volatile levels of employment on Clydeside.[52] There was an irony here. In the earlier period low wages were perceived as a key element in Scottish industrialisation. In the longer term, however, the low-wage system and the striking inequalities in income imposed powerful constraints on Scottish diversification by the later nineteenth century, when both the domestic consumer market and service industries were becoming more significant in mature economies elsewhere in Europe, England and North America.

That Victorian industry was not a source of general prosperity is confirmed by the examples of Scottish migration and housing in this period. Precisely at the time when manufacturing was achieving re-markable success in overseas markets the Scots were leaving their native land in huge numbers for the USA, Canada and Australasia. Not far short of 2 million people emigrated from Scotland overseas between 1830 and 1939, a rate of outward movement that was around one and half times that of England and Wales. This did not include another 600,000 who moved south of the border. The haemorrhage was so great that it placed Scotland near the top of the European emigration league, along with Ireland and Norway. In the years of massive outward movement, such as 1904–13, when more than 600,000 people left, Scotland achieved the unenviable position of topping this table, with the highest emigration rate of any country in Europe. Again, in the 1850s, the loss of young men through emigration was considerably greater than in the years of human

52. R. Rodger, 'The labour force', in W. H. Fraser and I. Maver (eds), *Glasgow*, vol. II: *1830–1912* (Manchester: Manchester University Press, 1996), pp. 163–85.

carnage during the First World War. Scotland was one of the few European countries which experienced both large-scale industrialisation and a great outward movement of population. Most other societies prone to high levels of emigration were poor rural economies. It seemed that many Scots were voting with their feet in the search for better prospects than were easily available to them at home.[53]

The condition of working-class housing in Scotland provoked endless investigation and comment by the early twentieth century. From these surveys it is abundantly clear that there was little real progress made between 1870 and 1914. Clive Lee has concluded that:

[B]y the eve of the First World War Scotland stood on the brink of a housing catastrophe. In 1911 nearly 50 per cent of the Scottish population lived in one or two roomed dwellings compared with just over 7 per cent in England. Rents were significantly higher north of the Border, 1905, 10 per cent greater than in Northumberland and Durham and almost 25 per cent higher than the other English midland and northern counties. Over two million Scots in 1914, nearly half the population, lived more than two persons to a room, the contemporary definition of 'overcrowding'.[54]

The housing problem reflected the reality of low and fluctuating incomes. For families on limited earnings it made economic sense to take small tenement flats at a rental sufficiently affordable to avoid arrears or eviction. The problem was not so much availability of reasonable housing as the ability of very many to pay for it. In 1914, for instance, in Glasgow alone there were over 20,000 unoccupied houses, or about a tenth of the city's total stock. The housing crisis was the most striking manifestation of the depth of Glasgow's acute problems of poverty in the very decade when it proclaimed itself the 'Second City of the Empire'.

The achievements of Victorian industry have to be acknowledged. It was indeed a remarkable feat for a small country to dominate key sectors of the world's economy for much of the nineteenth century. In addition, the huge expansion of manufacturing and mining provided countless new jobs for Scotland's growing population. But the limitations of the success should also be recognised. The low incomes and widespread

53. T. M. Devine, 'The paradox of Scottish emigration', in T. M. Devine (ed.), *Scottish Emigration and Scottish Society* (Edinburgh: John Donald, 1992), pp. 1–15.
54. C. H. Lee, *Scotland and the United Kingdom* (Manchester: Manchester University Press, 1995), p. 46.

poverty that prevailed despite industrial growth placed Scotland at a strategic disadvantage in the twentieth century when home demand for household goods, motor cars and cycles, furniture and electrical products became critical to continued economic growth. The weakness of consumer-based and service industries and the specialist concentration on ships, locomotives, bridges, rolling stock and iron work in the manufacturing areas of the west of Scotland proved with hindsight to be a fatal flaw in the Victorian economy, which had tragic consequences in the inter-war period.

Even before 1914, the structure seemed dangerously vulnerable. The country relied more on heavy industry than the United Kingdom as a whole. The 1901 Census of Production showed that 30.6 per cent of Scottish output was accounted for by shipbuilding, iron, steel and engineering compared to 21.3 per cent for the UK. Moreover, these heavy industries were all interrelated, geared to overseas demand, especially in the Empire, and clearly at risk from international competition from nations such as the United States and Germany. It was inevitable, given their population size and great resources, that they would in time become formidable industrial powers. When half a continent starts to develop, it can produce much more than a small country, no matter how skilled and innovative the latter might be. The threat was especially potent because Scots excelled in the manufacture of *basic* capital goods, many of whose production methods could be rapidly imitated by overseas competitors. In addition, the resource endowment which had helped to give Scotland a cutting edge was already weakening by 1914. In the 1870s, over 2 million tons of iron ore was being mined annually. By 1913 this had slumped to 590,000 tons per year. Coal supplies remained plentiful, but in Lanarkshire the richest seams were fast becoming exhausted. The result was higher costs. In the west of Scotland there was substantial investment in coal-cutting machinery, but even this failed to prevent a dramatic fall in labour productivity.

Problems also emerged in iron and steel. Scottish iron ore had a high phosphorous content and hence was not well suited to the malleable iron production essential for steel-making. It therefore became a feature of Scottish metal industries that iron production and steel-making were separate activities. In 1900 only three of fifteen steelworks were integrated with blast furnaces. The fragmented process of production and the weakness of integrated plants led to higher costs than those of competitors and hence to a structure which cost the industry dear in the 1920s and 1930s. Of greater concern was the position of shipbuilding because the orders for the steel mills and the engineering shops of the west of Scotland crucially depended on the prosperity of the Clyde yards. Superficially, all seemed well. In the years before 1914 record tonnages were launched and the reputation for technical innovation remained intact. But those historians who have scrutinised the business records of the big firms have detected two disturbing trends.[55] First, due to competition, not least from the north-east of England, many vessels were being constructed at a loss, and this condition of 'profitless prosperity' was becoming more common in the years before the First World War. Second, some major yards, such as John Brown's and Fairfield's, became committed to the building of battleships, cruisers and destroyers for the Admiralty. It was a profitable and apparently secure strategy in the era of the naval arms race, but it could prove much less sensible in different political circumstances. Both these problems could be contained in the short term. Grave problems might emerge, however, for the heavy industrial complex as a whole if shipbuilding, the foundation of the entire structure, suffered for a longer period. On the eve of the Great War that still seemed a remote prospect. In fact, it was a deep irony that, though wartime demand inevitably gave a remarkable stimulus to Scottish manufacturing in the short term, the longer-term consequences were much less benign.

During the years 1914–18 Scottish industry became a vast military arsenal for the greatest conflict in human history. Unrestricted submarine warfare later in the war destroyed the equivalent of nearly a third of the pre-1914 merchant fleet and generated a prodigious new source of demand for the shipbuilding yards of the Clyde. Engineering and metal production were diverted to the mass production of guns and shells. The linen and woollen districts of Scotland supplied huge amounts of canvas for tenting and clothing for troops. Trench warfare, the enduring image of the Great War, would have been impossible, for instance, without sandbags made from Dundee jute. By 1918 one thousand million of them had been shipped to the fronts in Europe. In the same year the Clyde Valley became the single most important concentration of munitions production in the United Kingdom with the great heavy industries of the region under government control, regulation or direction. Some areas of mining and manufacturing activity lost out. The Border tweed industry was hit when its sources of yarn in Belgium were cut off. The eastern coalfield, which had been enjoying dynamic growth before 1914, suffered through the loss of the German and Baltic markets and the Admiralty's decision to requisition the Forth coal ports.

Overall, however, the Great War intensified Scottish reliance on a narrow range of great industries which were often interdependent. A vulnerable economy had become even more exposed.[56]

FURTHER READING

Campbell, R. H., *Scotland since 1707: The Rise of an Industrial Society* (Oxford: Basil Blackwell, 1965).

Campbell, R. H., *The Rise and Fall of Scottish Industry, 1707–1939* (Edinburgh: John Donald, 1980).

Checkland, S. G., *The Upas Tree: Glasgow 1875–1975 – and After, 1975–1980* (Glasgow: University of Glasgow Press, 1981).

Fraser, W. H., and Maver, I. (eds), *Glasgow*, vol. II: *1830–1912* (Manchester: Manchester University Press, 1996).

Lee, C. H., *Scotland and the United Kingdom: The Economy and the Union in the Twentieth Century* (Manchester: Manchester University Press, 1995).

Lee, C. H., 'The Scottish economy and the First World War', in C. M. M. Macdonald and E. W. McFarland (eds), *Scotland and the Great War* (East Linton: Tuckwell Press, 1999), pp. 11–35.

Lenman, B., *An Economic History of Modern Scotland, 1660–1976* (London: B. T. Batsford, 1977).

Payne, P. L., *Growth and Contraction: Scottish Industry, c. 1860–1990* (Dundee: Economic and Social History Society of Scotland, 1992).

Slaven, A., *The Development of the West of Scotland* (London: Routledge and Kegan Paul, 1975).

Whatley, C. A., *The Industrial Revolution in Scotland* (Cambridge: Cambridge University Press, 1997).

56. C. H. Lee, 'The Scottish economy and the First World War', in C. M. M. Macdonald and E. W. McFarland (eds), *Scotland and the Great War* (East Linton: Tuckwell Press, 1999), pp. 11–35.

CHAPTER THREE

The Transformation of Agriculture: Cultivation and Clearance

T. M. Devine

INTRODUCTION

Industrialisation and agricultural transformation in Scotland were two sides of the same coin. So closely connected were the two movements that unravelling the complex texture of inter-relationships is a challenging task. On the one hand, the remarkable rise of industrial and urban employments in the eighteenth century created a much enlarged market of non-food producers, which in turn generated a massive new demand for the produce of Scottish farms. It was apparently this factor above all else which provided the crucial incentive for investment and innovation in the new husbandry from the middle decades of the eighteenth century.[1] Equally, however, agriculture itself was also one of the primary foundations of the Industrial Revolution. Without radical increase in the production of both foods and raw materials from within Scotland until the early nineteenth century, the whole process of rapid economic growth might have stalled.

In theory, of course, the emerging industrial communities could have increasingly purchased their vital food needs from abroad. By the 1790s, for instance, imports of oats and oatmeal from Ireland were reckoned to be feeding around 40,000 Scots (or 2.5 per cent of the population), most of whom lived in the industrialising west of the country.[2] But foreign imports were no panacea in these critically important early decades of

1. T. M. Devine, *The Transformation of Rural Scotland: Social Change and the Agrarian Economy, 1660–1815* (Edinburgh: Edinburgh University Press, 1994), pp. 35–41.
2. L. D. Cochran, *Scottish Trade with Ireland in the Eighteenth Century* (Edinburgh: John Donald, 1985), p. 97.

the economic revolution. For one thing, the outbreak of the French Wars meant that continental Europe ceased to be a significant source of grain supply for Scotland after 1795. For another, Ireland was never more than a marginal exporter of meal to the Scottish market and, occasionally, as in 1800, when the Irish ports were closed, ceased to have much real significance.[3] Only from the second decade of the nineteenth century did imports from overseas once again become important. Until then, at least, the success of the industrial economy depended in large part on the response of indigenous agriculture and its related activities. Vast increases in grain, animal and raw material production were delivered. Over a sixty-year period from the 1750s, the estimated output of corn and green crops in the Lothians doubled and that of slaughtered animals rose sixfold.[4] One other telling indicator of the cycle of growth in grain output was the spectacular advance in the quantity of malting barley charged for duty. In 1809–10, 784,527 bushels were produced in Scotland; by 1840 the figure was over 4.3 millions.[5] Pastoral farming was also remarkably buoyant, most notoriously in the Highlands, where the rapid expansion of sheep numbers was often marked by the widespread displacement of many communities. To take but one county example, Argyll had 278,000 sheep in 1800, 827,000 in 1855 and over a million by 1880.[6] The seas around Scotland were also exploited on an unprecedented scale. By the 1820s great fleets of over 3,000 boats would gather for the annual herring fishery along the east coast from the northern tip of Caithness to Buchan in Aberdeenshire. Catches rose relentlessly from over 100,000 barrels cured in 1812–15 to around 600,000 barrels by the early 1850s.[7]

This varied revolution in production brought many benefits to the process of industrialisation. More labour could now be released from the cultivation of food to the manufacture of goods and the provision of services. Grain prices did rise, especially between 1795 and 1812 and particularly in years of poor harvests. Crucially, however, food prices did not go through the roof. Indeed, as already shown in Chapter 2, real wages actually rose for the majority in most years between c. 1770 and

---

3.　T. M. Devine and G. Jackson (eds), *Glasgow*, vol. I: *Beginning to 1830* (Manchester: Manchester University Press, 1985), p. 231.
4.　L. J. Saunders, *Scottish Democracy: The Social and Intellectual Background, 1815–1840* (Edinburgh: Oliver and Boyd, 1950), p. 37.
5.　S. G. E. Lythe and J. Butt, *An Economic History of Scotland, 1100–1939* (Glasgow: Blackie and Son, 1975), p. 131.
6.　E. Richards, *A History of the Highland Clearances*, vol. I (London: Croom Helm, 1982), p. 176.
7.　M. Gray, *The Fishing Industries of Scotland, 1790–1914* (Oxford: Oxford University Press, 1978), pp. 39–58.

c. 1800, thus increasing the domestic market for producers of consumer goods. Furthermore, as a result of the energetic response from Scottish farmers, a rising and increasingly urbanised population had less need to rely on foreign food imports. Such a dependency might have placed pressure on the balance of payments by leading in turn to an outflow of cash to pay for grain, higher interest rates in the banking system and a general slowdown in economic activity.

The Scottish countryside was also a key source of raw materials for industry. Certainly, cotton and, to a lesser extent, linen, depended crucially on external supplies of wool and flax respectively but elsewhere indigenous supplies were vital. The woollen industry relied on the great sheep ranches of the Borders and the Highlands. Timber was used for building, internal furnishings, pit-props for the burgeoning mining industry and a host of other activities. The inland transport of goods and people would have been impossible without the thousands of horses bred on Scottish farms annually, not least the Clydesdale, regarded as the best heavy draught horse of its day. Animal carcasses provided hides for the tanners, bone for the glue-makers and fats for soap and candle manufacturers. Straw was universally used for packaging and as litter in urban stables. Taken together, all this represented a factor of strategic significance in industrial expansion. Without agricultural transform-ation, then, the Scottish economic miracle in general might have been jeopardised.

THE RURAL LOWLANDS: BEFORE IMPROVEMENT, 1700–C. 1750

In order to appreciate fully the scale and speed of agricultural trans-formation it is necessary to place it in historical context by providing a brief sketch of the traditional farming regime. Traditionally, Scottish agriculture before the era of widespread Improvement has had a bad press. It was seen as inert in structure, primitive in technique and wasteful of both land and labour. 'Improving' writers of the later eigh-teenth century waxed eloquent about the supposedly absurd defects of techniques such as the 'infield/outfield' system of cultivation, the basic form of agricultural organisation throughout the old order in Scotland. The infield was the best land, worked continuously and given an almost 'gardenly' care. Outfield land was poorer and more extensive, cultivated for shorter periods. But these later commentators were far from objec-tive. They had a vested interest in praising the new and condemning the old. Essentially, the 'improving' writers saw themselves as propagandists for more 'enlightened' farming practices and tended to select evidence skilfully to support and promote their cause.[8]

Modern research on estate archives and other contemporary sources has helped to provide a more realistic picture of traditional agriculture.[9] First, in broad terms, it met the essential food needs of Scottish society at the time. After the horrors of the 'Lean Years' of the 1690s, there were some difficult times in 1709, 1724–5 and again in 1740–41 but no major harvest crisis. Compare this with the record in Ireland, where famines in the early 1740s are reckoned to have killed an even larger proportion of the population than 'the Great Hunger' a century later.[10] Second, the cultivation methods so vehemently condemned by later writers had a basic rationale at the time. For instance, the universal practice of ploughing the land into long 'rigs' (or ridges), where the crops were grown and which were divided by deep furrows was essential for draining off surface water when there was no alternative system before underground tile pipes became common in the nineteenth century. Similarly, the splitting of land into strips and patches and the distribution of small plots to tenants, subtenants and cottars may have seemed illogical from a later perspective, but were vital in order to provide families with some ground for meeting their own needs for food. The communal working practices of the time, which involved everything from house-building to peat-cutting, were an effective way of pooling the labour power of men, women and children when virtually every job had to be done by hand and 'technology' was mainly confined to tools like the spade, sickle and flail. A communal approach was also favoured in the management of outfields. Each year, different parts rested as others were brought under the plough. The process could work effectively only if there were some planning and common controls, so that different tenants followed an agreed sequence each year of breaking land in or deciding to return it to pasture. A similar strategy was adopted to prevent overgrazing by allocating each tenant a given number of animals through the practice known as 'stenting' or 'souming'. Regulation and co-operation had to be at the heart of the old system.

Third, Lowland agriculture before the 1750s was far from being static

---

8. T. M. Devine, *The Scottish Nation, 1700–2000* (Harmondsworth: Allen Lane/The Penguin Press, 1999), pp. 124–5.
9. See, inter alia, Devine, *Transformation of Rural Scotland*, pp. 1–35; R. A. Dodgshon, *Land and Society in Early Scotland* (Oxford: Oxford University Press, 1981); A. Fenton, *Scottish Country Life* (Edinburgh, John Donald, 1976); I. D. Whyte, *Agriculture and Society in Seventeenth Century Scotland* (Edinburgh: John Donald, 1979). The following paragraphs are based on these key sources.
10. C. Ó'Gráda, *The Great Irish Famine* (Cambridge: Cambridge University Press, 1989).

or inflexible. In some areas, a changing balance developed between each part of the system, with outfield expanding at the expense of infield as farmers and proprietors took advantage of the booming droving trade to England and the Scottish towns to lay down more land to pasture for stock fattening. In addition, in the main arable districts of the Lowlands, especially the Lothians and Berwickshire, infield systems had become more sophisticated, with four-course rotations of wheat, bere (a hardy form of barley), oats and legumes. Liming had also steadily been adopted by more and more tenants during the seventeenth century; it helped to break down the acidity in the soil and was especially valuable in helping to open up areas of outfield to regular cultivation. The early systematic use of lime for this purpose can be traced back to the 1620s and, by the early eighteenth century, liming had become a common feature of Scottish Lowland agriculture. Through regular application, tenants in areas particularly well endowed for grain growing were able to expand their infields at the expense of outfields and specialise more in arable agriculture. Thus in Roxburgh and Berwick by the early eighteenth century, outfield cultivation had become much more intensive, with two-thirds under crop on some estates. In outline, this was a trend towards the unified pattern of cultivation which was eventually to become characteristic of improved agriculture.

Fourth, the social organisation of the old countryside was more complex than often suggested.[11] The basic community unit was the *ferm-toun*, small settlements of little more than fifteen to twenty households dispersed across a countryside virtually bereft of the hedges, ditches, dikes, roads or any of the other artificial constructions of the modern rural landscape. The touns varied widely in size. In more developed areas of the Lothians and Berwickshire they were big enough to seem like villages. Elsewhere, they were as few as half a dozen families living in settlements apparently randomly scattered across land where patches of arable were separated by bigger stretches of bog and moorland. These clusters of people all had their own internal hierarchies. The rent-paying élite were at the top and then ranked below them were subtenants and cottars (given patches of land in return for seasonal work in the larger holdings), together with full-time farm servants and a range of tradesmen, blacksmiths, weavers and shoemakers, who supplied many of the needs of the local community.

---

11. M. Gray, 'The social impact of agrarian change in the rural Lowlands', in T. M. Devine and R. Mitchison (eds), *People and Society in Scotland*, vol. I: *1760–1830* (Edinburgh: John Donald, 1988), pp. 53–7.

Significant changes were already taking place within this ancient structure before c. 1750. The tenant class was steadily contracting in size, with thrusting individuals bettering themselves at the expense of others by absorbing more land in the townships. The most significant illustration of this trend was the expansion of holdings held by one tenant and a fall in the number of farms possessed by several husbandmen. The enlarged single tenancy was geared more to serving markets and less constrained by communal working practices, and the farm under one master was to become the ideal of the Improvers later in the eighteenth century. A study of a wide sample of holdings in five Lowland counties suggests that more than half the farms were still in 'multiple tenancy' at the time of the Union of 1707.[12] However, in the next few decades this form of tenure was seen to be in rapid decline. Indeed, in most of the estates examined, single tenancy was overwhelmingly dominant by the 1740s, with only around one-fifth of all holdings now containing two or more possessors. Within the old world, therefore, an embryonic rural middle class was emerging in some areas.[13]

The impact of the 'new' tenantry was nowhere more apparent than in the Borders, where great sheep ranches with large areas of hill grazing and limited arable holdings in the valleys were already well established in the eastern counties by the late seventeenth century. One result of this territorial expansion was the unrelenting squeezing out of the rural population. Abandoned remains of touns which were inhabited into the early eighteenth century can be found throughout the Tweed valley and in Eskdale. Similarly, a number of the parish entries for this region in the *Statistical Account* of the 1790s describe once-populated settlements which were now visible only as mouldering remains. Over a hundred years before the Highland Clearances, the advance of the commercialised sheep farms in the deep south of Scotland was causing widespread depopulation. In the western Borders, for instance, Sir David Dunbar at Baldoon, near Wigtown, built a huge cattle park over two and a half miles long and one and a half in breadth to winter over a thousand beasts. Dunbar was only one of several Borders proprietors who let their estates to commercially minded tenants for specialist stock-rearing.[14]

There is considerable evidence, therefore, that the old farming had an intrinsic effectiveness, by and large served the food needs of the time

---

12. Devine, *Transformation of Rural Scotland*, pp. 4–29.
13. Ibid., pp. 25–9.
14. R. A. Dodgshon, 'Agricultural change and its social consequences in the Southern Uplands of Scotland, 1660–1850', in T. M. Devine and D. Dickson (eds), *Ireland and Scotland, 1600–1850* (Edinburgh: John Donald, 1983), pp. 46–59.

well and was also capable of flexibility and adjustment. It has to be remembered, however, that the vast majority of Scots still lived and worked in the countryside in this period. Most of the population were both food producers and consumers rather than (as was to be the case in the later era of urbanisation and industrialisation) simply consumers of farm produce. Even modest improvements in efficiency or marketing could therefore satisfy contemporary needs by adding to grain surpluses. This is shown clearly in the broad stability of meal prices in most years during the first half of the eighteenth century. In addition, despite advances in cultivation, crop yields remained relatively low. On the best infield lands, yields of four seeds to one might be obtained but on the outfields the averages remained well below three to one.[15]

Production for the market was on the increase but the subsistence needs of the family and locality still took priority in most areas. The preponderance of small farms of below 30 acres in size in many districts and the widespread custom of splitting land into small patches as sub-sistence plots for subtenants and cottars tends to confirm this pattern.[16] Further, despite some significant changes in the social structure of the farming communities, notably among the tenantry, the rural landscape had altered little in most areas outside the more favoured Lothians region. Estate maps of the 1750s still show the old familiar patterns of scattered infields and outfields, rig cultivation, absence of enclosed fields and large areas of moor and bog land. It was a landscape which had still more in common with that of earlier centuries than with the age of improvement when the countryside was transformed forever.

THE RURAL LOWLANDS: TRANSFORMATION

It was the historic changes in the markets for grain, animal products and raw materials which above all else shaped the transformation of the rural economy. The Scottish population rose by two-thirds from 1,265,000 in c. 1755 to over 2 millions by 1820. The unprecedented speed and scale of urban development, noted in Chapter 2, created a huge increase in the number of Scots who had to buy food rather than grow it for themselves. Rising living standards in the later eighteenth century, especially for the

---

15. A. J. S. Gibson and T. C. Smout, *Prices, Food and Wages in Scotland, 1550–1780* (Cambridge: Cambridge University Press, 1995), pp. 162–84; Devine, *Transformation of Rural Scotland*, p. 55.
16. I. D. Whyte and K. A. Whyte, 'Some aspects of the structure of rural society in seventeenth century Lowland Scotland', in Devine and Dickson (eds), *Ireland and Scotland*, pp. 32–45.

middle, artisan and professional classes, deepened market demand for rural produce and at the same time made it more diverse.[17] Grain prices soared, even in counties not at the centre of the new industrialism. For instance, average prices for oats in Fife for the years 1765–70 were 56 per cent higher than for the period 1725–50, while those for 1805–10 showed a further staggering increase of 300 per cent. There was now a much greater incentive for landlords and farmers to invest and experiment, especially since the revolution in rural transport, with the construction of parish and turnpike roads, canals and, eventually, railways, brought the new class of urban and industrial consumers ever closer to the producer.

But we also need to probe the reasons why the rural communities in the Lowlands managed to respond so vigorously to these market opportunities.[18] At least in the first phase of Improvement down to the early nineteenth century, landowners and their factors were at the heart of the process. Their basic advantage was that in most parts of the Lowlands, outside some districts in the south-west, land was worked through tenancies governed by leases. Peasant proprietors were few and far between. Scottish landowners therefore possessed full legal rights of eviction at the end of a fixed-term lease which gave influence not only over the changing composition of the tenantry but also the power to build in mandatory improving clauses which were enforceable at law. Contemporary court records show that many landowners routinely used legal muscle to force the adoption of new cropping practices. The very fact that the leaders of the old society as a class were such enthusiastic supporters and proponents of the new economic order was itself of profound significance because it lent a crucial legitimacy to the whole course of agrarian reform.

Perhaps three main reasons can be advanced to explain why Scotland's landed élites embraced the new agronomy so eagerly. First, the costs of landed status were rising steeply in the eighteenth century, an era which has been rightly described as one of competitive display when higher social position was increasingly defined by material status. The aristocracy and many of the lairds now aspired to standards of unprecedented splendour with grander houses, more elaborate furnishings and decoration and impressive estate parklands which were meant to convey the

17. S. Nenadic, 'The rise of the urban middle classes', in Devine and Mitchison (eds), *People and Society in Scotland*, pp. 111–13.
18. The following paragraphs summarise the arguments in Devine, *Transformation of Rural Scotland*, pp. 36–110, and M. Gray, 'Scottish emigration: the social impact of agrarian change in the rural Lowlands, 1775–1875', *Perspectives in American History*, 7 (1973), pp. 113–31.

special standing of their owners. To this Revolution of Manners was added new demographic pressures as landed families became bigger and both costs of education for sons and dowries for daughters rose accordingly. Scottish landowners, traditionally among the poorer élites of Europe, had to search for fresh sources of income.

Second, the Scottish intellectual revolution of the time fed through into agrarian reform as the rationalism of the Enlightenment helped to change humankind's relationship to the environment. No longer was nature accepted as given or preordained; instead, it could and should be altered for the better or 'Improved' by systematic intervention. Improvement became not simply a matter of vital material concern but an intellectual movement which soon attracted a veritable army of theorists, propagandists and commentators. A crucial conduit between the world of ideas in the universities and the practical business of radically changing farming routines was the new class of estate factors, many of them were university-trained lawyers who had sat in the lecture rooms of such giants of the Scottish Enlightenment as Adam Smith, Francis Hutchison, Adam Ferguson and John Millar and others.

Third, the role of new men and new money in the landed structure should not be underestimated. English historians are now generally sceptical about the central relationship between Empire and economic growth in this period. But the impact of imperial profits may have been more significant in Scotland, where alternative sources of income were still more limited than south of the border and where the involvement in empire of the sons of lairds, merchants and professionals was, on average, so much greater.[19] Many of these adventurers were sojourners who went overseas to try to make their fortunes and then return home with capital to buy land or invest in the estates of their own families. Some, probably a minority, did achieve great success. Thus by 1815, the counties around Glasgow were ringed by the properties of the city's tobacco lords and sugar princes while, in parts of the Borders, Highland and eastern Lowlands, returning Indian 'nabobs' were conspicuous and colourful figures. Precise evaluation of their role awaits further research.

At the same time, the long-term contribution of the landed classes needs to be kept in perspective. Current knowledge suggests that their intervention was critical in the first phase of the agricultural revolution, broadly from the 1760s to the end of the century. Even during this period, however, the tenants who actually worked the land were moving

---

19. Linda Colley, *Britons: Forging the Nation* (New Haven: Yale University Press, 1992), pp. 122–39; D. Allan, *Scotland in the Eighteenth Century* (Harlow: Longman/Pearson Educational, 2002), pp. 165–85.

to centre stage and they became the dominant force from the 1790s. As noted earlier, even within the old order, a developing but potentially powerful business class was emerging within the farming community as more holdings were merged and larger single tenancies became more committed to servicing the market. In the later eighteenth century this process accelerated and, at the same time, improved methods spread as landowners invested in enclosure, new roads, liming and better farmhouses in return for increased rents. The speed of adaptation was remarkable, even given regional and local differences, as higher produce prices in most years during the Napoleonic Wars demonstrated the handsome profits that the new systems could now secure for both proprietors and many, if not all, farmers. For instance, in more than a third of parishes in four typical Lowland counties (Angus, Fife, Ayrshire and Lanarkshire) the traditional scattered patchwork of strips of land had already been gathered in the 1790s into compact fields divided by hedge and ditch. The process of rapid dissemination must also have been aided by the impressive standards of literacy among the rural communities since so much of the new knowledge was spread in printed form through a profusion of books, pamphlets and journals, which poured from the press.

The revolution that was fashioned by these varied forces and responses had many different facets. Perhaps the most fundamental was the change in orientation. The old world of subsistence farming crumbled and finally collapsed while the market by the early decades of the nineteenth century established virtual total dominance in most Lowland areas. Farms throughout the region became geared to satisfying the cities and towns for grain, butter, cheese, eggs, meat and a host of other articles ranging from sour milk for bleaching to timber for construction. The Lowlands had long been a complex mosaic of different farming traditions. In the era of Improvement, the distinctions became even sharper as the demand from the towns and industrial districts encouraged farmers to specialise more in what they did best in the light of local climatic and geological circumstances. Thus the clay lands of Ayrshire, Renfrewshire and western Lanarkshire became more significant as centres of dairying with the growth of commercial cheese- and butter-making for the booming centres of the Industrial Revolution. Around all of Scotland's major cities market gardening for potatoes, hay, grain and turnips to feed the teeming populations of the expanding urban areas also became more common. The south-east, including the counties of East Lothian, Fife, Berwick and Roxburgh, were traditionally the richest arable districts in Scotland. Their capacity was further enhanced by the rapid adoption of the new rotations, allowing intensive cropping of wheat and barley. The Borders, reaching northwards to the southern parishes of Lanarkshire and Ayrshire, had long specialised in sheep farming in the eastern and central parishes and cattle-rearing in the west. Now the region became more closely integrated with arable areas to the north and east, where the stocks were fattened for sale. Again, in the hill country of the central and eastern Lowlands, the pastoral farms were growing bigger and in the process forcing the removal of small tenants and cottars. There was a stream of complaints from parish ministers in the 1790s that social displacement and de-population were widespread in some of these districts. In the north-east counties, the balance of agricultural activity was also altering as additional stretches of land were laid down to grass and more and more farmers became committed to cattle breeding and fattening. It was an early sign of this region's emergence as an international centre of excellence for stock-rearing later in the nineteenth century and the home of the celebrated Aberdeen-Angus breed.

But the revolution also transformed the visual appearance of the countryside. By the 1840s a recognisably modern landscape of trim fields, compact farms, new roads and rural villages had emerged from the confused assortment of strips, rigs and open moor which had characterised the Lowlands since time immemorial. The new patterns were designed to maximise the productive capacity of the soil by bring-ing the land into a regular sequence of continuous cultivation through systematic fallowing and more effective rotations of crops. At the heart of the process were sharp increases in grain yields. The average oat yields in a sample of counties in the 1790s were around 10 to 13, more than triple late seventeenth-century returns. As the agricultural reporter William Fullarton noted in some astonishment of Ayrshire in 1793, 'the third of the farms in crop supplied double or treble the yield which had formerly been taken from the whole'.[20]

The key to this new agriculture was the more intensive application of traditional methods, such as fallowing and the lavish application of lime, coupled with the more 'modern' and innovative use of sown grasses and turnip husbandry. In the old system, regular cultivation had been confined to the relatively small area of the infield because of the limited supply of manure. Sown grasses, such as clover, dramatically increased the amount of fodder, allowed more beasts to be kept and produced more dung to be spread as fertiliser. By 1800, according to the *Statistical*

---

20. W. Fullarton, *General View of the Agriculture of the County of Ayr* (Edinburgh, 1793), p. 21.

Account, the majority of farms in the central and eastern Lowlands were using rotations incorporating sown grasses. Turnips were less common in the later eighteenth century, but in the long run they were to have even greater impact. For the first time they provided a heavy feeding crop which could be eaten on the fields. It therefore became possible even for farms that specialised in grain production to bring in animals from outside to be fattened and at the same time fertilise the arable land. It was a virtuous circle in which more beasts producing more dung added to the productivity of the soil, on which still more fodder crops could be cultivated. The system particularly appealed in Scotland, which, for reasons of climate and terrain, had tended to be more committed to pastoral husbandry. Now the areas of hill country and cattle and sheep farming were combined effectively with the lower-lying districts of arable agriculture. Particularly in areas north of the Tay and across the north-east counties of Banff, Kincardine and Aberdeen, turnip husbandry and cattle fattening became the primary foundations of the new system.

The continued drive for profit and ever more efficient methods of working the land also had profound human consequences. Apart from the new, lighter two-horse ploughs pioneered by James Small and others and the threshing machine, invented in 1787, new technology was of little relevance to the agricultural revolution before 1850. Only in the second half of the nineteenth century did the coming of the mechanical reaper and other labour-saving devices affect some areas of farm work. Before then all tasks of the farm depended on exhausting human effort: the daily drudgery of clearing the land, sowing, ploughing, reaping, weeding, gathering, milking, lifting and a host of other jobs. There was, therefore, a major drive to increase the productivity of labour by altering traditional habits of working and transforming the social position of entire social groups in the rural communities. All of this, the Improving writers argued, would produce material benefits in the long-run. In the short-term, however, these drastic social changes must also have made life harder and less secure for many on the land.[21]

The trend pre-1760 to single-tenant farms now accelerated as the remaining multiple tenancies were eliminated and many individual holdings were brought together under one farmer. In addition, an even more radical development ran parallel with the consolidation of farms. The cottar system of allocating small patches of land in return for labour

---

21.   T. M. Devine (ed.), *Farm Servants and Labour in Lowland Scotland, 1770–1914* (Edinburgh: John Donald, 1984), pp. 1–8.

services came under widespread attack. The dispossession of the cottars was deeply significant, as in several districts in the Lowlands they had comprised between one-third and one-half of the total number of inhabitants. Fundamentally, this ancient structure was in conflict with the new agrarian order. The old system was well suited to a regime where demand for labour tended to concentrate in brief periods in the year around tasks such as grain-harvesting and fuel-gathering. It was useful in these circumstances for farmers to have a reliable pool of labour which could be called upon in busy seasons and then laid off without any cash cost until required again. However, the needs of improved agriculture were different. The more intensive cultivation of the land, thorough ploughing, the adoption of new crops and of innovative rotations ensured that the working year started to lengthen. There was, on the whole, an evening out rather than an accentuation of seasonal labour requirements within mixed farming. Inevitably, this development favoured the hiring of full-time workers. These were sometimes married servants hired by the year but, more commonly, in most districts, were single male and female servants employed for six months. Only these groups were suited to the regular toil increasingly carried out in improved Lowland farms. Ironically, the married-servant class was similar to the cottars in several respects. They obtained a house, garden, fuel, the keep of a cow and other privileges as part of the wage reward. The crucial difference, however, was that they were full-time workers, entirely under the masters' control during their term of employment, and could be dismissed at the end of it.[22]

This position of subordination was crucial. While the independence of cottars can be exaggerated – they did possess land, but only in mere fragments, and they had to obtain work in larger holdings in order to make ends meet – they were obviously less subject to the discipline of the masters than full-time servants. But the new agriculture demanded much higher levels of labour efficiency. Tenants were under pressure from two sources. First, landowners were forcing up rentals in dramatic fashion, and, second, wages of agricultural workers were also rising from the 1770s, and especially from the 1790s, as industrial and urban expansion lured many from the country districts to the towns. One important response was the enforcement of policies designed to enhance the productivity of labour. The removal of the cottars can be seen in this context. In the most improved districts, where the old Scots plough was being replaced by James Small's plough, using a team of one man and

22. Ibid.

two horses, the clearest effect can be seen. Gradually the whole work routine centred on boosting the efficiency of the horses. Hours of labour and number of workers were closely related to the number of horse teams and their workrate. Ploughmen took responsibility for a particular pair, and their entire routine from early morning to evening was devoted to the preparation, working and final grooming of the animals. This system required that the ploughmen be permanent servants, boarded within the farm steading or in a cottage adjacent or close to their animals. The part-time labours of the cottars were now redundant as it became possible to tailor requirements to the numbers actually required for specific farm tasks.[23]

The continued contraction in size of the tenant-farming class as a result of consolidation and the removal of the cottars (which was all but complete in most areas by the 1820s) created an entirely new social order, in which only a tiny minority of the population had rights to land. The single exception in the Lowlands was the counties of the north-east region, where the development of crofting from the 1790s maintained the land connection for many well into the later nineteenth century. Elsewhere, landlessness was predominant.[24] In the agricultural communities a small number of rent-paying farmers, holding a lease for a given period, employed landless servants and labourers who were dependent entirely on selling their labour power. The sheer scale and speed of social and economic change in the Scottish countryside in this period is remarkable and is probably unique in a European context at this time. By the 1840s, improved agriculture had triumphed throughout the Lowlands, and Scottish farming, criticised for its backwardness in earlier years, had now become internationally renowned as a model of efficiency for others to follow. The historiography of the other major Scottish region, the Highlands, is quite different in tone and emphasis.

THE HIGHLANDS: CRISIS AND CLEARANCE

There is a long tradition in Scottish history of treating the Highlands as a case apart. Poor natural endowment, the survival of a tribal clan-based social system into the eighteenth century and a land where the people spoke Gaelic rather than English all suggest that the region was differ-

---

23. M. Gray, 'North east agriculture and the labour force, 1790–1875', in A. A. MacLaren (ed.), *Social Class in Scotland Past and Present* (Edinburgh: John Donald, 1976), pp. 99–100.
24. I. Carter, *Farm Life in Northeast Scotland, 1840–1914* (Edinburgh: John Donald, 1979), pp. 10–75.

ent. In some ways, indeed, it might be argued that the Highlands became even more obviously idiosyncratic during the age of transformation after c. 1750. While the Lowlands prospered and flourished on account of industrialisation and improved farming, the Highlands can be depicted as a region of failure, as self-evident proof that economic growth does not necessarily result in change for the better in all areas. In the first half of the nineteenth century, the Highlands suffered the trauma of widespread eviction of local communities (the Clearances), mass emigration and, in the 1840s, large-scale famine, which for a time threatened many thousands with starvation. The analytical issue for the historian of the Highlands tends to focus not on the reasons for success but on the causes of failure.[25]

From another perspective, however, and especially when the eighteenth-century evidence is considered, there were some striking similarities with the patterns already described for the Lowlands. True, the south and east of Scotland did not have to endure the punitive measures imposed by the British state on the Gaels after the failure of the last Jacobite rebellion in 1746. That apart, however, the main reasons for economic and social change were common to both the Highlands and Lowlands. Furthermore, as will be shown below, the Highland region responded positively at first to the new opportunities. Down to the early nineteenth century there seemed good cause for optimism.

Like the Lowlands, significant changes were already underway before the 1750s. Clanship was not frozen in time. Where commercial relationships were developing, the increased marketing of black cattle, fish and timber was proceeding apace and the new consumerism of the clan élites was becoming ever more manifest.[26] Again, in the Highlands as elsewhere in Scotland, the urban and industrial markets were the power engines of more fundamental change after c. 1760. Demand for traditional staples boomed. Cattle prices quadrupled in the course of the eighteenth century and total exports of cattle from the region probably quintupled. In Argyll and, albeit to a lesser extent, further north, commercial fishing of herring became even more significant with, for example, some 600–800 boats engaged annually in Loch Fyne alone. Due to changes in government revenue legislation and enhanced

---

25. This was the thrust of the first major modern study of Highland economic history, Malcolm Gray's *The Highland Economy, 1750–1850* (Edinburgh: Oliver and Boyd, 1957). Later scholars have usually followed Gray's lead. For a more positive view of the economic potential of the Highlands see Allan Macinnes, 'Scottish Gaeldom: the first phase of clearance', in Devine and Mitchison (eds), *People and Society in Scotland*, pp. 70–90.

26. A. I. Macinnes, *Clanship, Commerce and the House of Stuart, 1603–1788* (East Linton: Tuckwell Press, 1996).

Lowland markets, demand increased persistently for illicit whisky, and the exploitation of Highland slate quarries at Easdale and Ballachulish and elsewhere, and of woodland on many estates, continued apace. Textile production began to expand in Highland Perthshire, Argyll and eastern Inverness and in parts of Ross and Cromarty and Sutherland, and the production of linen cloth stamped for sale in the Highland counties rose steadily, from 21,972 yards in 1727–8 to 202,006 yards by 1778.

Southern industrialisation had an insatiable appetite for Highland raw materials in the later eighteenth century and there-after, with wool being in special demand. The Lowland cotton industry quickly achieved abundant supplies of raw fibre from the Caribbean and then from the southern USA, but it was more difficult for the woollen manufacturers. Overseas supply from Europe was limited and erratic during the Napoleonic Wars and it was only when Australia started to export in volume from the 1820s that overseas sources became really significant. In the interim, the gap was increasingly filled by Highland sheep farmers. In 1828 Scottish wool accounted for just under 10 per cent of UK output and for 25 per cent by the early 1840s.[27]

Equally significant for a time, though in different ways, was the manufacture of kelp, a calcined seaweed extract used in the manufacture of soap and glass. Industrial demand grew, not least because cheaper and richer sources of foreign barilla were curtailed during the French Wars and kelp production seemed well suited to the western Highlands and Islands, where the raw material was abundant. A cheap and plentiful supply of labour was vital since the process of production, though essentially a simple one, was very arduous with a ratio of one ton of kelp to 20 tons of collected seaweed. Kelp manufacture began in the west in the 1730s but not until after 1750 did it really begin to take hold: 2,000 tons per annum output were reached in the 1770s and 5,000 in 1790, and thereafter the industry boomed, achieving a peak production in 1810 of about 7,000 tons. By that date its main centres had become clearly established as the Uists, Barra, Harris, Lewis, Skye, Tiree and Mull, and on the mainland there was also considerable activity in Arnamurchan and Morvern. To a considerable extent, however, kelp production was concentrated in the Hebrides, especially in the Long Island; and there it had profound social consequences.

These responses to external markets give the lie to any suggestion that the Highlands were a conservative society, wedded to tradition

---

27. Richards, *History of the Highland Clearances*, p. 174.

and incapable of dynamic change.[28] In fact, the pace of development was actually faster in Gaeldom than elsewhere in Scotland as traditional society moved from tribalism to capitalism over less than two generations. The unprecedented rise in rentals – Skye rents trebled between 1775 and 1800 while those in some Wester Ross estates jumped tenfold over the period 1776 to 1805 – confirms that regional income was rising sharply. The Highlands were achieving a comparative advantage in the production of wool, mutton, fish, whisky, slate and kelp. Significant gains in productivity in key sectors can also be identified. The big sheep ranches of the north-west were the equals of the Lothians farms in their efficiency. The carcass weight of the beasts increased by an average of 60 per cent between 1799 and 1884, while the fleece weight was reckoned to have doubled between the 1790s and 1830s.[29]

Moreover, Highland lairds seemed little different from Lowland proprietors in their enthusiastic embrace of Improvement. Recent research has shown, for instance, how active the Highland élites were in profit-making across the Empire in the East and West Indies and the American colonies, and how much of this capital was channelled home to support ambitious schemes of Improvement on family estates.[30] As in the Lowlands, farm reorganisation and tenurial change were also at the heart of the revolution. In the southern, central and eastern Highlands the innovations were a mirror-image of these which took place elsewhere in Scotland. Individual family farms of around 40 to 60 acres were created out of the old communal townships. Each had its complement of servants and labourers engaged in mixed husbandry. Large cattle and sheep farms existed throughout the region but the smaller holdings were more representative. Another key feature of many parishes here was the successful development of local non-agricultural activities, such as the booming herring fishery of the Argyll sea lochs and the linen manufacturers of Highland Perthshire. By and large, though life was hard, the region was one of modest comfort and economic resilience which managed to escape the disasters which were to overwhelm the rest of the Highlands later in the nineteenth century.[31]

28. T. M. Devine, 'A conservative people? Scottish Gaeldom in the age of Improvement', in T. M. Devine and J. R. Young (eds), *Eighteenth Century Scotland: New Perspectives* (East Linton: Tuckwell Press, 1999), pp. 225–37.
29. J. A. Watson, 'The rise and development of the sheep industry in the Highlands', *Transactions of the Highland and Agricultural Society of Scotland*, 5th series, 44 (1932), p. 23; Richards, *History of the Highland Clearances*, p. 176.
30. A. I. Macinnes, 'The Highlands in the age of Improvement', in A. Cooke et al. (eds), *Modern Scottish History, 1707 to the Present*, vol. I (East Linton: Tuckwell Press, 1998), pp. 180–6.
31. For assessment of the patterns of economic change in this region see Gray, *Highland Economy*, pp. 223–8; T. M. Devine, *The Great Highland Famine* (Edinburgh: John Donald, 1988), pp.

Along the western seaboards of Inverness-shire and Rosshire and the coasts of Sutherland, and including most of the inner and outer Hebrides, a quite different social order was taking shape amid the ruins of the traditional society. Over great tracts of the region, especially on the mainland before 1815, but extending over the islands in subsequent decades, large grazing farms devoted to the raising of Blackface and Cheviot sheep became dominant. But although the advance of pastoral husbandry caused immense social disruption and the clearance of many communities, it did not often result in this period in planned and overt expulsion of the inhabitants. Instead, relocation (and especially re-location in crofting townships) was the favoured policy, so that profit could be extracted both from the labour-intensive activities of the crofters and from the more extensive operations of the big flock-masters.

Thus, over less than two or three generations, as the joint tenancies were destroyed, the crofting system was imposed throughout the region. By the 1840s, at least 86 per cent and in most parishes 95 per cent of holdings were rented at £20 or less. These small tenancies, only a few acres in size, were laid out in 'townships' or crofting settlements and had certain common features because they were the product of an 'Improving' philosophy which was enforced by virtually all landowners in these districts. At the core was the arable land, divided into a number of separate smallholdings, and these were surrounded by grazing or hill pasture which was held in common by the tenants of the township. The most striking feature, however, was that the croft was not designed to provide a full living for the family. Sir John Sinclair reckoned that the typical crofter had to be able to obtain at least 200 days of additional work outside his holding in order to avoid chronic destitution. Crofts were in fact reduced in size in order to force the crofter and his family into other employments. The holding itself should provide only partial subsistence and, to make ends meet and afford the rental, the crofter and his family had to have recourse to supplementary jobs.

These non-agricultural tasks were usually seasonal in nature. The crofting system provided a convenient source of subsistence for a reserve army of labour that was required only at certain times of the year. Crofting, therefore, became the *sine qua non* for the rapid expansion of kelp manufacture (in which between 25,000 and 40,000 people were seasonally employed during the peak summer months in the Hebrides),

1–4; A. Mackillop, *'More Fruitful than the Soil': Army, Empire and the Scottish Highlands, 1715–1815* (East Linton: Tuckwell Press, 2000), pp. 103–29.

for fishing and for illicit whisky-making. Crofts were also used to attract recruits to the family regiments of the landowners, with tiny areas of land being promised in return for service. Throughout the process of transforming the joint tenancies into crofts there was one fundamental guiding principle: too much land would act as a distraction from other, more profitable tasks. The crofters were to be labourers first and agriculturists only second. In retrospect, this proved a disastrous policy for the people of the western Highlands and Islands.

Essentially, the whole social system of the region became bound up with the success of the by-employments which flourished down to the end of the Napoleonic Wars. But in the main these activities were ephemeral because, like kelp manufacture and military service, they often existed only on the basis of the transitory conditions of wartime. Moreover, in their heyday they had little positive effect on the crofting economy. Kelp, for instance, was noted for its volatile prices, but, because of the great market expansion of the 1790s, became the principal economic activity in the Western Isles by 1815. But the working population gained little from this short-term bonanza as landlords in the kelp islands achieved monopoly control over the manufacture and marketing of the commodity and the 'earnings' of the labour force were mainly absorbed by increased rentals, rising population and annual payments to proprietors for meal.

Because of the labour needs of so many activities, most landlords were content for a time to see the unregulated division of lands among cottars and squatters. But this pulverising of the holdings helped to tie the people to the land and, unlike the pattern in the south and east Highlands and the Lowlands, inhibited permanent migration. The impact of these policies can be clearly seen in the demographic statistics. Between 1801 and 1841 along the western seaboard and the islands, population increased by 53 per cent, while in the south and eastern Highlands, as a consequence of much higher levels of out-migration, the average was around 7 per cent. This was a key factor in that region's economic and social resilience. The reckless process of subdivision elsewhere also depended on an equally rapid increase in potato cultivation. Potatoes had been grown in the early eighteenth century but by 1750 were still relatively uncommon. It was only where the croft became dominant that potatoes became a central part in the diet, and during the crofting revolution of the later eighteenth and early nineteenth centuries cultivation expanded on a remarkable scale. The transformation of land structures and the adoption of the potato went hand in hand. Because of its very high yield, the potato became the key source of support for the dense communities of crofters, cottars and squatters that were building up to service kelp and fishing.[32]

The final failure of the potatoes in 1846 and for several years afterwards, was the catalyst for a mass exodus from the crofting region. Around a third of the population left between 1841 and 1861.[33] Starvation was avoided by state and charitable intervention but the mass clearances of destitute crofters and cottars and 'assisted' schemes of emigration to the New World accelerated on an unprecedented scale. The optimism and hopes for Improvement of the later eighteenth century lay in ruins. Instead, the Highlands became a 'problem' region where economic transformation had brought distress rather than benefit. This seemed all the more puzzling to contemporary observers, given some of its advantages for development. The Highlands possessed an expanding and cheap labour force, was surrounded by seas that were rich in fish and the potential of the region as a major source of raw materials had been amply demonstrated before 1815. The possibilities for capital accumulation were also very great because so much of the area's principal asset, land, was concentrated among a small group of proprietors. The Highlands were one of the few parts of Britain where, because of their strategic importance as a source of soldiers and sailors, the state invested on a considerable scale through the Commission for Annexed Forfeited Estates, the British Fisheries Society and an ambitious programme of road and bridge building in the early nineteenth century. But all this was to no avail; there was little long-term impact.[34]

Some blame the landowners for failure. Resolving that complex and emotive question is difficult because, as recent work has shown, the landed class was far from monolithic and strategies varied significantly. Some proprietors did try to fund fishing and industrial development while others were much less proactive and squandered their rental incomes outside the Highlands. On the other hand, money also poured into the region as new owners replaced most of the old élites.[35] The problem was that even the most imaginative schemes seemed to have little effect in the long-term. It should also be remembered that the region's landowners faced more formidable obstacles than their fellows elsewhere in Britain – above all, the poor quality of land, which inhibited

32. Devine, *Great Highland Famine*, pp. 12–18.
33. Ibid., pp. 192–211.
34. See references to the work of Devine, Macinnes and Richards cited above, at footnotes 31, 26 and 6.
35. T. M. Devine, 'The emergence of the new élite in the Western Highlands and Islands, 1800–60', in T. M. Devine (ed.), *Improvement and Enlightenment* (Edinburgh: John Donald, 1989), pp. 108–42.

the development of labour-absorbing arable farming and hence virtually forced the region's economy in the direction of large-scale pastoral farming, where the western Highlands did indeed have a comparative advantage. This response had an inherent economic rationality but had a devastating impact on the welfare of the people.

Whatever the truth of the matter, even the most determined and costly scheme of landlord investment was probably doomed to failure by the end of the Napoleonic Wars.[36] By then the north-west was virtually locked into an economic vice that was contracting inexorably. There were at least four major problems. First, by 1815 commercial forces had transformed the region into an economic enclave of British industry. In essence it had become a satellite, with its functions utterly subordinate to the production of foodstuffs, raw materials and labour for the southern cities. No longer were the people of the western Highlands dependent only on the climate, the price of cattle and the returns from the land; their fate was now also inextricably bound up with the fluctuation of distant markets for a range of commodities. Second, commercialisation had fashioned an insecure and vulnerable economic structure, centred on crofting, the potato and by-employments; and at the same time much grazing land, vital in the old society, had been absorbed by the new sheep farms, which also tended to channel most of their economic gains out of the region. Third, the Highlands, as an integral part of the British market economy, was fully exposed to the direct impact of competition from advanced centres of industry such as the west of Scotland and the north of England. The Highlands lacked coal reserves of any significance, had few towns and, like other British peripheral regions such as the west of Ireland and the south-east of England, its small-scale textile industries were soon remorselessly squeezed by competition from the manufacturing heartlands. It was forced to specialise in sectors where it had a comparative advantage within the new economic system, and these were confined largely to sheep farming and the provision of casual labour for the Lowland economy.

Fourth, the postwar recession spelt impending death for many of the by-employments which had allowed the crofters to scratch a living in previous years. Most areas of the British economy experienced some difficulty in the years after 1815, but in the north and west the outcome was disastrous. This was partly because in a recession peripheral areas tended to suffer worst, but it was also because so much of the Highland

---

36. These final paragraphs in this section summarise the arguments in T. M. Devine, *Clanship to Crofters' War* (Manchester: Manchester University Press, 1994), pp. 51–3.

boom was due to ephemeral wartime conditions, and much of the region's export economy fell apart with the coming of peace. Cattle prices halved between 1810 and 1830. Fishing stagnated, due to the erratic migrations of the herring in the western sea lochs, the withdrawal of bounties on herring in the 1820s and the decline of the Irish and Caribbean markets for cured herring. Kelp, the great staple of the Hebrides, suffered even more acutely when peace brought revived imports of foreign barilla, a cheaper and richer substitute. The reduction of the duty on foreign alkali combined with the discovery that cheaper alkali could be extracted from common salt also had a devastating effect. The price of kelp had already halved by 1820 and it fell further in later years. The coming of peace also led to the demobilisation of the vast number of Highlanders who had joined the army and navy, and before long even illicit whisky-making was also under severe pressure as a result of radical changes in revenue legislation in the 1820s. That decade was indeed a grim one for the people of the western Highlands as virtually the whole economic fabric which had been built up between 1760 and 1815 disintegrated. Even more ominously, though sheep prices stagnated they did not experience the collapse of other commodities: to many observers only commercial pastoralism, with all its implication for further clearance and dispossession, had a real future.

The profound economic weaknesses of the western Highlands and Islands were cruelly exposed when the potatoes failed in 1846. The blight lasted to a greater or lesser extent for almost a decade and had a devastating impact on the region. An Irish-type mortality disaster was indeed averted by charitable intervention, landlord assistance and some state aid. But the consequences of the potato failure were still traumatic. Destitution intensified and the bankruptcy of the small tenants triggered a new wave of clearances, especially in the Hebrides. Above all, a huge stimulus was given to mass emigration.[37] The Highland tragedy confirmed the uneven impact of the Agricultural Revolution in Scotland.

FLUCTUATING FORTUNES, 1850–1900

The 1850s and 1860s were in most years decades of prosperity in Scottish agriculture. Even in the Highlands, the catastrophes of the 1840s were followed from c. 1856 by an era of relative stability and

37. Devine, *Great Highland Famine*, passim; Devine, 'Highland landowners and the Highland potato famine', in Leah Leneman (ed.), *Perspectives in Scottish Social History* (Aberdeen: Aberdeen University Press, 1988), pp. 141–62.

recovery as cattle prices rose, the regional white and herring fishery enjoyed unprecedented expansion and temporary migration for work in southern industry, construction and farming assumed even greater significance.[38] Indeed, all sectors of the rural economy in Scotland responded to the escalating demand for food, drink and raw materials from the vast expansion of towns and cities whose needs could not yet be satisfied on any significant scale from overseas suppliers. In the 1840s under a third of the nation lived in urban areas of 5,000 or above. Thereafter, city and town growth was continuous and unrelenting. Scotland became the second most urbanised country in the world after England as the urban share of national population doubled between 1831 and 1911. By the latter year, 60 per cent of all Scots lived in towns of 5,000 or more inhabitants.[39]

Underpinning this market expansion was a parallel revolution in transport. The combination of the railway and the steamship had a decisive effect and the great potential of Scotland as a great cattle-fattening and breeding country was finally realised. Cattle intended for the English market had in earlier times to be sold lean to the drovers who took them south on the hoof. Then in the 1820s came the steamships followed in the 1850s by the railways. which opened up the huge London market to Scottish fat cattle. The most spectacular gains were achieved in the north-east which rapidly became a specialist centre of excellence for the production of quality meat. By 1870 beef from the region carried the highest premium in London markets. The Aberdeen Angus, developed by William McCombie of Tillyfour farm, evolved into a breed of world-wide reputation.[40] The railways also enabled the perishable products of milk and buttermilk to be brought into the expanding cities from further afield while affording farmers the enhanced opportunity to import feeding stuffs and fertilisers in huge quantity like guano and industrial phosphates. The result was even higher yields. Steam power was now used more for threshing, and by the 1870s the greater part of the grain and hay crop was being mechanically harvested in most areas of the Lowlands.[41] The physical face of agriculture also changed as larger, more elaborate and better designed farm steadings spread across the countryside. To this day, many of these impressive buildings remain

38. Devine, *Clanship to Crofters' War*, pp. 192–207; James Hunter, *The Making of the Crofting Community* (Edinburgh: Ian Donald, 1987), pp. 109ff.
39. R. J. Morris, 'Urbanisation in Scotland', in W. H. Fraser and R. J. Morris (eds), *People and Society in Scotland*, vol. II: *1830–1914* (Edinburgh: John Donald, 1990), pp. 73–102.
40. Carter, *Farm Life in Northeast Scotland*, pp. 33–60.
41. W. Howatson, 'Grain harvesting and harvesters', in T. M. Devine (ed.), *Farm Servants and Labour*, pp. 131–5.

as lasting memorials to the prosperous days of 'High Farming' in Victorian Scotland. Arguably, however, the greatest changes took place invisibly, below the surface of the land. Despite their innovations, the eighteenth-century Improvers had never really solved the crucial problem of drainage, a key issue in Scotland with its wet, maritime climate. The system of draining off surface water by the traditional rigs still remained common well into the Victorian period. This changed with the invention of the cylindrical clay pipe and the provision of government loans at low interest rates from the 1840s.

Landowners in this period did not simply gain from swelling rent rolls as grain and cattle prices rose steadily and investment in the land bore profitable fruit. Industrialisation also contributed handsomely to the fortunes of several magnates by affording them the opportunity to exploit mineral royalties. Among the most fortunate Scottish grandees in this respect was the Duke of Hamilton, whose lands included some of the richest coal measures in Lanarkshire, the Duke of Fife, the Earl of Eglinton and the Duke of Portland. That great symbol of the new industrial age, the railway, was warmly welcomed by the landed classes as a whole. This was hardly surprising since one enquiry by J. Bailey Denton in 1868 had concluded that the letting of farm land could increase by 5 to 20 per cent according to its proximity to a railway station. Landowners were heavily involved in railway financing and, indeed, before 1860 were second only to urban merchants as investors.[42] Some patrician families also benefited from considerable injections of capital from the Empire to which the landed classes had often privileged access through their background and the associated network of personal relationships and connections. In the north-east, for instance, one conspicuous example of the lucrative marriage between imperial profits and traditional landownership was the Forbes family of Newe. They had owned the estate since the sixteenth century, but its economic position was mightily strengthened and territory increased from the middle decades of the eighteenth century when the kindred of the family began merchanting in India. By the early nineteenth century the House of Forbes in Bombay was producing a flow of funds for a new country seat, enormous land improvements and the purchase of neighbouring properties in Aberdeenshire. Examples of the connection between imperial profit and landownership of the kind illustrated by the Forbes family could be found in every county in Scotland.[43]

42. Devine, *The Scottish Nation*, pp. 451–2.
43. R. F. Callander, *A Pattern of Landownership in Scotland* (Finzean: Haughend Publications, 1987), p. 75.

The good times came to an end in the later 1870s. An immediate problem was bad weather, which was at its worst in the winter of 1878/9. But the root causes lay elsewhere. There had been poor harvests in earlier times but these were often compensated by a rise in the prices of scarce crops. This did not happen in the later 1870s because a structural change was underway in the global supply of food. Free trade and the transport revolution which had brought great benefits to British agriculture were now radically altering world-wide supply systems. The railway and the steamship unlocked the vast grain-growing potential of the American prairies.[44] Scottish industry had long faced international competition in foreign markets. Now the nation's landowners and farmers were for the first time fully exposed to similar forces. In the two decades from the mid-1870s wheat imports to Britain almost doubled to nearly 100 million cwt while barley imports more than doubled to 26 million cwt. Then, the livestock sector, which escaped relatively unscathed at first, was hit by the arrival of refrigerated beef and lamb from North America and Australasia. Dairy farmers also experienced severe competition, not only directly through an expansion in the importation of American cheese but also indirectly as some European countries, notably Denmark, responded to the flood of cheap grain from the New World, by specialising even more in dairy products for the British market.[45]

It is true, nonetheless, that the impact of the 'Agricultural Depression' was complex, varying over time, place and between different sectors of the rural economy. In the Highlands, for instance, while sheep farming on marginal land was in crisis, the 'recreation economy' centred on the great sporting estates continued to thrive.[46] In addition, Scottish agriculture as a whole suffered less than the great wheat and corn counties of southern England. The greatest decline in prices was in wheat, which in Scotland was only a major crop in the south-east Lowlands. The tradition of mixed farming in Scotland gave the agrarian system considerable flexibility and the capacity to adjust to changes in the market. Also, the Scottish livestock farmers operated at the quality end of the trade, which gave a degree of protection against cheap overseas imports. Nevertheless, while Scottish agriculture was spared the worst effects of the Great Depression, the prosperity and confidence of the mid-Victorian era was still undermined. The average price of oats

44. C. S. Orwin and E. H. Whetham, *History of British Agriculture, 1846–1914* (Newton Abbot: David and Charles, 1964), pp. 240–57.
45. R. H. Campbell, *Scotland since 1707* (Edinburgh: John Donald, 1985), pp. 208–10.
46. W. Orr, *Deer Forests, Landlords and Crofters* (Edinburgh: John Donald, 1972).

in the 1890s was a quarter less than that of the 1870s. Even returns from the sale of quality fat cattle for the north-eastern counties show a big slide from the mid-1880s. The net result of this was a parallel decline in landlord rents. Even livestock areas were not spared as the countryside adjusted to the new reality that the halcyon days of high prices and low imports were over for good. In Morayshire, a prime stock-rearing county, rents of larger farms fell by a quarter between 1878 and 1894 and the pattern was even worse in less favoured grain-producing areas, where rents of between one-half to one-third were recorded. The misery was not spread equally, however, among estate owners. The smaller proprietors often found themselves in acute difficulty having to meet fixed obligations such as interest charges and family annuities from a reduced income. The larger estates faired better as their owners tended to have outside sources of income.[47]

The economic gloom experienced by some landlords was paralleled by adverse political developments, the most dramatic of which was the imposition of Estate Duty in 1894. Again, by the 1870s as game was being developed systematically the crops of tenant farmers increasingly suffered from the depredations of both ground game (rabbits and hares) and game birds. Farmers who killed game in retaliation could be prosecuted. The other and more serious source of tension was the law of hypothec which gave a landlord the position of a preferred creditor for the payment of his rent by giving him a general security over a tenant's moveable property. Some argued that this legal privilege allowed landowners to impose high rentals secure in the knowledge that arrears could be recovered from a tenant's assets. Tensions on these and other issues led to the creation of the Scottish Farmers' Alliance to press for land reform and resulted in a succession of defeats at the polls for landlord candidates in the general elections of 1865 and 1868. In the event concessions were made both on the game laws and hypothec. The 1883 Agricultural Holdings Act (Scotland) also gave tenants the right to compensation for agricultural improvements. All this helped to draw the teeth of discontent and prevented the tensions fuelling a full-scale revolt of the tenants.[48]

It was a different story in the Highlands. There, a series of popular disturbances in the 1880s, which have come to be known as the 'Crofters'

47.   Carter, *Farm Life in Northeast Scotland*, pp. 76–97; T. M. Devine, 'Scottish farm labour in the era of agricultural depression, 1875–1900', in Devine (ed.), *Farm Servants and Labour*, pp. 243–55.
48.   R. H. Campbell, 'The rural experience', in Fraser and Morris (eds), *People and Society*, pp. 65–6.

War' came together with an effective political campaign of land reformers, Gaelic revivalists and radical liberals to force the hand of the government.[49] A Royal Commission, chaired by Lord Napier and Ettrick, was soon followed by the passage of the Crofters' Holding (Scotland) Act. Security of tenure for crofters was guaranteed as long as rent was paid; fair rents would be fixed by a land court; compensation for improvements were allowed; and crofts could be bequeathed to a relative. The legislation was remarkable and has been widely hailed since as the Magna Carta of the Highlands. Clearances were now impossible; the sacred rights of private property were breached and legislative controls imposed on landlord–tenant relations.[50] In the words of one scholar, the Act provided the crofter with 'most of the advantages of ownership – security and power of bequest – without its drawbacks'.[51]

Other writers, however, are less impressed. They argue that in the longer term the 1886 Act became a powerful force for conservatism and condemned crofting society to a future of inertia and stagnation by freezing an existing structure of smallholdings and ensured by its constraints and limitations that any evolution of holding size as circumstances changed would be virtually impossible.[52] What compounded the problem was the loyalty the legislation inspired, which made any attempt at amendment politically unpopular and unattractive. The Act had provided the Crofters' Commission with powers to grant enlargement of crofts, but these were inadequate and resulted in only marginal changes. In addition, there was no provision at all for the creation of entirely new crofts. However, to judge this historic legislation by narrow economic criteria is perhaps misleading. The 1886 Act came about for pragmatic reasons as a response to the breakdown of public order in parts of the western Highlands. It was not designed to be a blueprint for economic recovery but a political solution to a social crisis. In the longer-run, nevertheless, the legislation heralded a new tradition of state intervention in the Highlands which became such a marked feature of the region's history in the twentieth century.[53]

49. I. M. M. Macphail, *The Crofters' War* (Stornoway: Acair, 1989).
50. Ewen A. Cameron, *Land for the People? The British Government and the Scottish Highlands, c. 1880–1925* (East Linton: Tuckwell Press, 1996).
51. A. Collier, *The Crofting Problem* (Cambridge: Cambridge University Press, 1953), p. 98.
52. Campbell, *Scotland since 1707*, p. 222.
53. Ewen A. Cameron, 'The Scottish Highlands: from congested district to Objective One', in T. M. Devine and R. J. Finlay (eds), *Scotland in the Twentieth Century* (Edinburgh: Edinburgh University Press, 1996), pp. 153–69.

CONCLUSION

The excellence of Scottish agriculture in Victorian times attracted foreign visitors who came from near and far to admire, to learn and often to imitate. They marvelled at the well-ploughed fields, the efficiency of technique and the pioneering innovations in both crop and animal husbandry. But this achievement was not inevitable. Scotland's land and climate were not intrinsically favourable to an advanced agriculture. As one commentator has memorably put it: 'Scottish earth is in most places – even in the more fertile south and east – a skin over bone'.[54] It was then human ingenuity, skill and great effort rather than geological advantage which fashioned the new agronomy. For over a century from the decisive changes of the decades after c. 1760 to the 'high farming' of the 1850s Scottish agriculture enjoyed remarkably high levels of land and labour productivity. An increased population was fed, thereby facilitating a huge shift in the national workforce from food cultivation to manufacturing and industrial employment. Improved agriculture underpinned all this and more, often at considerable social cost, most notoriously in the Highlands, but also, less visibly, in the break-up of the old rural communities of the Lowlands. By the later nineteenth century, however, some thought the golden years were over as the New World, with much greater advantages in natural endowment than Scotland, became enormous suppliers of grain and beef to European markets. As with Scottish industry, the threat of international competition loomed ever closer at the beginning of the new century.

FURTHER READING

Cameron, E. A., *Land for the People? The British Government and the Scottish Highlands, c. 1880–1925* (East Linton: Tuckwell Press, 1996).

Carter, I., *Farm Life in Northeast Scotland, 1840–1914: The Poor Man's Country* (Edinburgh: John Donald, 1979).

Devine, T. M., *The Great Highland Famine* (Edinburgh: John Donald, 1988).

Devine, T. M., *The Transformation of Rural Scotland, 1650–1815: Social Change and the Agrarian Economy* (Edinburgh: Edinburgh University Press, 1994).

Devine, T. M., *Clanship to Crofters' War: The Social Transformation of the Scottish Highlands* (Manchester: Manchester University Press, 1994).

Devine, T. M. (ed.), *Farm Servants and Labour in Lowland Scotland, 1770–1914* (Edinburgh: John Donald, 1996).

Gray, M., *The Highland Economy, 1750–1850* (Edinburgh: Oliver and Boyd, 1957).

54.   Neal Ascherson, *Stone Voices: The Search for Scotland* (London: Granta Books, 2002), p. 27.

Gray, M., 'Scottish emigration: the social impact of agrarian change in the rural Lowlands, 1775–1815', *Perspectives in American History*, 7 (1973), pp. 113–31.

Gray, M., *The Fishing Industries of Scotland, 1790–1914* (Oxford: Oxford University Press for Aberdeen University, 1978).

Orwin, C. S., and Whetham, E. A., *History of British Agriculture, 1846–1914* (Newton Abbot: David and Charles, 1971).

Richards, E., *The Highland Clearances: People, Landlords and Rural Turmoil* (Edinburgh: Birlinn, 2000).

Sprott, G., *Farming* (Edinburgh: National Museums of Scotland, 1995).

CHAPTER FOUR

The Establishment of the Financial Network

C. H. Lee

THE FINANCIAL CRISIS OF THE LATE SEVENTEENTH CENTURY

One of the principal and universal characteristics of modern societies is the reliance upon a network of financial services that are provided by many interconnected institutions. Such structures are so pervasive that they can pass with little notice and their significance can easily be over-looked because of the fact that many of their operations are intangible. But no economic system can grow or flourish without the support of an underlying financial network to co-ordinate its activities, provide the stability essential for the pursuit of commerce, and facilitate the movement of capital to its most productive uses. Finance has played an extremely important role in the growth of the Scottish economy. Part of that has been recognised. In the introduction to his study of Scottish banking, Sydney Checkland noted the importance of Scottish pioneering activity in banking, in the introduction of limited liability, the extension of note issue, the development of agency and branch outlets, and the invention of the overdraft so that it became a model for other systems. English banks subsequently adopted features such as joint stock companies, branch banking, and the payment of interest on deposits.[1]

The purpose of this chapter is twofold, to explore the development of the financial network itself and to examine its contribution to the wider issues of economic growth in Scotland. The process of creating the modern financial structure certainly starts with the establishment of the Bank of Scotland in 1695. But this could equally be claimed as an

---

1. S. G. Checkland, *Scottish Banking: A History, 1695–1973* (Glasgow: Collins, 1975), pp. xvii–xviii.

appropriate starting point for the economic modernisation of Scotland. Indeed, the foundation of the Bank reflected both the current weakness of the Scottish economy at the end of the seventeenth century and the possibilities that existed for future economic progress. The foundation of the Bank of Scotland was designed to address these problems. It was also the first component of the Scottish financial network.

The principal stimulus for the establishment of the Bank of Scotland was a chronic shortage of liquidity, that is notes and coin for exchange, in the Scottish economy towards the end of the seventeenth century. The shortage of money became a greater problem as the economy expanded, and as merchants progressively abandoned a system based on periodic exchange at fairs and markets, several times per year, in which barter still played a part. This system might be satisfactory with regard to goods that were consumed locally but it was not suited to the growth of international commerce. But there were other underlying difficulties in the early eighteenth century. Scotland's marketable produce was largely confined to raw materials and foodstuffs, sheep and cattle, fish, grain and coal. In exchange manufactured goods were imported, of a higher quality than could be produced domestically. But such an exchange in which cheap products are exported and expensive ones imported inevitably generates a deficit in the balance of trade. In 1704, for example, Scottish imports were almost double the value of Scottish exports.[2] This deficit obviously affects payment, and in economies reliant on gold and coin it implies a loss of specie. Other problems are also created. If payment is made by the discount, or acceptance, of bills of exchange, an adverse trade balance would increase the premium paid to have such bills accepted by as much as 10–15 per cent of their value.[3]

Perhaps the most serious aspect of the dearth of liquidity related to the government's finances. The main source of revenue at this time lay in customs and excise duties. But many Scots found that smuggling enabled them to avoid such payments and the geography of the country, with many isolated but accessible beaches and harbours, was helpful to such evasion. The capacity of the economy to generate revenue for the government was too slight to counteract the shortage of gold and silver. Scotland had a much smaller tax base per head than England, and the collection of duties was hampered by inefficiency and corruption. In consequence the government was unable to raise sufficient revenue to

2. Ibid., p. 11.
3. R. Saville, *Bank of Scotland: A History, 1695–1995* (Edinburgh: Edinburgh University Press, 1996), p. 60.

pay for the army and even had to ask for help from the English Admiralty for help in protecting Scottish vessels from French privateers. Shortage of coin particularly hit tax collection, since a successful collection was capable of denuding a locality of coin. To make things worse, the obvious outcome of such a shortage of cash was a punitively high rate of interest that discouraged economic activity.

The beginnings of modern banking, towards the close of the seventeenth century, in Britain reflected the effects of a growing economic system pushing against the restraint of increasingly inadequate supplies of cash and credit. In England the immediate problem was different from that faced by the Scots. It was the result of extensive military commitments abroad that had pushed the cost of defence beyond the normal capacity of taxation. The establishment of the Bank of England in 1694 was designed to deal with the problem. The Bank was authorised to raise capital worth £1.2 million, subsequently to be offered as a loan to the government, so that the Bank of England occupied thereafter a central role within the public finances and the metropolitan financial market. While the shortage of the state for funds lay behind this development, the foundation of the Bank of Scotland in the following year reflected the need for cash and credit in the Scottish economy, and for a means of exchange to facilitate trade with both England and mainland Europe. Its establishment was profoundly important for the future of the Scottish economy.

THE ESTABLISHMENT OF THE FINANCIAL STRUCTURE:
THE PUBLIC BANKS

Financial structures, their creation, multiplication and interweaving, constitute the characteristic signs of economic development. Without such a support network, no economy can survive or prosper because these networks are the conduits through which business is transacted, credit sought and provided, investment mobilised, and the security of commercial activity established. Completion of the transition to a modern trading economy required the introduction of a stable and expandable financial structure based on banking. The base upon which the Scottish financial system was constructed comprised four public institutions, all established between 1695 and 1746, and initially brought together in political and economic struggle against each other. The first of these public bodies was Bank of Scotland. The charter allowed Bank of Scotland to raise a capital of £1.2 million Scots, and the first directors decided to have 10 per cent of this paid up by the opening date in March 1696. There were 172 subscribers or adventurers. Of these, 63 were primarily landowners in Lowland Scotland and were together responsible for about £400,000 worth of stock. Another group were merchants, about 25 in number and based along the east coast from Edinburgh to Aberdeen and they raised £300,000. Many of these merchants had overseas interests, in the Baltic ports and continental Europe and London. Lawyers, medical practitioners and goldsmiths were prominent among those who contributed the balance. The strength of the mercantile community, in skill as well as in finance was essential for the new bank, for they provided technical expertise relating to the conduct of international business.[4]

Despite the fact that they were founded within a year of each other, the Bank of Scotland and its English counterpart were essentially different. While the Bank of England was devised primarily to lend to the government, its Scottish counterpart was forbidden to do so. It was a business corporation, aided by the fact that its dividends were to be free from taxation for 21 years and that it enjoyed a monopoly of public banking in Scotland for the same period. But there was an expectation that the Bank would act in the public interest and, accordingly, its activities were restricted to banking, and at least two-thirds of its shares had to be held in Scotland. There were important restrictions on lending. Advances had to be secured against the security of land through heritable bonds, personal property or commodities.[5] The Bank could increase its capacity to lend by borrowing or by issuing notes. Most of the lending undertaken by the Bank in its earliest years went to individuals with substantial wealth in land, property or mineral rights. This maintained the financial security of the Bank and serviced precisely those interests that had called for its establishment.

The early years of business were fraught with problems for the Bank of Scotland that stemmed from both commercial rivalry and financial uncertainty. Both problems merged in conflict with the Company of Scotland, the second of the public companies that was set up to fulfil the ambitious and glamorous aim of setting up a base in Central America at Darien to develop Scottish trade with America, Africa and the Indies. Its aim was to insert itself within the Spanish colonial empire at the isthmus of Panama and to establish an entrepot that would give the Scots a key position in linking the trade of the Atlantic with that of the Pacific and

---

4. Ibid., pp. 2–3, 7–8.
5. Checkland, *Scottish Banking*, p. 30.

give them 'the door of the seas and the key to the universe'.[6] By virtue
of incorporation the Company of Scotland had limited liability, and a
lengthy period of monopoly as well as the right to engage in banking.
This company thus became a rival to the Bank for the modest amount
of potential investment that could be raised in Scotland. When the
Company of Scotland distributed its banknotes throughout Scotland in
1696, the immediate effect was to create a substantial demand for cash to
buy them. Bank of Scotland notes were cashed in, exerting a pressure on
its resources that required guarantees and support from the nobility and
the government to ensure survival. This experience was characteristic of
early banking. The essence of commercial banking lay in the issue of
notes as a promise to make payment, and all banks increased their note
issue well in excess of the value of the reserves of coin or gold they kept
to honour requests for payment. The most obvious way to drive a
competitor out of business, therefore, was to collect his banknotes and
then present them in large numbers demanding repayment in gold or
coin for sums exceeding the bank's reserves. The Company of Scotland
offered a wider threat to economic stability in seeking to devote a much
higher share of its resources to speculative investment than might be
usual or prudent in a relatively poor society. But it soon ran into
difficulties, the occupation of Panama proved to be brief, due to a
shortage of money, an inhospitable environment in Darien, and powerful
opponents, notably the East India Company and the Spanish colonists.
The Company of Scotland lost its entire working capital, after attracting
a substantial share of Scottish investment, and thus brought the national
economy to the brink of ruin.

The Bank of Scotland survived the first challenge to its existence,
although the defunct Company of Scotland had still one final attack to
make. The Act of Union 1707 contained an agreement that Scotland
would be compensated for possible losses incurred as a result of entering the Union. This included an immediate cash payment, called the
'Equivalent', and supplementary payments or an 'Arising Equivalent'.
The latter was to be paid from increases in taxation revenue that would
flow from the Union, and included compensation to the value of
£230,000 for shareholders and creditors of the Company of Scotland.[7]
In the event, it proved impossible to satisfactorily meet all the claims,
especially as the tax revenues fell for several years. Creditors were given
debentures, promises by the government to pay at some future time. By

6. Ibid., p. 17.
7. Ibid., p. 44.

1713 several hundred of the debenture holders formed themselves into a committee to seek redress. This group included a number of the Darien projectors, including William Paterson, the Duke of Argyll, the Earl of Islay, Campbell of Monzie, later Lord Monzie, and Lord Belhaven. They were soon to become the most powerful political interest group in Scotland and closely allied to the Walpole administration at Westminster. The route to recovery of assets and acquisition of power for this group lay in supplanting the Bank of Scotland. In 1724 an Act of parliament incorporated the holders of the Equivalent debt into the Society of the Equivalent Company, with a capital of almost £250,000. Three years later the Society was granted a charter to operate as bankers in Scotland and to use the funds of the 'Equivalent' as capital.[8] Almost half of the stock of the Society of the Equivalent Company was invested in the new bank, so that it could be claimed that the residual vestiges of the Darien Company were reincarnated in the new institution. Thus the Company of Scotland was partly embodied in the Royal Bank of Scotland, whose first commitment as the 'new bank' was to destroy or take over the 'old bank'. Once established, the Royal Bank attacked its rival in the customary fashion by collecting its notes to demand specie in exchange.

The conflict between the two public banks lasted for almost two decades. The principal vehicle for the conflict was through the note issue that remained the key to profitability and liquidity. Following the initial and unsuccessful attack of the new bank, both institutions maintained a cautionary reserve of the other bank's notes. By the middle of the eighteenth century, a new development brought the two public banks together as joint leaders of the Scottish financial system. But before then a third chartered institution had appeared, and was another political triumph for those who now controlled the Royal Bank of Scotland. Lord Milton had a substantial interest in the Board of Manufactures that had been established in 1727 to support the linen industry. The royal charter establishing the British Linen Company in 1746 allowed the company to raise £100,000 capital, half of which was to be devoted to the expansion of linen cloth and yarn. But it soon became apparent that banking functions naturally developed from the core activity as the Company issued its own notes in return for supplies of flax, and in response to a shortage of liquidity. In effect it became the first provider of branch banking facilities. The banking part of the business was sufficiently successful to justify the abandonment of textile manufacture in 1763.

8. Saville, *Bank of Scotland*, pp. 84–94.

Many of those prominent in the affairs of the Royal Bank had an interest and a role in the British Linen Company. As might be expected, the finance for the three great public banks came from landed, mercantile and political élites, including Scots based in London. They drew upon the resources and skills of the limited élite of wealthy citizens.

By the middle of the eighteenth century, the Scottish financial system was firmly established on the base of the three public banks. The structure of the Scottish system was also completely different from that established in England, and this helped and, indeed, encouraged the separation of the two financial systems. In the first half of the eighteenth century, the Scottish public banks had considerably extended the money supply and credit facilities. It has been estimated that the addition to banking facilities in the 50 years following the foundation of Bank of Scotland was an increase of £280,000, representing a sixfold increase. This pre-dated the main increase in agricultural and industrial change, and was an important facilitating agent for it.[9] Despite the advances made in creating a financial network to support commercial development, there remained, in 1750, one principal weakness. The public banks were all based in Edinburgh and the further geographically that one went from that hub, the weaker and less cohesive were the financial services. The response to that problem, in the appearance of new banks, eventually galvanised the two major banks into action and into collusion with each other.

The challenge came from Glasgow and from the effects of the tobacco trade, and was a manifestation of the still unsatisfactory level of banking support outside the capital city. In 1749 six Glasgow businessmen established themselves as a private bank under the aegis of the Bank of Scotland. This became known as the Ship Bank from the illustration on their notes. They represented funds accumulated in the tobacco trade and a need for banking services in the west. The Banking Company of Aberdeen appeared at the same time, and was motivated by the same needs of financial services in a growing urban area some distance from Edinburgh. The Glasgow Arms Bank, the name derived from the use of the city's coat of arms on its notes, brought together another group of Glasgow merchants. The conflict became serious when the two Glasgow banks opened agencies in Edinburgh with the possibility of note redemption there. The response was agreement between the two major banks that they would never again organise a run against the notes of the other bank, that they would act in mutual defence against any other party

9. Checkland, *Scottish Banking*, p. 85.

that sought to impose such a strategy, and that they would accept each other's notes but not those of any other institution. This established the joint leadership of the two major public banks over the Scottish financial system.

THE EXTENSION OF THE BANKING COMMUNITY

The public banks were brought into existence to provide liquidity that was essential for commercial growth. The same pressures determined the expansion of the banking system after 1750 in the context of increasing economic activity. The proliferation of banking fell into two phases that reflected the process of growth. The first phase from the middle of the eighteenth century until the 1830s was characterised by the emergence of the provincial banks. Before then the services of the public banks were supplemented by a group of private banks, based principally in Edinburgh and Glasgow, and offering services that grew naturally from their mercantile activities. The first of these was John Coutts of Edinburgh, a corn merchant and general commission agent who conducted business in association with his brother, who was based in London. Together they secured the contract to transmit the revenue from the Scottish excise to London. Other prominent private bankers included William Alexander, who financed much of the tobacco trade, and several tobacco merchants in Glasgow. The early private bankers mixed a variety of commercial activities with the banking services they supplied. They discounted bills, offered loans but did not issue notes.

The provincial banks appeared first in the middle of the eighteenth century, a manifestation of economic growth, and filling a local void in the provision of banking facilities. Most of the provincial banks were set up by local merchants in order to aid the operation of the business community and especially to allow the expansion of trade. They provided a link to the Edinburgh banks and offered credit and banking and discounting facilities locally. As the prospectus for the Dundee Banking Company stated, it was:

> sensible of the great inconveniency which the merchants and manufacturers of this part of the country lie under by reason of their distance from Edinburgh, and the difficulty of procuring loans and negotiating cash accounts with the Banks there established.[10]

10. C. W. Munn, *The Scottish Provincial Banking Companies, 1747–1864* (Edinburgh: John Donald, 1981), p. 16.

In 1787 the promotional literature for the Perth Banking Company stated its aim as:

> promoting Trade, Manufactures, Agriculture and Industry, and in facilitating every branch of Commerce in Perth and for many miles around ... [by] ... Issuing Notes of Hand payable at our office in Perth, Lending money on Cash-accounts, bills and permanent securities, purchasing Bills of Exchange, and discounting of Bills and Notes.[11]

The proposal for the Eastern Bank of Scotland stated that:

> the capital of the present local banking companies in Dundee is now too small ... The only remedy for this defect in the present system is the establishment of a Bank of large capital having a widely spread interest and connection with the district.[12]

Eighteenth-century banks were small operations and usually had less than twenty partners and represented local interests. In the rather unstable economic environment it is not surprising that many of these provincial banks were formed and re-formed many times. The Perth Banking Company survived several 21-year contracted terms before merging with the Union Bank of Scotland in 1858. While most of the provincial banks were small and local in their interests, some sought to operate on a larger scale. The Aberdeen Banking Company, founded in 1767, had agencies in Thurso, Inverness, Huntly, Keith, Portsoy and Banff, while the Paisley Union Banking Company, started in 1788, had agencies stretching from Oban to Carlisle and Berwick. But it was one of the largest provincial banks that illustrated the perils of banking and experienced humiliating collapse. The Ayr Bank was founded in 1769 with 136 shareholders subscribing a capital of £150,000. This bank had substantial support in south-west Scotland, including an impressive sprinkling of landed gentry with land holdings estimated at £3–4 million.[13] The Ayr Bank issued notes on a massive scale, established branches throughout Scotland and raised additional funds by borrowing on the London market to support its overtrading. Its ebullient policy

11. R. S. Rait, *The History of the Union Bank of Scotland* (Glasgow: John Smith and Son, 1930), p. 134.
12. J. M. Reid, *The History of the Clydesdale Bank, 1838–1938* (Glasgow: Blackie, 1938), p. 119, quoting from the Dundee *Advertiser*.
13. Munn, *Scottish Provincial Banking*, p. 30.

brought collapse within three years, when the bank found itself borrowing at a higher rate of interest than it was receiving from its own advances. The bankruptcy of the Ayr Bank in 1772 was shared by many private bankers in Edinburgh who were ruined when payment on bills of exchange that they were holding was stopped.[14]

The provincial banking companies were soon overtaken by economic growth as they had insufficient resources to provide the framework for large-scale business. They gave way to joint stock banks in the expansive period following the end of the Napoleonic Wars in 1815. These banks took business from the provincial banks because they were larger and thus more secure. The provincial banks had had an average capital of £50,000 while the joint stock banks, by the 1820s and 1830s, averaged £400,000.[15] Amalgamation offered the only route for the provincial banks to transform themselves into joint stock operations, and many took this option. The growth of joint stock banking also heralded a change in the geographical balance of finance in Scotland. Glasgow and the industrialising western Lowlands had been relatively underprovided financially in the eighteenth century. After 1825 the great burst of joint stock bank formation was heavily, although not exclusively, concentrated in the west. The Glasgow Union Banking Company, founded in 1830 with a nominal capital of £2 million, started a branch system that reached Carlisle and Penrith. Two years later, the Western Bank of Scotland, with a nominal capital of £4 million, commenced trading. This bank created branches at an unprecedented rate and by 1850 had 72, far more that any other Scottish bank. An alternative expansionary strategy was adopted by the Glasgow Union Bank, that of amalgamation. The Thistle Bank was bought in 1836, followed by the Edinburgh private bank of Sir William Forbes and Company, and the Paisley Union Bank. Before the decade was out a further new joint stock bank appeared, the Clydesdale Bank in 1838. There was also a major new development in the shape of the North of Scotland Bank based in Aberdeen. The joint stock banks grew by merger and acquisition. The Clydesdale Bank absorbed the Greenock Union Bank in 1843, and the Dundee-based Eastern Bank of Scotland in 1863. It also built a network of branches that by 1901 had reached Aberdeen to compete with the North of Scotland Bank on its own territory, a move that was followed by the establishment of branches at Peterhead, Forfar, Elgin, Buckie and Fraserburgh by 1914.

14. Rait, *Union Bank*, pp. 164–6.
15. C. W. Munn, *Clydesdale Bank: The First One Hundred and Fifty Years* (Glasgow: Collins, 1988), p. 19.

There was one further banking development of great significance. The appearance of savings banks early in the nineteenth century extended banking services down the social scale to include the more prosperous and thrifty of the lower orders of society. The savings banks were designed to encourage both thrift and preparation for old age on the part of those who were most likely to become a burden on the community. The first savings bank was started at Ruthwell in Dumfries in 1810. In 1814 the Edinburgh Provident Bank was begun by the local Society for the Suppression of Beggars, and emulated by forty others within a year. The hope was that making regular savings bank deposits would encourage the poor to take responsibility for their welfare, make it harder for them to fritter resources on drink, and ease the burden on the Poor Law. By 1835 there were 100–120 savings banks in Scotland with about 40–50,000 savers. The Glasgow National Savings Bank was founded in 1836, supported by major local employers such as Charles Tennant, James Findlay and Robert Napier. By the end of the first year of operation there were 2,000 accounts still open and the clientele included printers, weavers, factory workers, mechanics and domestic servants. The Perth Savings Bank showed a predominance of accounts held by weavers, mechanics, artificers and domestic servants.[16] By the late nineteenth century there remained over fifty savings banks in Scotland but six of them held 90 per cent of the deposits. As might be expected, they were in the larger urban centres: in the four cities together with Perth and Paisley. By the early years of the new century there were more than half a million accounts open in Scotland, one for every nine people, and with a total value of deposits of £18.2 million in 1905.[17] From the 1850s new agencies encouraged small savers, notably the penny banks and the Post Office deposits. The latter was more successful south of the border for, in Scotland, savings banks retained popular support. The savings banks customarily deposited with other banks. The Paisley Provident placed its funds with the Paisley Banking Company and the Glasgow Union Bank. But the Greenock Provident deposited its funds with the trustees of the Greenock Harbour Board, with the Greenock Water Board and with the Town Council. Most savings banks took advantage of the 1835 legislation that enabled them to lodge deposits with the Commissioners for the Reduction of the National Debt. Depositors were able to buy government annuities through the agency of the savings banks.

16. M. Moss and A. Slaven, *'From Ledger Book to Laser Beam': A History of the TSB in Scotland from 1810 to 1990* (Edinburgh: TSB Bank Scotland plc, 1992), pp. 28, 32.
17. Ibid., p. 52.

NEW FINANCIAL INSTITUTIONS: INSURANCE AND INVESTMENT

While the development of the financial system in Scotland in the eighteenth century was largely confined to banking activity, the further growth and proliferation of activity after 1815 was manifest in the creation of a range of different types of financial institution. Most obvious, and of great importance, were the insurance companies. This type of business had been concentrated in London from the early eighteenth century when business had focused on marine and fire cover. There was some growth of provincial insurance in England in the second half of the eighteenth century. Then a burst of new companies in the early years of the next century included two Edinburgh companies, the Caledonian in 1805, and the North British Insurance Company in 1809. They were followed by Scottish Widows in 1815, the Scottish Union and National Insurance Company in 1824, the Life Insurance Company of Scotland, which later became known as Standard Life, in 1825, and Scottish Amicable in 1826. The West of Scotland Fire Insurance Company started business in Glasgow in 1823, as did the Forfarshire Insurance Company in Dundee and, two years later, the Aberdeen Assurance Company. Growing urbanisation increased the risk of fire and provided a demand for the earliest popular form of insurance. Rising prosperity and the need to provide for premature death or illness increased the need for life assurance. Scottish Widows' Fund Life Assurance Society started, as its name suggests, in order to accumulate funds to purchase annuities, but the company soon found that life assurance offered greater business opportunities. By 1850 the total of Scottish bank deposits was only slightly larger than the policies of Scottish life assurance offices, £36 million as against £34 million. Both increased substantially in the second half of the century.[18]

It became clear in the first half of the nineteenth century that life-assurance policies offered more attractive business opportunities even than marine and fire insurance. Initially Standard Life concentrated on providing such policies for the landed gentry, who could offer the security of their estates. This offered the assurance company security for the loan offered because in the event of non-payment of interest and/or the capital it could lay claim to the land. In both Scotland and Ireland this business offered good opportunities for Standard Life. But the famine of the 1840s undermined the policy. To flourish, life assurance had to attract a wider range of clients. By the 1850s policies were

---

18. Checkland, *Scottish Banking*, p. 368.

purchased by an increasing and diverse clientele, including public officials, teachers, clergy, doctors, lawyers, clerks and farmers. These policies were mainly for sums between £100–500, and were taken out in middle life by those aged between 30 and 45.[19] Business at this time was still modest. The merger with Colonial Life, the separate overseas arm of Standard Life, increased the number of life policies to 1,820 from 1,428 in 1865.[20] By the late nineteenth century the life policies outstanding against the security of landed estates were causing increasing difficulty, especially in Ireland. The bankruptcy of the Earl of Kenmare, owing Standard Life £146,000, placed the company in a situation in which it was obliged to manage the estate in Limerick when no purchaser could be found. There were similar problems on this side of the Irish Sea. Skibo Castle was repossessed from Ewan Sutherland, who had lost heavily after speculating in Highland Railway shares, and in 1886 the Earl of Glasgow's loans were called in, with the result that he had to sell his estates and four homes.[21] Despite these setbacks, very large loans to the aristocracy were provided throughout the Victorian era. Some insurance companies faced the collapse that overcame some of the banks. In 1869 the Albert Life Assurance Company and the European Assurance Society both failed, the result of an aggressive selling policy and the accumulation of large debts.[22]

The growth of the international economy in the nineteenth century offered business opportunities throughout the world for insurance companies. One notable feature of the insurance companies was their early entry into world markets. By the 1830s Standard Life, with strong Irish links, was operating in Dublin and Cork. But it also had an office in Quebec, and by mid-century its subsidiary company, Colonial Life, was established in North America, particularly in Canada, in the West Indies and Ceylon. For much of the nineteenth century Canada remained the principal overseas market, and by the eve of the First World War North America had become a major centre for both life business and investment.

In the 1830s the first joint stock companies for overseas investment were established, notably in Aberdeen in the form of the Illinois Investment Company. Australia, Canada and the United States were prime markets for such developments, and these activities increased later in the century, attracted by the security of land and the high interest rates that

19. M. Moss, *Standard Life, 1825–2000* (Edinburgh: Mainstream, 2000), p. 83.
20. Ibid., p. 95.
21. Ibid., pp. 110–11.
22. Ibid., p. 100.

indicated a shortage of capital. This type of activity greatly increased in the last quarter of the century. The Dundee Land Investment Company was formed in 1878 to purchase land for resale in small lots, as did the Scottish Manitoba and North-West Real Estate Company founded in Edinburgh in 1881. But there were great risks involved, and the latter company lost 33 per cent of its capital stock in twelve years as land depreciated.[23] Other Scottish investment companies placed their funds in cattle ranching in the 1880s as mortgage investment in the American west became a Scottish speciality. The Edinburgh-based Prairie Cattle Company, formed in 1880, was the first large-scale joint stock venture undertaken by British capital in Texas. Edinburgh and Dundee interests were predominant in investment trusts by the turn of the century.

A step change in the financial markets was brought about by the flotation of railway companies that required far greater investment than any previous activity. An obvious manifestation of this, and an important step in the increasing formalisation of financial markets, was the establishment of local stock exchanges. Further, the growth of trade in railway stock effectively created stockbroking as a distinct activity. Several Glasgow-based brokers began to handle railway-company flotations in the 1830s and 1840s. Stock exchanges were established in both Glasgow and Edinburgh in 1844, and in Aberdeen in the following year but amalgamation, forced when the boom collapsed, left a single stock exchange in each city. But there were 46 railways in Scotland with a combined capital of £5.7 million. Many of the railway companies were oversubscribed sometimes by six or seven times by 1845.[24] By 1910, Scotland had a total railway investment of £136.4 million.[25] Several large investment companies were also floated in the 1830s, such as the Illinois Investment Company with a capital of £100,000, and the North American Investment Company with a capital of £213,000.

Scottish stock exchanges adopted specialist interests from the 1870s. By then the stock exchanges were dealing in property companies that accepted small loans and made advances to speculative builders on property. By 1877 Edinburgh had seventeen companies with loans worth £4 million. The collapse of the City of Glasgow Bank in 1878 brought down many of these firms.[26] At the same time there appeared mortgage and investment companies raising funds in Scotland that were lent in

23. R. C. Michie, *Money, Mania and Markets: Investment, Company Formation and the Stock Exchange in Nineteenth-Century Scotland* (Edinburgh: John Donald, 1981), p. 157.
24. Ibid., pp. 92, 95.
25. E. Crammond, 'The economic position of Scotland and her financial relations with England and Ireland', *Journal of the Royal Statistical Society*, new series, 75 (1912), pp. 157–75, at p. 164.
26. W. A. Thomas, *The Provincial Stock Exchanges* (London: Frank Cass, 1973), p. 302.

the United States at 8 per cent interest. Edinburgh focused on railways, mining and finance while Glasgow concentrated on railways and mining. Some speculative ventures led to grief. The Glasgow Stock Exchange was closely involved in the gold-mining speculation in India in 1879–81. By 1883 many firms were in liquidation and the shares had lost all value. Glasgow was also engaged in the South African land and mining boom of the 1890s and the financing of rubber plantations in 1909–10. Apart from their international interests, the stock exchanges retained a strong interest in local activities, shale oil in the case of Edinburgh and Glasgow, fishing in Aberdeen and jute, fishing and shipping in Dundee. By the 1890s the level of business was falling, as markets became increasingly integrated through improved communications and stock exchange business became increasingly concentrated on the London Stock Exchange.

One financial institution that fared relatively poorly in Victorian Scotland was the building society. Between 1845 and 1978 Scotland produced only 19 building societies out of a United Kingdom total of 339. Scotland's share of building society assets fell consistently below its share of population, and was only 2.9 per cent of the total in 1913 and 0.4 per cent by 1978.[27] This particular weakness reflected the low rate of owner occupancy, especially before 1914, by which date the vast majority of British societies had been established.

In the course of these two centuries Scotland had developed a complex and highly integrated financial structure that had close links to the London financial markets and metropolitan institutions that represented the heart of the international financial network. This, in turn, linked the Scottish financial network to the world economy. While this was true of banks and insurance companies in the English provinces, they were so much closer to London and therefore more easily subsumed within the metropolitan network. Scotland was sufficiently far removed to maintain a partial independence and to develop a coherent and specifically Scottish structure. The greatest possible importance in the creation of that structure must be accorded to the public banks, which, from the earliest days of the formation of the financial structure, had been operative in establishing a distinctly Scottish and partially separate structure. When the era of institutional consolidation arrived following the First World War, financial institutions that were part of the Scottish network had a much better chance of maintaining their independence

---

27. G. Davies, *Building Societies and their Branches: A Regional Economic Survey* (London: Franey and Co., 1981), p. 36.

than might have been the case in different circumstances. So, while the process of amalgamation continued to whittle away at the number of joint stock banks and insurance houses, Scottish financial institutions survived with greater success than their counterparts in many other sectors of the economy.

THE SUPPLY OF CAPITAL TO THE FINANCIAL INSTITUTIONS

The financial network provided a mechanism for the mobilisation and reallocation of capital. The first stage of that process was the supply of necessary investment to enable the institutions to commence and build their businesses, and thereby to become the conduit for the movement of capital. Subsequent upon the attraction of investment to commence business, additional resources came from the commercial activities themselves. So bank deposits and insurance premiums determined the sums available for investment, both for protection against loss and as a source of additional profit. An indication of the growth of the system is provided by Checkland's estimates of the scale of the banking system in terms of assets/liabilities at several benchmark dates, as shown in Figure 4.1. This was relatively modest until the conclusion of the Napoleonic Wars and substantially more rapid thereafter. The inclusion of non-banking parts of the financial network would have considerably increased the scale and growth rate of the financial system in the nineteenth century. The records of the Clydesdale Bank, showing deposits and advances, as indicated in Figure 4.2, confirms the impressively upward trend of Victorian finance. The increasing ratio of deposits to advances towards the close of the century is indicative of the growing financial security of the most successful institutions.

The largest organisations needed a government charter to allow shares to be transferred, and the chartered banks needed government permission to increase the size of their capital stock, and periodically did so. Not surprisingly the two great public banks drew their resources from the landed and commercial interests in the eighteenth century. The provincial banks that appeared about the middle of the eighteenth century were characterised by a small number of partners and strong local interest. Only 6 per cent of the shareholders in the Aberdeen Banking Company and 5 per cent of subscribers to the Dundee Assurance Company were not resident in those particular localities.[28] The

---

28. Michie, *Money, Mania and Markets*, p. 7.

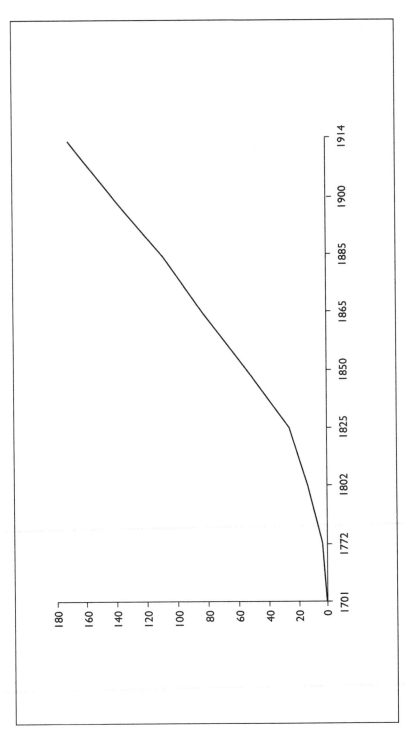

Figure 4.1. Scottish banking system. Assests/Liabilities (£m).

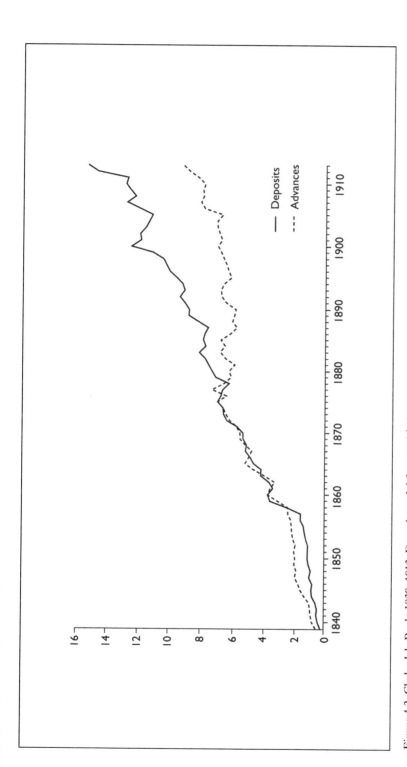

Figure 4.2. Clydesdale Bank, 1839–1913. Deposits and Advances (£m).
Source: Charles W. Munn, *The Clydesdale Bank: The First 150 Years* (Glasgow: Collins, 1988), pp. 338–40.

Paisley Banking Company, founded in 1783, had nine partners, five of whom were local merchants, three of whom were Glasgow merchants, and one was a local landowner. The Dundee Banking Company had thirty-six partners, primarily local traders but included eight members of the landed gentry. The Paisley Union Banking Company, established in 1788, numbered among its partners landowners, mine owners, merchants and cotton manufacturers. The Falkirk Banking Company, founded in 1789, reflected the town's position as an important market for agricultural produce by including malting and distilling interests among its partners. The Aberdeen Banking Company reflected wider trends as the composition of its partners changed in the course of the eighteenth century, and as lawyers and merchants replaced landowners. It was a relatively large undertaking with 197 partners and a proposed note issue of £100,000.[29] Some of these small banks fell victim to their specialist interests. The Falkirk Bank collapsed in 1816 as the farmers and distillers who had been both partners and the best customers of the bank for loans fell into commercial difficulties. The same fate overtook the Stirling Banking Company a decade later when agricultural depression undermined grain dealers, maltsters and distillers. The Shetland Banking Company that operated between 1821 and 1842 was closely tied to the mercantile interests of its partners. Poor crops and bad fishing led to the demise of this bank.[30]

In the nineteenth century small co-partnerships in banking were supplanted by joint stock companies. They were able both to raise much larger capital and, thereby, to offer greater security. Joint stock bank shares offered an attractive investment with a good chance of realising a substantial premium in five years. There were other advantages in that shareholders could borrow against the security of their shares, and were offered new share issues at below-market price. Shareholders of the Clydesdale Bank were allowed to borrow the equivalent of half their paid-up shares at a reduced rate of interest.[31] But there was a high risk because of unlimited liability. Apart from the collapse of the Ayr Bank in 1772, there were two other spectacular and costly failures in Scottish banking. Both were the result of allowing the accumulation of a very large debt by a small number of commercial creditors. The collapse of the Western Bank in 1857 was the consequence of five companies together accumulating a debt of £1.6 million. When three of the companies, with a combined debt of £1.2 million, went bankrupt, the

29. Checkland, *Scottish Banking*, pp. 112, 115.
30. Munn, *Scottish Provincial Banking*, pp. 43, 71, 85–8.
31. Munn, *Clydesdale Bank*, p. 45.

Western Bank followed, leaving its shareholders with losses of £3 million and without the protection of limited liability. The City of Glasgow Bank collapsed in 1878, when three companies together owed £5.4 million out of a total lending of £12 million. A criminal trial for fraud, by the issue of false balance sheets, resulted in prison sentences for some of the principals of the company.[32]

The first of the large joint stock banks to be established was the Commercial Banking Company of Scotland, founded in Edinburgh, in 1810. Its authorised capital was £3 million, the equivalent of the two major public banks combined at that time. By 1815 the bank had 673 shareholders, many more than any other bank. In 1825 the National Bank of Scotland, in Edinburgh, and the Aberdeen Town and County Bank appeared. The National Bank had 1,300 shareholders and a nominal capital of £5 million. The Aberdeen Town and County Bank had an authorised capital of £750,000 divided into 1,500 shares. Holders included a wide range of Aberdeen interests from the Principal of King's College to innkeepers, chandlers, brewers, builders and ironmongers. The Glasgow Union Banking Company started with 517 shareholders, while the Western Bank attracted 430 and, in Aberdeen, the North of Scotland Bank had 1,563 shareholders.[33] The Clydesdale Bank advertised its shares widely in the press in Scotland and the north of England prior to its formation in 1838, although the bulk of shares eventually went to subscribers located in Glasgow and Edinburgh. The venture attracted almost 1,000 subscribers, all of whom were vetted to ensure their 'respectability and circumstances'.[34] Investors were usually local. By the nineteenth century businesses were larger and the number of shareholders increased. In 1830 the Scottish Union Insurance Company had 5,000 shareholders and in 1836 the North of Scotland Insurance Company had 1,000 shareholders. By 1840 there were 14,000 owners of bank shares in Scotland, over half of them resident in Edinburgh and Glasgow.[35]

The ownership of financial institutions and their capital base came in the eighteenth century from the landed and mercantile élite. As that élite grew in size and wealth, so it became increasingly able and willing to invest more widely. By the nineteenth century the scale of capital required necessitated the shift from partnerships to joint stock companies, so that the ownership became dispersed. But such investment

32. Checkland, *Scottish Banking*, pp. 468–70.
33. Ibid., pp. 287, 307, 326–7, 347.
34. Munn, *Clydesdale Bank*, p. 15.
35. Michie, *Money, Mania and Markets*, p. 66.

did not constitute the entire capital at the disposal of the financial institutions; their commercial operations were intended to generate such resources. For financial institutions there are two sources of such funds. The first is the profits on business conducted, for banks the interest on loans, and fees for financial services such as discounting bills, while for insurance companies the surplus of premium income over payment for policy claims was an important element in their capital accumulation. But financial institutions have a further advantage in that they hold, often for extended periods of time, the funds of their clients in bank deposits, insurance premiums, or building society deposits. These accumulated deposits enabled the financial institutions to become important sources of investment and this marked the real significance of their role in fostering economic progress.

CAPITAL AND INVESTMENT

The suppliers of financial services contribute to the growth of the economy in a variety of ways but most obviously by the provision of loans, credit and investment. In the eighteenth century provincial banks helped local industry. The Aberdeen Banking Company gave credit facilities to develop Aberdeen harbour in 1774 and again in 1812, and for Peterhead harbour at the earlier date. The Perth Banking Company and the Perth United Bank supported the Stanley mills with short-term credit and capital investment. Town councils, faced with a growing demand for infrastructure developments, relied on the banks. The Dundee Banking Company gave advances to Dundee town council in the late eighteenth century, while the Perth banks provided loans for gas lighting, the local hospital, civic buildings, street paving and lighting and a prison, while the Glasgow Waterworks negotiated a credit worth £30,000 from the Glasgow Banking Company in 1830.[36] The iron industry was especially reliant on banking support. This took a variety of forms. The Dalnottar Iron Works had a credit for £1,000 while the Cramond Iron Works secured £2,000 on a heritable bond. The celebrated Carron Iron Works borrowed from the Thistle Bank and the Ayr Bank. Following the collapse of the latter, Carron obtained a loan from the Royal Bank of Scotland. The Royal Bank advanced credit to the Forth and Clyde Navigation, while the Crinan Canal obtained finance from the British Linen Bank. The public banks supported the con-

36. Munn, *Scottish Provincial Banking*, pp. 208, 217–18.

struction of new docks at Leith and infrastructure developments in Edinburgh.[37]

The capacity of the banks to lend was determined by the sums they attracted in deposits. The growth of deposits held by Scottish banks increased from £15 million in 1825 to £132 million by 1914, representing a very substantial increase. The banking community provided investment through loans and overdraft credit facilities. The Clydesdale Bank gave advances to a wide range of industrial concerns, including William Teacher, a wine and spirit merchant at the time who later became a distiller, the Cunard Shipping Company, the Irrawaddy Flotilla and Burmese Shipping Company, the Leeds Waterworks, Glasgow Academy, the City Improvement Trust and the Glasgow Abstainers' Union. The Clydesdale Bank lent to several major shipping and ship-building companies, to engineering and iron manufacturers. It also supported several Cumberland iron and steel companies from its branches established in the north-west of England in the 1870s. The Bank was involved in funding the major infrastructure developments in the Victorian period, including railway companies like the London, Chatham and Dover Railway and the West Highland Railway and tramways in Glasgow, Dundee, Paisley and Kirkcaldy. The Clydesdale Bank also had an extensive list of football club accounts, including Celtic, Rangers, Falkirk, Dundee, Carlisle United and Workington.[38]

The advent of the railway brought a distinctive jump in the scale of capital needed and mobilised. Prior to that development, the principal source of borrowing had been the state, especially in wartime, and there had been a substantial increase in the public debt during the Napoleonic Wars. The railway boom soon became an international phenomenon that had the effect of integrating capital markets throughout the United Kingdom and far beyond into a single system. By the start of the railway age finance was moving freely between Scotland and England. By 1849 it was estimated that 77 per cent of the capital for the North British Railway had been raised in England, and 67 per cent of the finance for the Edinburgh and Glasgow Railway came from the south. But finance also flowed south, Glasgow investors being prominent in the sub-scriptions to the London and Southampton Railway as early as the 1830s. Railway stock continued to be popular. By 1887 Scottish railway companies had £101.8 million invested in their stock, including 12,930 debenture holders, 27,981 ordinary shareholders and 33,861 preference

37. Checkland, *Scottish Banking*, pp. 232–3.
38. Munn, *Clydesdale Bank*, pp. 128–9, 136, 235.

shareholders. Thus about 75,000 shareholders held an average investment of £1,350 in Scottish railways at that date.[39]

The substantial holdings of financial resources by insurance companies and banks meant that these institutions became important
investors. The accumulation of premium income with a lengthy period
before any payment was due gave insurance companies control of assets
that offered an opportunity for profitable investment, as well as a
means of offsetting the risk embodied in the policies they had issued. But
investment opportunities were less obvious before the railway boom.
Standard Life started buying land in the 1850s because interest rates
were low. It bought debentures in the Glasgow, Paisley and Greenock
Railway and in the Edinburgh and Glasgow Railway, as well as in the
Edinburgh, Perth and Dundee Railway. But the latter soon fell into
financial difficulties and this discouraged the company from further
railway investment for some time. However, in 1866 the company gave
a loan of £30,000 to the Highland Railway on the security not of the
railway itself but of its directors who were local landowners. The
directors of Standard Life were also worried about property development and the threat of fluctuating prices, although they did lend to
the Kelvinside Estate Company in 1856 to develop suburban Glasgow.
A further loan was granted to the same company in 1869 as was an
investment in the Castle Hill Estate in Ealing in west London.[40] Standard
Life was much more inclined to support the provision of public utilities,
and lent to Liverpool Corporation for the construction of a new prison,
to Manchester Corporation for slum clearance, to the London Hospital
for Women, to the Edinburgh Water Company, to the Peebles Poorhouse
and to the Darlington Union Workhouse. But some industrial investments were attractive, such as the financial support given to Merry
and Cunninghame for the purchase of the Glengarnock iron works in
1872.

Despite its earlier reservations about railway projects in Britain,
Standard Life built a substantial portfolio of investments in railways
overseas in the late nineteenth century, including stock in the East
Indian, Great Indian Peninsular and Tasmania Railways.[41] The Scottish
Widows' Fund Life Assurance Society also changed policy towards the
end of the century, replacing mortgages on land with investments
overseas. By 1913 the company had investments worth £21.5 million

39. Michie, *Money, Mania and Markets*, pp. 67, 117, 159.
40. Moss, *Standard Life*, pp. 76–7, 97.
41. Ibid., pp. 77–9, 97–8.

with considerable sums in overseas stocks and railway bonds.[42] By the eve of the First World War, Standard Life had investments in railways in North America, Europe, Africa, India and Burma. In 1891 Standard Life adjusted its investment strategy to include state bonds and railway stock from around the world, including the Santa Fé Railway, the Canadian Atlantic Railway, and the Grand Trunk Railway in Canada. In the first decade of the new century Standard Life invested substantially in farm mortgages in the American and Canadian west. By 1912 it had 23 per cent of its investments in Canada and 22 per cent in the United States, a total investment worth £6 million. Scottish Widows, with an investment of £2.8 million, and Scottish Provident, with an investment of £2.7 million, were also substantial investors in North America.

Personal investment usually requires a trade-off between the desire to exploit fully all available opportunities to increase wealth with the need to curb the risks entailed to avoid substantial loss. The larger the investment portfolio, the greater is the capability for risk reduction if not elimination. Investment trusts may be regarded as forerunners of unit trusts in allowing subscribers to invest on a scale of their choice and without excessive risk. Scotland provided the only investment trusts formed outside London in the early years of these financial instruments. Robert Fleming played a major part, initially in Dundee, and later in London. In 1873 he established the First Scottish American Investment Trust for investment in American railway mortgage bonds. Together with two other issues, in 1873 and 1875, a total of £1.1 million was raised. These investments were intended to be low risk. The bond was split between thirty and sixty different securities and no security had more than 5 per cent of the total investment. Security was augmented by the selection of the highest quality bonds in land. Other Scottish companies stuck to the same formula. The Scottish American Investment Company of Edinburgh confined itself to government stocks, land and railways in the United States and Canada. The Northern American Trust Company of Dundee remained loyal to railway bonds.

The opportunities of the international financial markets were considerable for many of the major Scottish financial institutions. The evidence of Standard Life's investment policy illustrates this, as shown in Figure 4.3. There was a marked increase in investments in the decades prior to the First World War that involved a clear restructuring of the investment portfolio. Much of the increase was brought about by the

---

42. Sir Herbert Maxwell, *Annals of the Scottish Widows' Fund and Life Assurance Society* (Edinburgh: R. and R. Clark, 1914), pp. 116, 131.

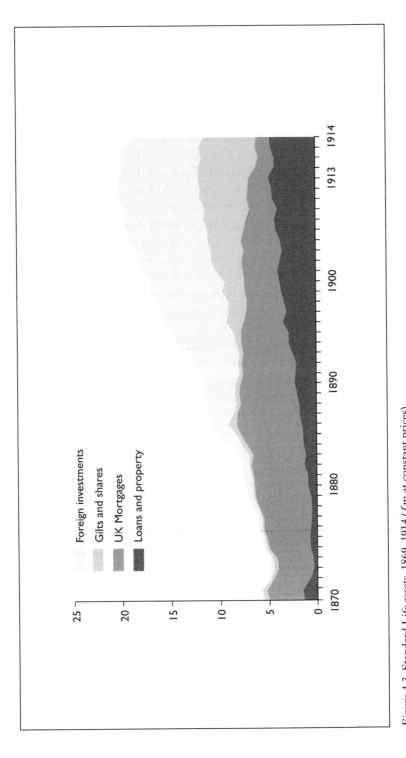

Figure 4.3. Standard Life assets, 1869–1914 (£m at constant prices).
Source: Michael Moss, *Standard Life, 1825–2000* (Edinburgh: Mainstream, 2000), pp. 386–7.

increase in overseas mortgages and foreign government stocks. It was the boom in international markets that enabled Standard Life and other companies to expand. This factor was especially important because it released them from reliance on the domestic Scottish or even British economy. This locational flexibility would become even more important in the twentieth century when the domestic economy faced a series of severe economic difficulties.

FINANCE AND THE SCOTTISH ECONOMY

By the eve of the First World War, the large financial institutions had become major components of the Scottish economy. A survey of business structure in 1904/5 identified 108 companies in Scotland that enjoyed a value of share capital in excess of £300,000. Of these companies, eight were banks, fourteen were insurance companies, and twenty-two were investment or property companies. Only railway companies possessed more financial power than the financiers. The Scottish economy was dominated financially by the North British Railway, with a capital of £47 million, and the Caledonian Railway, with a capital investment of £42 million. Only the Glasgow and South West Railway and J. & P. Coats, the thread manufacturer, among the non-financial companies enjoyed a capital greater than £5 million. But seven banks had deposits in excess of £10 million, four insurance companies had funds between £10–17 million in their responsibility, and five investment companies each had capital in excess of £1 million.[43]

Furthermore, the financial companies stood at the heart of the interlocking networks of companies, reflected in multiple directorships. The hub of the economy lay in two networks, one based in Edinburgh and including the Royal Bank of Scotland, the British Linen Bank, and the North British Railway as its central elements, and the other based in Glasgow and focused on the Clydesdale Bank, the Caledonian Railway and the Tennant family chemical and steel empire. Scottish Widows, Standard Life and the Union Bank of Scotland were also important components of the network of commercial and financial influence. The majority of these links developed and were perpetuated through individuals. The founder and first chairman of the Clydesdale Bank was James Lumsden, partner in a family stationery and publishing company

43. J. Scott and M. Hughes, *The Anatomy of Scottish Capital: Scottish Companies and Scottish Capital, 1900–1979* (London: Croom Helm, 1980), pp. 11, 18, 64.

based in Glasgow. He also participated in the founding of the City of Glasgow Life Assurance Company and the City and Suburban Gas Company. He invested in the new railway companies, in the Glasgow Union Banking Company and was a partner in a Clyde river steamer. In public life, he served for twenty years on the Glasgow Police Commission, and as Lord Provost of Glasgow from 1843 to 1846. His son, Sir James Lumsden, joined the family business and later joined the board of the Glasgow and South West Railway, serving as deputy chairman and then chairman for a total of seventeen years. He, too, served as Lord Provost of Glasgow from 1866 to 1869.[44] Sir James King was chairman of the Clydesdale Bank between 1882 and 1911, with two short breaks. He was also the chairman of the Caledonian Railway, and held directorships in J. & P. Coats, the Lothian Coal Company, the Coltness Iron Company, Young's Paraffin Light & Mineral Oil Company, and Tharsis Sulphur and Copper. He too served on Glasgow City Council as Dean of Guild and Lord Provost.

There is no suggestion in the historical literature that the Scottish economy as a whole was disadvantaged by shortage of investment prior to 1914. Existing accumulations of finance appear to have been sufficient for developmental purposes except for the earlier decades of the eighteenth century immediately after the losses incurred in the Darien scheme. Indeed, the substantial flows of capita abroad in the quarter-century before the Great War suggests a possible surplus. It is important to remember that the purpose of investment by individuals or institutions is to improve the welfare of those shareholders. Any benefit to the economy as a whole is an unintended derivative. There is at least one area of economic and social importance that has been identified as suffering from insufficient investment in this period. Housing did not attract adequate investment to accommodate satisfactorily the majority of the population because they were unable to earn incomes that would pay the rent required if the cost of construction was to be recovered. The gains made by the prosperous minority through international investment may, therefore, represent a further effect of the highly skewed distribution of income and wealth in Scotland before 1914.

44. Reid, *Clydesdale Bank*, pp. 156, 186.

FURTHER READING

Checkland, S. G., *Scottish Banking: A History, 1695–1973* (Glasgow: Collins, 1975).
Michie, R. C., *Money, Mania and Markets: Investment, Company Formation and the Stock Exchange in Nineteenth-Century Scotland* (Edinburgh: John Donald, 1981).
Moss, M., *Standard Life, 1825–2000* (Edinburgh: Mainstream, 2000).
Munn, C. W., *The Scottish Provincial Banking Companies, 1747–1864* (Edinburgh: John Donald, 1981).
Munn, C. W., *Clydesdale Bank: The First One Hundred and Fifty Years* (Glasgow: Collins, 1988).
Saville, R., *Bank of Scotland: A History, 1695–1995* (Edinburgh: Edinburgh University Press, 1996).

CHAPTER FIVE

Economic Progress: Wealth and Poverty

C. H. Lee

INTRODUCTION: WHAT IS PROGRESS?

Studies of economic growth tend naturally to focus on the processes by which that growth is achieved, what economists call the supply side of the economy. There is ample justification for this focus, but it is worth remembering that the purpose of economic advance is determined and driven, at least equally, by the demand side of the economic system, reflecting the needs, wants and desires of all members of society. Economic activity is seldom undertaken as an end in itself but as a means to increasing personal prosperity. At the lowest level and in the poorest society, this is a struggle to produce sufficient food, clothing and shelter to ensure survival. In a modern and relatively prosperous society, it is driven by the desire for greater affluence, status symbols or the fruits of office. Few societies, if any, have ever enjoyed either universal prosperity or perfect equality between citizens. Far more typical has been the existence of wide variations in prosperity between groups or classes of citizens within a general level of prosperity that, apart from the most recent past, has been low but improving slowly through time. That has been the characteristic state of Scottish society during the past three centuries.

Given this general context, the extent and strength of economic advance can be seen to depend on two critical factors, the aggregate rate of economic growth by which society as a whole becomes richer, and the distribution of those additional benefits between citizens. In the process of economic advance characteristic of modern industrialisation two further features have added their influence. Economic change has brought structural change that involved both the creation of new activities and the decline of traditionally established forms of work. Further, an important characteristic of modernisation, of particular importance in the Scottish experience, was the growth of population. These are the essential variables that determined the size and the distribution of economic progress.

THE PATTERNS OF ECONOMIC CHANGE

Ideally, indicators of progress and prosperity should be measured so that their scale and relative influence may be accurately determined. Unfortunately, the era of abundant and relatively reliable statistics does not extend further back in time than the Second World War. For a century before that event, there exists a more limited and less secure set of statistical data. Before about 1840 data are increasingly patchy in availability and uncertain in quality. These general rules of thumb should be borne in mind when evaluating statistical information.

Without doubt the best available indicator of the dimensions of economic advance lies in estimates of population growth, principally because they are available for a long period of time and in generally reliable form. The growth of population has been a universal characteristic of economic progress, an indicator of increasing capability to generate affluence or to diminish poverty, and a stimulus to further advance by providing additional workers and consumers. For Scotland the Census of Population provides estimates for each decade from 1801 onward. Prior to that date, there is Dr Webster's celebrated estimate for 1755 together with a few occasional estimates and suggestions that have produced a consensus opinion that the population of Scotland in 1701 was about 1.1 million persons. In the eighteenth century there was modest growth, but the increase of 46 per cent between 1701 and 1801, assuming the population was 1.1 million at the former date, represents an average increase of less than half of 1 per cent per annum, or five additional people for every thousand people. In the twentieth century there was little growth at all, less than 15 per cent between 1901 and 2001, an addition of fewer than two people per thousand. In sharp contrast, the nineteenth century witnessed substantial increase so that there were almost three times as many Scots in 1901 as there had been a hundred years earlier.

An alternative way of expressing long-term population growth is in the form of an index, as shown in Figure 5.1, in which population

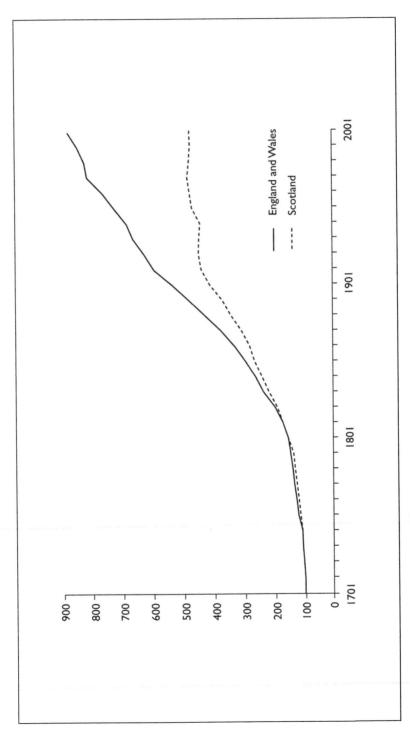

Figure 5.1. Index of population (1701 = 100).

growth is described as proportionate to a base year, here taken to be 1701. This shows clearly the three phases of Scottish demographic change. This figure also provides a comparison of Scottish population growth with the experience of England and Wales, a comparison that highlights two principal characteristics. In the early phase of development, from 1701 to approximately 1820, the population growth patterns of the two economies were almost identical. Thereafter there was a sharp divergence as the Scottish population growth levelled off at a rate of increase well below that of its southern neighbour.

The substantial differences in population growth in different historical periods were mirrored in considerable variations within Scotland. Webster's estimates suggested a relatively even spread of population, in that the six regions identified in Figure 5.2 were attributed very similar shares of the total population. This does not, of course, imply that population was spread evenly across the face of the country. Some regions, notably the Highlands, covered a much greater land mass than other regions and included considerable tracts of inhospitable terrain, and consequently would always have had fewer persons per acre than Lowland regions with significant urban centres. The process of population increase had a profound effect on the distribution of population within Scotland. The rural areas in the north and the south grew slowly until the mid-nineteenth century but declined thereafter. The great bulk of the population increase was concentrated in the central Lowlands between the estuaries of the Clyde and the Forth, but spilling southward into the counties of Ayr and Lanark and northward into Stirling and Fife. Modest increase in Grampian, centred on Aberdeen, and Tayside, centred on Dundee, does not seriously modify the conclusion that central Scotland completely dominated population growth, especially in the great expansion of the nineteenth century.

The census of population also provides another principal indicator of economic change in the form of employment structure. While these data contain their own limitations and elements of uncertainty, they can be accepted as providing an accurate broad-brush outline of the main economic activities probably from the 1841 survey onward. Earlier changes have to be inferred from backward extrapolation from the mid-nineteenth century, and supplemented by other evidence. Thus the Victorian period will be discussed prior to the century that preceded it. Since this period coincided with the greatest increase in Scottish population, it would be expected that employment would also grow. The recorded workforce of Scotland, according to the respective censuses of 1851 and 1911, was 1.3 million and 2.1 million, but this change included

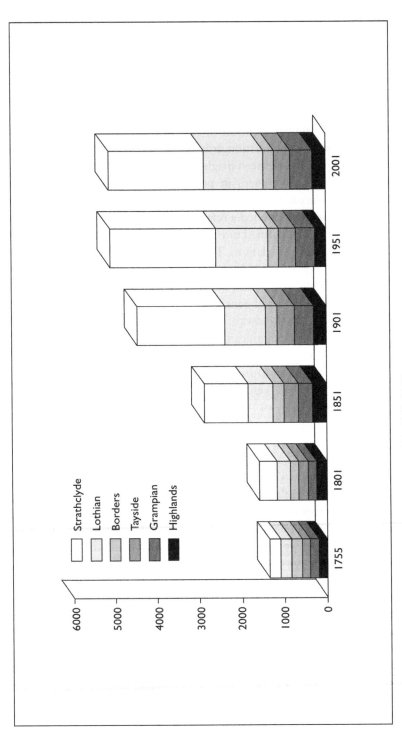

Figure 5.2. Scottish population (000s) (1755, 1801, 1851, 1901, 1951, 2001).

both an increase in some activities and contraction in others.[1] A decline in the labour force usually indicates one of two causes, an increase in efficiency so that fewer workers are required or a decline in competitiveness so that work moves elsewhere. There were two main areas of decline in Scottish employment during this period. Agriculture and related activities fell from a peak of 316,000 in 1851 to 218,000 by 1911, the result certainly of increased productivity and possibly also of some loss of competitiveness in the face of cheap food imports from abroad. Textile and clothing employment fell from a peak of 363,000 in 1851 to reach 305,000 by 1911, a development that largely reflected the greater comparative advantage of some English regions in cotton and woollen manufacture, although Scotland remained successful in specific niche markets such as thread and jute.

Given the fact that employment in Scotland doubled between 1851 and 1911, compensation for these losses was provided by growth in other sectors. This was the period in which Scottish heavy industry enjoyed its greatest expansion, encompassing the entire range of production process from coal-mining and iron-ore excavation to iron and steel manufacture, heavy engineering and shipbuilding. These activities together added 300,000 jobs to the Scottish economy during this period. The growth of this industrial network of activities had to be supplemented and supported by transport and commercial infrastructure that added in excess of another 200,000 jobs, while other manufactures added another 100,000 jobs and the professions almost 200,000 jobs. In this period, the Scottish economy was able to compensate with ease for the loss of jobs in sectors that were either declining or achieving productivity gains.

Observations on the century and a half before 1851 must be more circumspect. Given the modest rate of growth of population, a reasonable assumption seems to be that employment would have increased at a similar rate. The fact that agricultural employment, and textiles and clothing, both experienced growth in the 1840s, suggests both that they peaked in 1851 and that they had expanded during the previous century. The fact that, in 1841, agricultural activities accounted for 24.3 per cent of Scottish employment, and that textiles and clothing accounted for a further 25.9 per cent of the total, indicates their overwhelming importance in the earlier period. The only other significantly large employment category, personal services, which were mainly domestic services, added a further 17.5 per cent to the workforce. It seems highly probable, there-

---

1. C. H. Lee, *British Regional Employment Statistics, 1841–1971* (Cambridge: Cambridge University Press, 1979).

fore, that eighteenth-century development comprised substantially of the modest expansion of existing and pre-modern activities supplemented by the new trade opportunities offered in the New World.

This outline of Scottish population and employment change can be regarded as being generally accurate. But equally important in this period was the fact that regional variations within Scotland were substantial and the experience of those regions exhibited wide diversity. This should not be a cause of particular surprise. Scotland covers a very large and varied geographical area with a great diversity of landforms and natural resources. Data limitations, greater for Scottish regions than for the national economy, restrict statistically supported exposition. Population data again provide the best general outline of change. Within the context of modest eighteenth-century growth and more rapid nineteenth-century growth, there were two distinctive regional experiences. The rural peripheral regions reached a peak of their growth in the Victorian period, Dumfries and Galloway together with the Highlands in 1851, and the Borders in 1891. Thereafter their populations were static or falling. Other regions continued to grow, but the greatest differential increase was recorded in the west of Scotland in the greater Clydeside area that later became defined as Strathclyde region. These population changes were mirrored by changes in the employment structure. The rural regions lost jobs in agriculture, and the Highlands and Grampian regions lost work in the clothing and textile trades. Aberdeen had been a substantial centre for textile manufacture, using wool produced in its rural hinterland. But the economic collapse in the city in 1848, linked to financial speculation that came to grief, and brought ruin to many eminent citizens who were engaged in the manufacture of textiles.[2] As for the growth of heavy industry in the Victorian era, it was concentrated in the emergent 'central belt' of industrial activity joining the estuaries of Clyde and Forth, but spilling outward from Glasgow at its centre. By inference, the more modest growth prior to 1850 probably saw employment creation in most if not all regions. Even the Highlands enjoyed increased activity for a while, partly as a result of the creation of the crofting community.

It is a commonplace of present-day economic analysis to use national income or the stock of national wealth as the essential indicators of relative prosperity between nations or regions, as well as for each jurisdiction over time. Unfortunately, estimates for national income or wealth are

---

2. R. Perren, 'The nineteenth-century economy', in W. H. Fraser and C. H. Lee (eds), *Aberdeen, 1800–2000: A New History* (East Linton: Tuckwell Press, 2000), pp. 80–2.

as infrequent as they are uncertain for any time before the twentieth century. The national wealth of Scotland was estimated in 1798 at £120 million and, perhaps more meaningfully, as constituting 12.5 per cent of the wealth of Great Britain. Dudley Baxter estimated that the average Scottish wage for those in employment in 1867 was 86.9 per cent of the average for England and Wales, while Leone Levi's estimates for 1866 and 1885 respectively gave relative proportions of 90.1 per cent and 88.6 per cent.[3] By 1910, according to Edgar Crammond's estimate, it had risen to £1,451 million or £305 per head of population. This indicated that Scotland enjoyed 9.1 per cent of the wealth of the United Kingdom at that time. The national wealth for England and Wales was estimated at £383 per capita, suggesting that Scotland enjoyed a relative stock of wealth of almost 80 per cent of its southern neighbour. However, alternative methods of estimation, on the basis of estates liable to estate duty or Scotland's share of tax revenue, as compared to the capitalisation of assets adopted by Crammond, suggested a higher share of British wealth for Scotland. These were, respectively 10.4 per cent and 10.3 per cent, both close to Scotland's share of United Kingdom population of 10.5 per cent.[4] Estimates of national income are equally elusive. The estimate for 1910 produced a figure of £173.5 million, indicating a per capita income of £36 for Scotland, compared to £48 for England and Wales. A limited analysis of the growth of Scottish capital and income over time is afforded by comparison of Crammond's estimates with those of Robert Giffen for 1885.[5] These figures show the restructuring of the resources of the economy towards public companies and overseas investment and away from land, farming and fishing.

Crammond's estimate is lower than the series of national income figures estimated by A. D. Campbell that commence in 1924. But Campbell's estimate is not directly comparable since it expresses Scottish per capita income as a proportion of the United Kingdom average within which Scottish income is also included, approximately 96 per cent.[6] On the basis of such figures, Scottish national income would be estimated at approximately 90 per cent of that for England and Wales. The statistical evidence, albeit very limited, indicates clearly that Scotland enjoyed population increase and employment growth through-

3. A. L. Bowley, *Wages in the United Kingdom in the Nineteenth Century* (Cambridge: Cambridge University Press, 1900), p. 65.
4. E. Crammond, 'The economic position of Scotland and her financial relations with England and Ireland', *Journal of the Royal Statistical Society*, new series, 75 (1912), pp. 157–75, at 168–9.
5. R. C. Michie, *Money, Mania and Markets: Investment, Company Formation and the Stock Exchange in Nineteenth-Century Scotland* (Edinburgh: John Donald, 1981), p. 137.
6. A. D. Campbell, 'Changes in Scottish incomes, 1924–49', *Economic Journal*, 65 (1955), p. 231.

out these two centuries. There was also structural change as some activities declined while others grew substantially. These changes thus brought marked adjustments in the regional balance of activities. However, this progress seems to have fallen short of that achieved by England and Wales, leaving a deficit in per capita income of between 10 and 25 per cent by the beginning of the twentieth century.

THE BENEFICIARIES OF ECONOMIC PROGRESS

Economic progress does not simply appear with spontaneous convenience, except perhaps in the form of a newly discovered natural resource. Rather, it is the product of individual and corporate efforts to secure increased prosperity. It is not surprising that the radical changes that induced improvements in Scottish farming should be driven by the aspirations of landowners and tenants, nor that the contentious Act of Union of 1707 should be underpinned by the commercial ambitions of some Scots who sought untroubled access to English and colonial markets. There is an abundance of evidence demonstrating opportunities for increasing incomes in eighteenth-century Scotland. Perhaps the most obvious were Glasgow's 'tobacco lords', who prospered in the colonial trade, making and losing fortunes as prices fluctuated. They were few in number. Only 163 merchant burgesses were directly and consistently engaged in the trade between 1740 and 1790. Most came from established merchant families and borrowed capital from their peers in trade in the west of Scotland through the issue of bonds. A sample of such investors taken from the 1760s included landowners, booksellers, goldsmiths, factors, physicians and the Town Clerk of Glasgow.[7] Thus the fruits of the tobacco trade became widely spread through the west of Scotland. At least sixty-two landed estates were purchased between 1770 and 1815, and investments made using proceeds from the tobacco trade included boot and shoe manufacture, iron works, glass works and textile manufacture. This is the virtuous circulation of prosperity in creating further economic advance.

The distribution of the benefits of progress is of critical importance, influencing both the extent of social inequity and the generation of sustained economic growth. Whether or not inequality is helpful or disadvantageous to growth is, of course, a matter of live dispute.[8] There

7. T. M. Devine, 'The golden age of tobacco', in T. M. Devine and G. Jackson (eds), *Glasgow*, vol. I: *Beginnings to 1830* (Manchester: Manchester University Press, 1995), pp. 156–7.
8. J. R. Williamson, 'The historical content of the Classical labour surplus model', *Population and Development Review*, 11 (1985), pp. 183–7.

is ample evidence to suggest that Scottish wealth was very unevenly distributed, with much of it concentrated in the hands of a small number of large-scale landowners before the main onset of industrialisation. This is a common feature of pre-industrial societies. One of the earliest estimates of Scottish wealth is Lee Soltow's study of land valuations based on periodic surveys from 1770 to 1872–3. In 1770 only a little more than 2 per cent of adult males were actually owners, although it has been argued that the addition of some joint ownerships might increase this to 5 per cent.[9] Scottish land was concentrated in few hands, and included very large holdings by the Duke of Buccleuch, the Duke of Hamilton and Sir Lawrence Dundas. Indeed, a small group of ninety-two individuals owned the bulk of the landed estates in 1770. Comparisons with data for 1800, 1825 and 1854 reveal similar levels of inequality.

There exists more specific evidence of great individual prosperity accumulated in the nineteenth century, and catalogued in the records of estates changing hands, as revealed by William Rubenstein's extensive investigations. Between 1809, when records began, and 1914 probate records delineate the estates of the most prosperous citizens. This survey identified 162 millionaires who died within the period, 446 half-millionaires and 238 lesser wealthy. In Scotland there were 16, 40 and 5 representatives in the respective groups. The great majority of these rich Scots came from Clydeside. The list of largest fortunes, each over £2 million, included seven Scots in the total of forty. These included the Duke of Sutherland, first in the list but who included extensive landed interests in England as well as Scotland, the Marquess of Bute, also a landowner with interests outside Scotland, Sir Charles Tennant, representing the Glasgow chemical dynasty, William Baird and William Weir, Lanarkshire ironmasters, and Peter Coats and Sir James Coats of the Paisley thread-manufacturing firm.[10] In view of the fact that Scotland accounted for about 10 per cent of the British population, these figures seem to indicate a reasonable level of representation, with almost 10 per cent of millionaires, almost 9 per cent of half millionaires and 17.5 per cent of the super rich. Only in the category of the lesser wealthy was Scotland poorly represented. These fortunes represented a blend of old wealth, vested in land, and new wealth created from the opportunities offered by industrial development.

Rich citizens, and even the moderately prosperous, were a small

9. L. Soltow, 'Inequality of wealth in land in Scotland in the eighteenth century', *Scottish Economic and Social History*, 10 (1990), pp. 38–60, at 40–1.
10. W. D. Rubenstein, 'The Victorian middle classes: wealth, occupation, and geography', *Economic History Review*, 2nd series, 30 (1977), pp. 602–23, at 609–11, 614.

minority of the members of society throughout these centuries. While the middle class was clustered within the main urban centres, only 15 per cent of the population of Glasgow in 1800 were so defined.[11] The new tax on incomes, introduced to defray the costs of the Napoleonic Wars and targeting the most prosperous sections of society, was imposed on only about 20,000 Glaswegians, the city's tax burden amounting only to one-third of its share of Scotland's population. By the middle of the nineteenth century the situation had changed substantially, and in 1865 Glaswegians paid 1.5 times the Scottish average income tax. But only 10 per cent of them achieved a level of income that provided real security, and many of those with the greatest wealth derived substantial income from rents on land and property or interest on investments.[12]

The growth of a modestly prosperous group among the middling orders of society is reflected in the emergence of the savings bank movement. It started in 1810, but generated a flurry of new formations in its first decade, and was intended to encourage saving among those with limited resources. By mid-century it had been supplemented by penny banks, intended as vehicles for starting the saving habit en route to a savings bank account. Subscribers to the Glasgow Savings Bank included printers, weavers, factory workers, mechanics and domestic servants. In Perth weavers, mechanics, artificers and domestic servants predominated, but agricultural workers and labourers also contributed.[13] A list of new accounts opened in Edinburgh in 1907 showed that over half were opened by females, mainly married women, minors and domestic servants, while accounts were opened by men who were primarily mechanics, schoolteachers, or shopkeepers. By then there were approximately 500,000 accounts open in Scotland, one for every nine individuals.[14] This suggests that it was the middling ranks of society that contributed to savings banks. The fact that deposits did not decline sharply in the heavy unemployment of the 1920s may also be an indicator that those most liable to suffer unemployment were not always those who took the precaution of preparing for such an eventuality.

For those who were able to prosper in industry or trade, an increasing array of additional opportunities were emerging that enabled wealth to be protected and used to generate further income. One of the most

11. Stana Nenadic, 'The middle ranks and modernisation', in Devine and Jackson (eds), *Glasgow*, vol. I, pp. 279–82.
12. Stana Nenadic, 'The Victorian middle classes', in W. H. Fraser and Irene Maver (eds), *Glasgow*, vol. II: *1830 to 1912* (Manchester: Manchester University Press, 1996), pp. 271–2.
13. M. Moss and A. Slaven, *'From Ledger Book to Laser Beam': A History of the TSB in Scotland from 1810 to 1990* (Edinburgh: TSB Bank, 1992), pp. 28, 32.
14. Ibid., pp. 52, 74.

significant and impressive facets of Scottish economic development in these two centuries lay in the great increase in overseas investment in the last quarter of the nineteenth century. Lenman estimated its growth from £60 million in 1870 to £500 million by 1914.[15] Crammond's estimate for a Scottish national income suggested that £14.5 million or 8.4 per cent of the total in 1910 came from income generated from overseas investments.[16] In conjunction with Giffen's estimate for 1885, this suggests that 44 per cent of the increase in Scottish capital between 1885 and 1910 took the form of overseas investment. The share of new income devoted to foreign investments during the same period was over 31 per cent. Apart from the increase of income and capital added to public companies, overseas investment demonstrated the largest increase. Groups of businessmen with money to invest identified the opening of the west in North America as a prime opportunity. The North of Scotland Mortgage Company, one of the pioneers and run by a prominent Aberdeen businessman and MP James Barclay, lent in Canada, where capital was scarce and interest rates high, and where plentiful land offered an excellent security. The Texas Land and Mortgage Company was based on London but had strong Aberdeen-shire connections with 74 per cent of the shares held in the county.[17]

The Prairie Cattle Company was founded in 1880 in Edinburgh to finance ranching in Texas, although one-third of the funds came from Dundee investors. In fact, Dundee became celebrated for pioneering investment trusts that were established by Robert Fleming, starting, in 1873, with the First Scottish American Investment Trust, specialising in American railway bonds.[18] The scale of activity was reflected in the merger in 1889 of the Dundee Mortgage Company with the Dundee Investment Company to form the Alliance Trust. At the time of merger, the combined assets of the two companies comprised £963,000 in mortgages, £110,000 in real estate and £163,000 in reserves and securities. The new company remained active in the mortgage business until the 1920s when it became an investment trust.

The attractions of the American west for investors were clear in the combination of high returns and low risk, because capital was in short supply and the security of land and real estate could be used to minimise

15. B. Lenman, *An Economic History of Modern Scotland, 1660–1976* (London: B. T. Batsford, 1977), p. 193.
16. Crammond, 'Economic position of Scotland', p. 168.
17. W. G. Kerr, *Scottish Capital on the American Frontier* (Austin: Texas State Historical Association, 1976), pp. 50–2, 69.
18. H. Burton and D. C. Corner, *Investment and Unit Trusts in Britain and America* (London: Elek Books, 1968), p. 20.

risk. But there were risks involved. The depreciation of land values cost the Scottish Manitoba and North-West Real Estate Company, founded in Edinburgh in 1881, one-third of its capital within twelve years. By the late 1880s the market for land and ranching was glutted and prices fell. The North American land boom had been a brief window of opportunity. By the end of the First World War competition from insurance companies and a better flow of capital had reduced interest rates and returns on investments. The list of investors numbered many prominent in Victorian business circles. They included Archibald Coats of the Paisley thread-manufacturing dynasty, William John Menzies, writer to the signet and founding member of the Scottish American Investment Trust, George and David Carmichael, prominent Dundee engineers, William Ogilvie Dalgleish, a Dundee financier, and James Guthrie, from Brechin, a banker and subsequently chairman of the Alliance Trust. In Dundee, especially, local business leaders were prominent in investment enterprises. The management of the Dundee Mortgage Company was dominated by local worthies who represented a diverse range of business interests. William Lowson, who served as vice-chairman and later chairman of the company, was engaged in the family canvas-manufacturing business and held directorships in the Dundee Bank, the Dundee and Arbroath Railway, the Scottish North-Eastern Railway, and the Dundee and London Shipping Company. Another director, Thomas Cox, was a member of the Cox Brothers firm, the largest jute-manufacturing company in Britain.[19] While large investors dominated shareholding, there were smaller holdings that were purchased by railway clerks, small farmers, schoolteachers and tradesmen. In the Scottish American Mortgage Company these small shares were estimated to comprise 20 per cent of the total value of shares but over 60 per cent of the shareholders.[20]

It is quite clear that the Scottish economy in the eighteenth century, and more impressively in the nineteenth century, offered a variety of opportunities for making fortunes, large and small. It is equally clear that a range of ancillary activities emerged designed both to protect accumulated assets and to generate opportunities for further income. There were also opportunities for wealth to be lost through poor investment, unwise or unfortunate speculation or as a consequence of the downswing of the market. Increasingly, these opportunities were related to the emergence of an international economy that vastly increased the range

19. Kerr, *Scottish Capital*, pp. 23, 174–5.
20. Ibid., p. 105.

of potential money-making activities. That Scots played a full part in exploiting these opportunities is not in doubt, but whether Scotland as a whole prospered is less apparent.

WORK AND PAY

For the vast majority of Scots the world of work represented a struggle for survival, an environment in which low pay and intermittent employment meant that financial and personal disaster remained a constant threat. Information on wages is always difficult to interpret and wage rates are not a particularly reliable indicator since they have meaning only in the context of the reliability and continuity of work and local living costs. Certainly economic growth improved wages in some areas. A survey of agricultural wages in the 1790s showed that payment was best in the core area of the central Lowlands, close to the growing urban centres, and that wages declined as they moved away from this central region to the north and the south.[21] A similar pattern was revealed in the evidence collected for the Royal Commission on the Poor Laws in the 1840s.[22] There were variations between areas, the western Highlands faring especially badly, and between employment groups. General labourers fared worst, together with handloom weavers, whose trade was in rapid decline. The chronicler of the demise of handloom weaving estimated that cotton weavers' wages fell by 38 per cent in the two decades after 1820.[23] Even so, many Irish immigrants joined the ranks of the handloom weavers, an activity characterised by one assistant commissioner for handloom weavers as 'the common sewer of all unemployed labour'.[24]

There is also a lengthy literature describing Scotland as a low-wage economy. As early as 1770 John Gibson described Glasgow as a town with very low wages, while James Cleland estimated in 1831 that almost one-quarter of the city's employed population was subject to low pay and irregular work. Devine noted that a massive surplus of unemployed, underemployed and poorly paid persons had accumulated in Glasgow

21. Valerie Morgan, 'Agricultural wage rates in the late eighteenth-century Scotland', *Economic History Review*, 2nd series, 24 (1971), pp. 181–201, at 200.
22. Ian Levitt and Christopher. Smout, *The State of the Scottish Working-Class in 1843* (Edinburgh: Scottish Academic Press, 1979), pp. 173ff.
23. N. Murray, *The Scottish Handloom Weavers, 1780–1850* (Edinburgh: John Donald, 1978), p. 115.
24. R. H. Campbell, 'The making of the industrial city', in Devine and Jackson (eds), *Glasgow*, vol. I, p. 197.

after 1815, boosted by those returning home at the end of the Napoleonic Wars.[25] For the later part of the nineteenth century, there exist a variety of wage rate estimates that support the thesis that Scotland was primarily a low-wage economy, especially when compared to England and Wales. Baxter's survey of national income for 1867 suggested that differentials between skilled and unskilled were greater in Scotland than England, and that overall Scottish incomes were 16–19 per cent less than those in England in the 1860s.[26] Campbell concluded from the evidence of the 1886 Wage Census that Scotland had relatively low wages, although Hunt argued that by the time of the 1906 Wage Census, central Scotland had caught up.[27] Differences between trades provide some support for each interpretation. Baxter's wage estimates for 1867 suggested that the average Scottish wage was 86.9 per cent of the average for England and Wales, while Leone Levi's estimates for 1866 and 1885 gave relative proportions of 90.1 per cent and 88.6 per cent.[28] But too much reliance should not be placed on wage rates, as many employees did not work long enough to receive the full rate, some estimates were inflated and, as Richard Rodger has shown, rents and living costs were relatively high in Scotland. Surveys undertaken by the Board of Trade in 1905 and 1912 found that prices in Scotland were higher than in England for foodstuffs such as flour, butter, cheese, eggs, tea and beef, representing a 10 per cent disadvantage in real income.[29]

Labour markets prior to 1914 were less structured and co-ordinated than their modern counterparts so that unemployment was a frequent experience for many workers and underemployment was endemic. The survey taken in connection with the Royal Commission on the Poor Law, published in 1845, found unemployment present in most districts. Serious unemployment, prolonged or substantial, was found primarily in the western Highlands or the industrial west. The most serious contemporary instance concerned the collapse of textile employment in Paisley, where many small independent workers served as a reserve army for manufacturers. A change in fashion, which made the Paisley shawl less popular, and the onset of a depression in 1841 brought a surge of

25. James Cleland, *Description of the City of Glasgow* (Glasgow: John Smith and Son, 1840); T. M. Devine, 'The urban crisis', in Devine and Jackson (eds), *Glasgow*, vol. I, pp. 407–8.

26. W. W. Knox, *Industrial Nation: Work, Culture and Society in Scotland, 1800–Present* (Edinburgh: Edinburgh University Press, 1999), p. 90.

27. R. H. Campbell, *The Rise and Fall of Scottish Industry, 1707–1939* (Edinburgh: John Donald, 1980), pp. 191–4; E. H. Hunt, *Regional Wage Variations in Britain, 1850–1914* (Oxford: Oxford University Press, 1973), pp. 47–56.

28. Bowley, *Wages in the United Kingdom*, p. 65.

29. R. Rodger, 'Crisis and confrontation in Scottish housing, 1880–1914', in R. Rodger (ed.), *Scottish Housing in the Twentieth Century* (Leicester: Leicester University Press, 1989), p. 32.

bankruptcies and growing unemployment that reached 15,000 by 1843. By this time one-quarter of the citizens of Paisley were living on charity. In the general collapse the town corporation was bankrupted, including among its losses £20,000 entrusted to it by the local savings bank.[30] Local charitable efforts proved insufficient and it took contributions from the rest of the United Kingdom and from overseas to see the town through the crisis.

In 1907 the Glasgow *Herald* stated, with regard to underemployment, that 'the evil is too familiar to require proof'. The Rev. J. C. Pringle's report, published in 1910, described a pattern of work in the west of Scotland in which short periods of employment were interspersed with long periods out of work. Some industries used casual labour as a matter of policy. Bakeries in Glasgow supplemented their full-time workforce with casual workers at weekends. Casual labour was characteristic of dock labour, and the erratic swings in demand, depending on the time of arrival of vessels for unloading, created a very large reserve of workers, so that by 1908 in Glasgow half of them were subject to chronic unemployment. Indeed the Clyde employers had abandoned the practice of retaining a number of permanent labourers in 1889 on the grounds that a fully casual workforce was more flexible and less costly. The building trades were another focus for underemployment as noted by the Glasgow *Herald* such that 'a large number of men ... are always underemployed, loitering in a stagnant pool about certain large centres of unemployment'.[31] The practice of payment for piecework, linking payment to output, also reflected a labour market that favoured the employer. In engineering some 40 per cent of fitters and turners in the west of Scotland were paid in this way by 1914.[32]

Scottish trade unions had a difficult time in the Victorian period. The problems commenced with the defeat of the Cotton Spinners' Association in its 1837 strike, followed by a prolonged trade depression. The trade union lost members and suffered a shortage of funds as it used its financial resources to pay off debts that had been incurred during the industrial action. Throughout the century, phases of economic recession were exploited by employers, cutting wage rates and adjusting the terms and conditions of work. By the 1890s Sidney and Beatrice Webb's survey painted a gloomy picture of the level of trade-union membership and activity in Scotland. In 1892 only 20 per cent of the Scottish working population were trade-union members, a level that was only half of that

30. Levitt and Smout, *State of the Scottish Working-Class*, pp. 156–8.
31. J. H. Treble, *Urban Poverty in Britain* (London: Batsford, 1979), pp. 58, 63.
32. A. McIvor, *A History of Work in Britain, 1880–1950* (Basingstoke: Palgrave, 2001), pp. 69–70.

recorded in major industrial centres in England and Wales with similar industrial structures. A plethora of small organisations committed to the protection of craft skills, and negotiating pay and conditions at individual plant level, reduced the capacity for industrial action. The divisions by craft, gender and ethnicity carried over into political activity. The skilled working class remained loyal to the Liberal Party, and the Labour Party found difficulty in bringing together Protestant artisans and Roman Catholic unskilled workers.[33] Worse was to follow as the Amalgamated Society of Engineers was successfully locked out in a dispute in 1897. This was another major confrontation that constituted a major setback for the trade-union objective of a standard eight-hour working day. The weakness of the trade unions is consistent with a plentiful supply of labour, and with wild swings in the trade cycle for heavy industries that witnessed some spectacular levels of unemployment. In 1884, for example, there were 12,000 out of work in Glasgow and most of the shipyards were idle. In 1908 unemployment rates in the city reached 19.8 per cent of skilled engineers and 24.1 per cent of shipbuilding workers.[34]

This evidence is consistent with labour markets characterised by an abundance of labour, despite the reduction of potential workers by emigration. Low pay, underemployment, the widespread use of casual employment and piecework are consistent with such a market structure. As might be expected, such an environment was conducive to poverty. Indeed, manifestations of deprivation provide even more compelling evidence than the data relating to pay and working conditions.

POVERTY AND SOCIAL DEPRIVATION

The level of social affluence, before the times when national-income figures can be summoned to provide a reliable general indicator, has to be inferred indirectly from a range of alternative indicators for which evidence does exist. Housing and health standards, together with welfare provision to ensure a minimum socially acceptable standard of support, can be used as evidence for the period before 1914. Much has been written about Scottish housing, partly because it has many unique and specific features, partly because it provides a sharp contrast to its

33. William Knox, Alan McKinlay and James Smyth, 'Industrialisation, work and Labour politics: Clydeside, c.1850–1990', in Rainer Schulze (ed.), *Industrial Regions in Transformation* (Essen: Klartext Verlag, 1993), p. 213.
34. W. H. Fraser, 'The working class', in Fraser and Maver (eds), *Glasgow*, vol. II, pp. 321, 334.

counterpart in England and Wales, and partly because it provides a graphic and irrefutable picture of the extent of poverty and social deprivation in Scotland before the Great War.

Scotland had a poor record of housing, as revealed graphically in the devastating conclusions of the Royal Commission on Scottish Housing, which reported in 1917. This indictment ranged through all areas of Scotland from 'incurably damp labourers' cottages on farms, whole townships unfit for human occupation in the crofting counties and islands … [to] … groups of lightless and unventilated houses in the older burghs, clotted masses of slums in the great cities'.[35] The difference in housing provision almost certainly represented the greatest discrepancy between the quality of life in Scotland as compared to that of its southern neighbour. In 1911, while 73.8 per cent of houses in England and Wales had four rooms or more, in Scotland the proportion was only 26.5 per cent. The improvement in Scottish housing in the previous half-century had been manifest primarily in the decline of the single-roomed house, from 34.0 per cent of the housing stock in 1861 to 12.8 per cent in 1911. In its place, accommodation was increased in two- and three-roomed houses, together increasing from 48.4 per cent to 60.7 per cent of the housing stock.[36] Furthermore, Scottish housing was largely characterised by tenement blocks of flatted properties where privacy was highly restricted. In many areas basic amenities such as a water supply and rudimentary sanitation were available only to a minority.

The housing problems that became evident towards the close of the nineteenth century were the product of the process of building whereby the more prosperous moved out of urban centres and were replaced by those lower on the social ladder. But they often occupied properties that were subdivided or 'made down' to create more houses from the same building. This process created some deplorable slum dwellings with living conditions made worse by the lack of a water supply or sanitation. By the late nineteenth century, local authorities had been given powers to remove slums. In Aberdeen, the influential Medical Officer of Health Matthew Hay prevailed upon the City Council to carry out the clearing of some of the worst slums in the harbour area. But the process of slum clearance had to be slowed down, and some families were rehoused in the properties from which they had been evicted, because there was a shortage of alternative accommodation.[37] Like many other local auth-

---

35. Parliamentary Papers, *Royal Commission on the Housing of the Industrial Population of Scotland Rural and Urban*, Cmd 8731 (1917), p. 346.
36. *Census of Population, Scotland* (London: HMSO, 1911), vol. II, pp. 566–7.
37. N. J. Williams, 'Housing', in Fraser and Lee (eds), *Aberdeen, 1800–2000*, pp. 305–6.

orities, Aberdeen, before the Great War, was cautious and reluctant to become involved in the provision of public-sector housing. By the end of the Great War, it was estimated that Scotland needed between 100,000 and 250,000 new houses. But the fact that 13,000 properties in Glasgow were untenanted in 1914 has been identified as a clear indication of a disjuncture in the housing market between rents affordable by potential tenants and rents required by landlords.[38]

Scottish housing, for the poorer sections of society living in urban areas, meant being part of a tenement block. This implied a high density of living conditions that was compounded by equally high levels of overcrowding of individual households. The Medical Officer of Health for Aberdeen, investigating an outbreak of typhus in 1882, found one room intended for single occupancy being inhabited by eight people, and three families living in four rooms between them.[39] It is not surprising that typhus, scarlet fever, measles, typhoid, tuberculosis and smallpox thrived in such an environment. Infant mortality, death in the first year of life, has long been accepted as a prime indicator of social well being, and has been associated with some of the best and worst signs of affluence and deprivation. In the modern era, certainly from the middle of the nineteenth century, declining infant mortality represented a signal indicator of improving social conditions. In 1861 some of the worst rates exceeded 150 deaths per 1,000 live births, while, by the end of the twentieth century, a universal rate of about five deaths per 1,000 live births had been attained.[40] In Scotland the decline of infant mortality came both later in time and slower in process than in England and Wales. Only after the turn of the nineteenth century was improvement in Scotland clearly evident. Victorian infant mortality was far higher in urban industrial areas, including the coalfields, than in rural parts of the country, indicating the high cost of industrialisation. But Scotland's comparative disadvantage cannot be explained just in terms of industrialisation, which was just as characteristic of the English economy. The major difference lay in housing. Statistical tests for regional variations in infant mortality in Great Britain, conducted on data for 1921, confirmed the importance of population density in the determination of infant mortality. High infant mortality was associated with a high level of

38. S. Damer, 'State, class and housing: Glasgow, 1885–1919', in J. Melling (ed.), *Housing, Social Policy and the State* (London: Croom Helm, 1980), p. 90.
39. Williams, 'Housing', in Fraser and Lee (eds), *Aberdeen, 1800–2000*, p. 303.
40. C. H. Lee, 'Regional inequalities in infant mortality in Britain, 1861–1971: patterns and hypotheses', *Population Studies*, 45 (1991), pp. 57–8; National Statistics, *Regional Trends*, 35 (2000), p. 105.

population density, defined as the proportion of population living in three rooms or less, and varied inversely with a low level of population density, defined as the share of population living in seven rooms or more.[41] By then only three of forty-two English regions housed over half their populations in three rooms or less, London and the mining counties of Durham and Northumberland. But in Scotland only· the rural regions of Dumfries and Galloway and the Highlands attained this level. R. A. Cage's investigation into infant mortality in Glasgow confirmed this conclusion that small and densely populated housing, far more prevalent in Scotland than any other part of the United Kingdom, was a major influence in maintaining high infant-mortality rates. His statistical estimates for 1911, based on a data set for twenty-eight districts of Glasgow, showed that the main determinants of a high infant-mortality rate were single-roomed houses, and houses set within multiple-occupancy dwellings. 'Glasgow's single-ends were death traps, and as long as they existed, medical advances were unable to provide further reductions in infant mortality rates.'[42]

It might be thought that a society with so many citizens living more or less permanently close to crippling poverty would have developed some support against such real possibility of disaster. This was largely true in the eighteenth century when harvest failure could create a state of famine together with greatly inflated prices. In response to such problems some parishes devised a system of food subsidy. This could take the form of importing grain to sell at reduced prices, as in Midlothian in the 1740s, or a direct supplement to income from Poor Law funds. By the late eighteenth century there appeared, both in Scotland and England, publications opposing the increasing burden of the poor. A Church of Scotland report produced in 1820 indicated an increase in the burden since 1790 of 20 per cent in real terms.[43] For most of the nineteenth century, it was generally assumed that the inequalities in society were part of the natural order, and views about poverty and welfare derived from it. The Scottish Poor Law, far harsher than its English equivalent, operated on the totally unrealistic assumption that those who wished to work could find employment. This had been the conclusion of the majority report produced by the Royal Commission on the Poor Law 1845, recommending that the current system should not be changed,

41. Lee, 'Regional inequalities', pp. 62–3.
42. R. A. Cage, 'Infant mortality rates and housing: twentieth century Glasgow', *Scottish Economic and Social History*, 14 (1994), pp. 87–9.
43. Rosalind Mitchison, 'Who were the poor in Scotland, 1690–1830?', in Rosalind Mitchison and P. Roebuck (eds), *Economy and Society in Scotland and Ireland, 1500–1939* (Edinburgh: John Donald, 1988), pp. 141–5.

a prescription that was embodied in subsequent legislation.[44] The only acceptable solution to severe deprivation lay in the charitable inclinations of friends and fellow-citizens. In cases of extreme situations, as when the destruction of the potato crop devastated the Highland counties, such charitable intervention was organised and did have a substantive effect, drawing on resources of Edinburgh and Glasgow in particular. However, even in such extreme circumstances, recipients of charitable largesse were often required to demonstrate their worth by undertaking some physical labour in breaking stones, laying roads or digging trenches. The provision of welfare relied heavily on charitable institutions from dispensaries to soup kitchens, and all depended on the largesse of the prosperous minority.

THE FUNDAMENTAL WEAKNESS IN THE SCOTTISH ECONOMY

This chapter has explored the performance of the Scottish economy in generating growth and sustaining the quest for increased prosperity. The record is extremely chequered, comprising impressive advances in production and productivity, resulting in the accumulation of great fortunes, juxtaposed against extensive poverty and deprivation. An explanation of this particular combination should reveal the essential determinants of the evolution of the Scottish economy. It was argued above that an excess supply of labour in many markets was extremely influential in ensuring a regime of low wages, and that this was a principal reason for widespread poverty. This poses the question as to why there was an excess of labour, especially when migration was prevalent through much of these two centuries and was occasionally very substantial. The argument to be put forward is that the fundamental weakness of the Scottish economy lay in the inability to accommodate sufficient of its growing population in work, and that situation sustained the low-wage economy and the resultant poverty despite very considerable migration. This requires an exploration of the mechanics of demographic change.

The two basic components of population change are additions through births and deletions through deaths. Together they comprise natural increase, and in a closed society these forces would completely determine the rise and fall of population. But in an open society, as Scotland has always been, population can be added by immigration or lost by emigration. There has been a long debate among historians and

---

44. Levitt and Smout, *State of the Scottish Working-Class*, p. 161.

demographers about the relative importance of births and deaths in determining natural increase, particularly in the period of early industrialisation. Both the birth rate and the death rate, both measured per 1,000 population, have experienced a long secular decline, and that process was already taking place in the 1850s, when official Scottish records for such information were first kept.

The decline in the death rate has been generally associated with the improvement in the standard of life in the modern era. This has included the reduced frequency of outbreaks of plague diseases, which were notably fewer in the eighteenth century than they had been in the seventeenth century due to improvements in food and housing, the slow decline of infectious disease and of the illnesses of childhood. The bubonic plague paid its final visit to Scotland in 1649, and the disappearance of a disease that carried a 50–75 per cent mortality rate had a significant effect on mortality crises. Smallpox, with a relatively modest fatality rate of 15 per cent, peaked in the eighteenth century before falling due to Jenner's vaccine, which became available at the close of the century. The declining frequency and severity of these crises were further supported by better harvests, although the experience of Aberdeenshire in 1782, when the deficiency was estimated at 75 per cent of the normal crop, was a reminder that this kind of crisis had not completely disappeared. Furthermore, the local organisation of charity may have helped reduce the effectiveness of illness and natural hazards. Michael Flinn and his colleagues concluded that 'the main influence on population growth was a spontaneous decline in the frequency or virulence of infectious disease manifested first in the eastern parts of Lowland Scotland'.[45]

The mortality rate, the number of deaths per 1,000 people, is difficult to estimate prior to the introduction of recorded statistics in 1855. Estimates based on Webster's figures suggest the high but plausible rate of 38 for the mid-eighteenth century, while figures for the 1790s suggest a rate of about 24. This is close to the much more reliable figure for the 1860s of 22. It is possible that the rate increased in the early decades of the nineteenth century when rapid urbanisation, growing ahead of the necessary infrastructure of sanitation and water supply, created conditions favourable for cholera, typhus, typhoid and similar diseases. In the short term, this increased the death rate in major urban centres. Estimates for Glasgow experienced a death rate higher than 30 between

---

45. M. W. Flinn (ed.), *Scottish Population History from the 17th Century to the 1930s* (Cambridge: Cambridge University Press, 1977), p. 248.

1830 and 1864, which rose above 38 in the decade 1845–54.[46] Thereafter there was steady and sustained decline.

The birth rate was more susceptible to human decision and social pressure than the mortality rate. The age of marriage or the willingness to conceive children outside wedlock represented important determinants of the capacity of women to produce children. In the eighteenth century, it does not seem to have shown significant change. While Webster's data give the relatively high figure of 42 per 1,000, estimates for the 1790s indicate a rate of 35, the same as was later reported for the 1860s.[47] It is also possible that there might have been an increase in the early nineteenth century, as a response to increased mortality. But the general assumption made by demographers has been that birth rates were adjusted by social preference, including delayed marriage and, later, contraception, in the light of current death rates, especially of children.

Combining these early estimates for birth and death rates shows that modest improvements in health, housing and cleanliness could induce a sustained population growth. The difference between Webster's birth- and death-rate figures suggest a natural increase of four per 1,000 population, while subsequent estimates for the 1790s and 1860s suggest a natural increase rate of 11 and 13 respectively. Small changes in the demographic structure effectively explain the growth of Scottish natural increase. This experience was not unique, but the erosion of natural increase by outward migration does set the Scottish experience apart as distinctly different. Emigration from Scotland was evident in the eighteenth century especially in the 1760s, with America and the West Indies the principal destinations. Emigration from the Highlands in the 1770s raised, possibly for the first time, the issue of overpopulation, the shortage of good quality farmland and the anxiety among landowners that they might be left short of an adequate labour supply. Many migrants headed to central Scotland and Highlanders comprised 30 per cent of the population of Greenock in the last quarter of the eighteenth century, as compared to 6 per cent in its first decade. But prior to the 1820s emigration does not appear to have made serious inroads into the growth generated by natural increase, possibly a loss of 2,000 people per year compared to a natural increase of 12,000–15,000 persons.[48]

46. Ibid., p. 377.
47. J. G. Kyd (ed.), *Scottish Population Statistics, including Webster's Analysis of Population 1755* (Edinburgh: Scottish Academic Press, 1975); Flinn (ed.), *Scottish Population History*, pp. 259, 270.48.
48. Flinn, *Scottish Population History*, p. 443.

However, in parts of the Highlands the situation was already be-coming difficult. Estimates from Morvern parish in Argyll show a decline in the rate of natural increase from 1811 onward, the date of the first estimate, together with out migration in every decade until 1931, and resulting in sustained population loss from 1841 onwards. Another estimate for Tiree and Coll showed natural increase declining from 1851, and net outward migration in every decade between 1811 and 1931, so that there was a net loss of population from mid-century onward.[49] The pressure of population on resources in the Highlands was eased by migration, by raising cattle, by the introduction of kelp manufacture as a part-time employment, and by the introduction of the potato. Nevertheless, by the middle of the nineteenth century, and following the disasters of the 1840s when the potato crop failed, the Highland counties were struggling to provide employment for their growing populations. Already for more than a century there had been temporary migration from the Highlands for seasonal work in fishing and farming, and for more prolonged absence for textile workers and domestic servants to provide essential supplements to the family income. Irish immigrants were providing competition for seasonal work in the Lowlands to under-mine one of the supports of a fragile economy. After the middle of the nineteenth century, emigration grew to become a great surge out of the northern counties so that natural increase was exceeded by population loss in every decade until the Second World War. Similarly in the southern border counties of Scotland, agricultural progress meant a reduced demand for workers and a reduction in employment, and this also led to migration.

The outflow of population from the rural areas was cumulative in its effect. Migration has always disproportionately attracted the young, able and ambitious. The loss of eligible males through migration left an excess of marriageable women and a falling marriage rate. The loss of population from the Highland counties was reflected in falling birth rates. Many of those who took part in the rural exodus remained in Scotland and the counties of the central belt enjoyed modest net inward migration in the second half of the nineteenth century. By the First World War there was a manifest loss of population through migration even from the central industrial belt. A variety of explanations have been proposed. Devine has drawn attention to the changes in land ownership in the Highlands in the first half of the nineteenth century, during which period some 60 per cent of estates larger than 5,000 acres changed hands.

49. Ibid., p. 310.

The new owners, lawyers, financiers and merchants, possessed greater resources than their predecessors and thus greater capability to remove tenants, perhaps though assisted passages.[50] In the Lowlands, the importance of heavy industry, subject to cyclical trade fluctuations, has been attributed with having a causal effect on migration, while Malcolm Gray pointed out the disparity between shortage of farming land and low wages in Scotland as compared to abundant land and high wages in the Americas.[51] But all these elements of change were duplicated in England without stimulating a similar outflow. The thesis that the Scots were somehow predisposed towards migration, as an unusually mobile society, seems plausible but not essential. One obvious alternative explanation is that it was the lack of opportunities at home that caused such a huge and persistent outflow of Scots from their native land, a shortage of opportunity that was reinforced by low wages and endemic poverty.

Scotland has experienced only two significant phases of immigration during the past three centuries. In the final three decades of the twentieth century, the oil industry in the North Sea brought workers from all parts of the world to contribute to that most international of industries. More important historically was the substantial inflow of population from Ireland, so that there were 207,000 people born in Ireland living in Scotland by 1851, most of them having crossed the Irish Sea in the previous three decades, and many as a result of the potato famine of the 1840s. Virtually all were impoverished and were effectively driven out of a society where population increase had also not been matched by new employment opportunities. Even worse, the textile industries were in difficulty, new manufactures were not emerging and agricultural change based on subdivision of holdings had increased poverty. Thus, it seems highly probable that emigration from Ireland was driven by economic necessity similar to those effective in the Highlands. J. R. Williamson has observed that the impact of the Irish on the British economy was insignificant.[52] This is a reasonable judgement, but it is not true of Scotland. By 1851 the Irish migrants had added some 7.7 per cent to the Scottish population and, it seems likely, a similar number to the workforce. Most of them stayed in central Scotland, in a belt running from Dumfries and Galloway in the west to Tayside in the east. On the assumption that the Irish remained in those regions, the

---

50. T. M. Devine, 'Landlordism and Highland emigration', in T. M. Devine (ed.), *Scottish Emigration and Scottish Society* (Edinburgh: John Donald, 1992), pp. 86, 89.
51. Malcolm Gray, 'The course of Scottish emigration, 1750–1914: enduring influences and changing circumstances', in Devine (ed.), *Scottish Emigration and Scottish Society*, pp. 20–2.
52. William, 'Historical content of the Classical labour surplus model'.

addition to population there would have been 10.8 per cent.[53] This represents a substantial increase to the labour force, particularly in locations like Dundee, where textile production constituted a prime attraction. The Irish immigrants were largely impoverished and un-skilled. Some joined the ranks of handloom weavers as they became technologically redundant. But the Irish substantially augmented a labour market already characterised by low pay and plentiful workers. For employers, the Irish confirmed their strength in the labour market. For everyone else, they compounded an already desperate situation, supplanting other migrant workers in reaping the Lowland harvest, and gravitating towards any opportunities for work.

The critical change in Scottish population growth appeared in the period immediately after the Napoleonic Wars when it adopted a distinctly lower trajectory than that of England and Wales. Several factors were present during that period of adjustment. The labour force was boosted by men returning from war service, and by the flow of migrants from Ireland. At the same time, handloom weaving entered a phase of significant decline and, in the 1840s, the potato famine undermined the fragile economy of the Highlands. By mid-century structural change reduced employment in agriculture and textiles, further weakening the Highland economy. After 1851 the outflow of migrants from Scotland became an inherent part of the process of economic change as economic opportunity was swamped by the weight of numbers.

UNEVEN ECONOMIC PROGRESS

The substantial growth of overseas investment undertaken by Scots in the last quarter of the nineteenth century has great significance as well as size. One estimate for 1914 suggested that overseas investment was equivalent to £110 for every Scot compared to an average of £90 for the United Kingdom as a whole.[54] This indicates, as there is neither evidence nor complaint of investment shortages in Scotland before 1914, that the process of growth had generated a considerable accumulation of capital. That it should seek outlets abroad to take advantage of better returns

---

53. Brenda Collins, 'The origins of Irish immigration to Scotland in the nineteenth and twentieth centuries', in T. M. Devine (ed.), *Irish Immigrants and Scottish Society in the Nineteenth and Twentieth Centuries* (Edinburgh: John Donald, 1991), pp. 1, 8.
54. C. Harvie, *Scotland and Nationalism: Scottish Society and Politics, 1707–1994*, 2nd edn (London: Routledge, 1994), p. 70.

is completely reasonable. It is clear evidence of the success of Scottish economic advance in producing such a surplus, sufficient to account for over 8 per cent of national income as its return on those investments. But from a different perspective it further confirms the deep and inherent inequality in prosperity in Scotland. The investors were primarily men of substance who had made fortunes or at least a good income in business or the professions. While the aspiring middle classes were able to add their own modest savings, the vast majority of the less prosperous were excluded by their poverty. Unfortunately for them, investment in housing construction, especially for those on the lowest incomes, constituted a much less attractive investment opportunity than ranching or real estate in North America. The market forces that guided these funds abroad further exacerbated the economic and social divide within Scotland. There can be little doubt that the national income of Scotland, plausibly estimated as falling well below that of England and Wales, was also more inequitably divided between its citizenry. An obvious explanation for these features of Scottish development relating to inequality in the distribution of benefits lies in the abundance of employable labour and the resultant low-wage regime. Soltow indicated some surprise that writers about Scotland had paid little attention to inequality:

> We do find statements of the problem, but not often. The
> Reverend William Thom of Govan stated in 1772 'It is I believe
> an uncontroverted maxim, that in whatever country the whole
> property is engrossed by a few, there the people must be
> wretched; and this was the case in Scotland.'[55]

Reservations about the effectiveness of market forces in producing both individual liberty and a socially acceptable standard of living for the poorest citizens began to emerge, not surprisingly, from commentaries on housing conditions. Matthew Hay, Medical Officer of Health in Aberdeen between 1888 and 1923, observed in 1902 that:

> The sole motive guiding the private builder may not unfairly,
> and without aspersion, be said to be profit, and as much profit
> as possible. He will not build merely to provide accommodation
> for the displaced occupants of slums. There is no legal or moral
> obligation resting upon him. He will move only if he has hope

---

55. Soltow, 'Inequality of wealth'. p. 55.

of sufficient gain ... For these and other reasons I am clearly of opinion that the Corporation should obtain power to provide themselves the accommodation required for the displaced population.[56]

This view was endorsed by the authors of the Royal Commission on Scottish Housing who stated that:

We are driven to the conclusion that the sources and forces that were available for the provision of working-class houses had ... failed to provide anything like a sufficiency of houses, and that in particular they had failed to provide houses of a reasonable standard of accommodation and habitability.[57]

For the most deprived members of Scottish society, and those who represented them, rejection of the market mechanism became an inherent part of their diagnosis and solution for the problems of inequality. The market mechanism failed the poor because their economic power was so weak in the market place. For the same reason trade unions in Scotland were enfeebled. The excitement generated by 'Red Clydeside' during the rent strikes in the First World War was occasioned by the fact that at last, and briefly, the balance of power had swung in the favour of workers, who were now in short supply for munitions work. After the war a prolonged period of very high employment provided a reminder of the more enduring reality. Attempts to alleviate poverty, and the quest for a less inequitable distribution of economic benefits, shifted from the market place to the political sphere in the twentieth century and set Scotland on a highly distinctive development path.

FURTHER READING

Campbell, R. H., *The Rise and Fall of Scottish Industry, 1707–1939* (Edinburgh: John Donald, 1980).
Devine, T. M. (ed.), *Scottish Emigration and Scottish Society* (Edinburgh: John Donald, 1992).
Devine, T. M., and Jackson, G (eds), *Glasgow*, vol. I: *Beginnings to 1830* (Manchester: Manchester University Press, 1995).

56. Williams, 'Housing', in Fraser and Lee (eds), *Aberdeen, 1800–2000*, p. 306.
57. Cmd 8731, p. 292.

Flinn, M. W., *Scottish Population History from the 17th century to the 1930s* (Cambridge: Cambridge University Press, 1977).

Fraser, W. H., and Mavor, I. (eds), *Glasgow*, vol. II: *1830 to 1912* (Manchester: Manchester University Press, 1996).

Fraser, W. H., and Lee, C. H. (eds), *Aberdeen, 1800–2000: A New History* (East Linton: Tuckwell Press, 2000).

Knox, W. W., *Industrial Nation: Work, Culture and Society in Scotland, 1800–Present* (Edinburgh: Edinburgh University Press, 1999).

Lenman, B., *An Economic History of Modern Scotland, 1660–1976* (London: Batsford, 1977).

Rodger, R. (ed.), *Scottish Housing in the Twentieth Century* (Leicester: Leicester University Press).

Soltow, L., 'Inequality of wealth in land in Scotland in the eighteenth century', *Scottish Economic and Social History*, 10 (1990), pp. 38–60.

Part II
1914–2000

CHAPTER SIX

The Regional Economies of Scotland

David Newlands

INTRODUCTION

For a small country, Scotland has a very distinctive regional structure: largely rural areas in the Highlands and the Borders and a highly industrialised and urbanised central belt in between. At the beginning of the twentieth century, shipbuilding and engineering made Clydeside the dominant region of Scotland in economic terms. By the end of the century, the discovery of North Sea oil and the increased importance of services, particularly the financial sector, had led to an eastern shift in the centre of gravity.

This chapter is concerned with the evolving relationship between the Scottish economy and its constituent regions over the course of the twentieth century. It begins by considering the mechanisms by which regional economies prosper or stagnate. This prompts a series of questions. Have regional economic disparities in Scotland narrowed? Have regional economies become less distinctive? To what extent has the issue of regional disparities within Scotland been recognised and acted upon by public policy makers? What, in turn, has been the impact of policy upon the regional economies of Scotland?

These thematic questions are analysed over four time periods. A snapshot of the regional economies of Scotland at the beginning of the twentieth century is given to provide a description of the economic structures inherited from the Victorian era. The processes of structural change which were at work between 1914 and 1945 are analysed next. These processes continued after the Second World War and gradually transformed the regional distribution of economic activity. Changes are discussed in the period up to 1975, this date chosen as marking the end of the long postwar boom, the first production of North Sea oil and the creation of the Scottish Development Agency. Finally, developments over the last quarter of the twentieth century are discussed. The chapter ends with a short concluding section.

REGIONAL DIVERGENCE, REGIONAL CONVERGENCE

At the beginning of the twentieth century, there was already a developed market economy in Scotland, one that was well integrated into the UK and global economies of the time. As the century progressed, market forces strengthened and the integration of the Scottish economy increased. Neither development was smooth, however. At various times, particularly during the two world wars and the heyday of Keynesian interventionism, government has played a significant role in framing or directing the economic decisions of individuals and businesses. The growth of Scottish trade has fluctuated as well, faltering during wartime and also during the protectionism of the 1930s.

According to mainstream economic theory, the development of an integrated market economy should lead to a reduction in the degree of regional economic inequalities. The principal characteristic of mainstream or neoclassical economics is the equalising role of prices within the market mechanism. In a regional context, factor mobility will equalise wage rates and rates of return on capital. People will move from low-wage areas to high-wage areas. Capital will move away from regions with high-wage rates and low rates of return to create new employment in low-wage regions. Firms will move physically, but also, and often more importantly, investors will move financial capital. Some equalising forces, leading to a degree of economic convergence, were at work in twentieth-century Scotland. There was certainly movement of people within Scotland in search of higher wages and some evidence of movement of capital, although this is less visible. Improved transport and communication not only made migration easier but also facilitated the development of commuting. Differences in wages and employment between regions narrowed as a consequence.

These equalising forces leading to regional convergence act slowly. Meanwhile, new disruptions occur constantly. Wars and world depressions are such disruptions but there are numerous, more minor 'accidents'. Two Scottish examples of such chance happenings are the discovery of oil in the waters off Aberdeen and the growth of Silicon Glen from the foundations of Ferranti in Edinburgh. The neoclassical argument that market forces lead to regional convergence does not imply that regional economies necessarily become less distinctive. Indeed, the logic of neoclassical economic theory is that survival in a market economy requires specialisation.

In contrast to neoclassical growth theory, so-called theories of cumulative causation suggest that the operation of a market economy leads to greater not less regional inequality, regional divergence not regional convergence. These theories stress the importance of motor or key industries, industries which generate considerable external economies, and the development of concentrations of firms within industrial districts or clusters. External economies arise as a result of the geographical concentration of firms within an industry. This allows greater specialisation. It facilitates research and development. It creates a pool of labour with a wide range of skills and experience upon which all firms can draw. Transport facilities develop and educational and training institutions may offer tailored courses. A wide range of business services, such as lawyers, accountants and financial institutions, are available. The shipbuilding–engineering complex on Clydeside in the early twentieth century and the concentration of thousands of oil supply firms in and around Aberdeen in the late twentieth century are examples of industrial clusters.

Other factors contribute to the concentration of growth. Internal economies of scale permit firms to reduce costs, gain a competitive edge over rivals and expand at their expense. More recently, the importance of technical progress has come to be appreciated. Growing areas with profitable firms can finance research and development into new products and production processes. Firms experience favourable demand and supply conditions, thus improving the prospects of continued relative prosperity. For all these reasons, growing areas are likely to attract both labour and capital and experience a 'virtuous circle' of continued expansion. In reverse, areas without successful industrial clusters experience a vicious circle of decline or at best stagnation.

The neoclassical and cumulative causation theories represent very different views of how a market economy operates, but of course there has been no period in modern history when the state has not played some role in determining the regional distribution of economic activity. Government can formally and informally influence the location of particular firms or industries. Numerous examples are given in the course of this chapter but one with momentous consequences was that to relocate Ferranti from Manchester to Edinburgh during the Second World War. In years to come, this provided the foundation for the growth of Scotland's electronics industry in Silicon Glen. As the twentieth century proceeded, more and more of these decisions were taken within Scotland as the Scottish Office gained increased powers, powers now inherited by the Scottish Parliament. These powers included control over regional development agencies, semi-autonomous bodies which have played an important role in addressing regional disparities within Scotland. Local government has also had a part to play, although its scope for making a difference to the economies of tits areas has steadily diminished under the twin forces of globalisation and central-government controls.

Just as significant, and in some ways more significant than explicit regional policy measures, were the appearance and growth of a comprehensive welfare state during the twentieth century. Certainly in terms of eradicating the most extreme differences in living standards in different parts of Scotland, it was the social-security system and state provision of housing, health care and education which was of most importance. The corollary of this is that with the erosion of a generous, universal welfare-state system, together with privatisation, legislation to reduce the power of trade unions and a general renewal of faith in the market, regional disparities within Scotland have begun to increase again.

THE SCOTTISH REGIONS AT THE BEGINNING OF THE
TWENTIETH CENTURY

The regional economic structure of Scotland at the beginning of the twentieth century to a large extent reflected the impact of industrial developments a century earlier. The development of the coal and iron resources of Lanarkshire and the ports of the Clyde provided the foundation for the growth of the railway and steel industries and the specialisation in engineering and shipbuilding. Other regions of Scotland had their own concentrations of employment – but often in industries which were already beginning to stagnate. Agriculture and fishing accounted for nearly half of male employment in the Highlands and a third of male employment in Grampian, Dumfries and Galloway, and the Borders. Textiles and clothing were significant employers in Tayside – notably jute production in Dundee – and the Borders – with the Galashiels economy for example highly dependent on woollens. Most regions of Scotland were relatively poorly provided with service-sector employment. This had serious implications for spending power not least because some service-sector employment – such as the professions – was relatively well paid.[1]

1. C. H. Lee, *Scotland and the United Kingdom: The Economy and the Union in the Twentieth Century* (Manchester: Manchester University Press, 1995), pp. 39–40.

In the mid-nineteenth century, shipbuilding was fairly widely dispersed around Scotland. The concentration of shipbuilding on the Clyde was the result of the early adoption there of various innovations, such as screw propellers, but most of all the shift from wooden to iron hulls. Nevertheless, a significant shipbuilding industry survived in other parts of Scotland, such as Leith, Dundee and Aberdeen, into and for much of the twentieth century. While shipbuilding, with its strong linkages with coal, iron and steel, and the engineering industries dominated the economy of west central Scotland, it was not a leading sector for all of Scotland. It did not even dictate the development of the whole coal industry because while many of the coal mines in the west were owned by iron manufacturers, many of the eastern pits had a strong export orientation, especially those in Fife.[2]

Fife was not the only regional economy of eastern Scotland during the Victorian period to pursue a very different economic path to Clydeside. Aberdeen, for example, had several flourishing industries. Granite quarrying and polishing expanded to the point where imports of stone were required. The paper industry in Aberdeen and Inverurie prospered despite its remoteness from major markets. However, the most spectacular growth in late nineteenth-century Aberdeen was of steam trawling. By 1914, Aberdeen was the largest fishing port in Scotland (and the third largest in Britain). Aberdeen trawlers specialised in white fish, primarily cod and haddock, being well placed to exploit the Faroese and Icelandic fisheries. Herring fishing shifted to other ports such as Fraserburgh and Peterhead. The expansion of both the white and herring fisheries helped compensate for the continuing decline of the east-coast whaling industry.

Whisky was already a major industry but was located in two very different types of area, depending on whether production was of malt or blended whisky. Malt whisky was mainly produced in the Highlands and in relatively small quantities. Blended whisky included some malt but was mainly composed of spirit distilled from imported grain. Accordingly, blended-whisky production tended to be concentrated in the major ports, particularly Leith and Glasgow. The largest producer was the Distillers Company, formed in Edinburgh by an amalgamation of six firms.

The railways, which had been such a crucial factor in the growth of the Victorian economy, continued to shape Scotland in the twentieth century. The railways opened up new markets: for example, for the fish

---

2. B. Lenman, *An Economic History of Scotland, 1660–1976* (London: Batsford, 1977), pp. 181–2.

landed at north-eastern ports. They facilitated the development of commuting and the mobility of the labour force more generally. The operation of the railways was an important source of employment in its own right but also the stimulus to a range of other industries, including the banking sector, iron and steel, and the manufacture of locomotives. The production of locomotives was concentrated in and around Glasgow, at St Rollox, Cowlairs and Springburn. In the early twentieth century, Glasgow was the largest locomotive-manufacturing centre in Europe.

There were new industries, but the short-lived shale oil industry at Bathgate was unusual in not having been established by a foreign concern. The dynamite works set up by Nobel at Ardeer in Ayrshire in 1873 grew into a major chemical works. American capital established the North British Rubber Company in Edinburgh in 1856 and, perhaps most significant of all, the American Singer Company, which in the 1880s built a large factory at Clydebank to manufacture sewing machines. Sewing machines were precisely the sort of new, mass-produced consumer durable which Scottish entrepreneurs were very slow to adopt. Scottish industry remained concentrated on the production of heavy capital goods and traditional textiles. This was not because Scotland lacked a banking system capable of mobilising the funds required for new investment. The reverse was the case. The Scottish banking system was well developed.

Many of the foundations of the later growth of the financial sector in Edinburgh were laid in the later nineteenth century in the boom period of Scottish overseas investment. As Clive Lee has noted, much of this investment was in the United States, in the railways, the rebuilding of Chicago after the fire of 1871, mining and cattle ranching. However, there was also significant investment in Australia, New Zealand, India, Ceylon and Burma. Nor was it just Edinburgh investors who were involved. Glasgow, Aberdeen and Dundee were also sources of investment capital. Indeed, investment trusts developed in Dundee after the formation of the Scottish American Investment Trust in 1873. Nevertheless, the concentration of financial companies in Edinburgh was already evident. The banking sector in Glasgow never fully recovered from the failures of the Western Bank and the City of Glasgow Bank in the nineteenth century and, with the takeover of the Union Bank by the Bank of Scotland, only the Clydesdale was left in Glasgow. There were similar developments in Aberdeen. Two Aberdeen banks first merged with each other and were then taken over by the Clydesdale Bank. In addition to the banks, Edinburgh had a number of insurance companies and other financial institutions, such as investment trusts, with numerous links at board level between these various companies.[3]

The urbanisation of the Scottish population continued throughout the later nineteenth century and early twentieth century, reinforcing the dominance of central Scotland. Scotland's population increased by 44 per cent between 1871 and 1931, from 3.36 million to 4.84 million but most of the Lowland counties grew more rapidly. The population of the counties of Lanark, Dunbarton, Renfrew and Ayr increased by more than 80 per cent and of the three Lothians, Stirling and Clackmannan by more than 60 per cent. The population of the counties of Angus, Fife, Kinross, Perth, Aberdeen, Banff, Kincardine, Moray and Nairn grew but at a lower rate than the population of Scotland as a whole. Population fell in other areas of Scotland, most sharply in the seven crofting counties, by over 20 per cent between 1871 and 1931. The fall in the counties of Dumfries, Kirkcudbright, Wigtown, Berwick, Peebles, Selkirk and Roxburgh was 5–10 per cent.[4] The population decline of the Highland counties was one indicator, along with other signs such as a reduced animal population and a reduced acreage of arable land, of the persistence of the Highland problem, despite some improved security of tenure arising from the crofting legislation of the late nineteenth century.

STRUCTURAL CHANGE AND THE SCOTTISH REGIONS, 1914–45

Most of Scotland's heavy engineering and textiles industries experienced boom conditions and continued prosperity during and immediately after the First World War. This was true for example of the jute industry centred on Dundee and shipbuilding on the Clyde. There was a brief economic downturn in the early 1920s, but most industries survived that. One exception, however, was what remained of the cotton textiles industry in Glasgow and the west of Scotland. Apart from a few specialised sectors, such as the production of thread in Paisley, it experienced terminal decline. In contrast, Scottish woollen manufacturers concentrated on very high-quality tweed exports to the United States although this sector was then very hard hit by the high American tariffs introduced in 1930. The experience of the other Scots luxury product dependent on American markets, whisky, was almost the

3. M. Gaskin, *The Scottish Banks* (London: George Allen and Unwin, 1965).
4. R. H. Campbell, *Scotland since 1707: The Rise of an Industrial Society* (Oxford: Basil Blackwell, 1965), pp. 299–300.

opposite of tweed. The 1920s were the depressed decade because of Prohibition while the 1930s saw a recovery of exports.

With the depression in the 1930s and subsequent collapse of world trade, many of Scotland's heavy capital goods industries, being export-oriented, were extremely vulnerable. Unemployment rose sharply in many industries and regions. In shipbuilding, the 'unfinished hull of what was to become the *Queen Mary* became symbolic of the state of Scottish industry in general, and of Clyde shipbuilding in particular'.[5] The steel industry witnessed closures, for example of the Mossend and Calderbank works, the move of Stewarts and Lloyds to Corby in 1932 and a rash of amalgamations which saw the formation of Colvilles, soon to dominate what remained of the industry in Scotland.

Dundee was even harder hit than Clydeside. Unemployment in the jute industry rose above 70 per cent in 1931 and 1932. The experience of the jute industry was repeated, albeit in less extreme fashion, across Scotland. The industries in which Scotland specialised were hit by technical changes, shifts in consumer demand and stagnant export markets. The Scottish economy was thus ill prepared to capitalise on those industries which were expanding in the 1920s and 1930s. Most of these new industries were focused primarily on domestic markets, since they produced consumer durables. Throughout the inter-war period, the rate of unemployment in Scotland was well above the UK average, with the result that purchasing power was low compared to the south and midlands of England, which provided the largest domestic market. The spread of electrical power meant that there was less and less advantage to locations near coalfields. In addition, the south and midlands of England already had nuclei of several of the new industries. As a result, new centres of concentration developed in these regions and their expansion was subsequently further reinforced by the growth of component and ancillary industries and services.

A number of the new industries existed in Scotland but did not thrive in the 1920s. The classic example is motor manufacturing. There were several attempts to establish a motor-car industry in Scotland before the First World War, but most businesses just lasted a few years. The Albion Company lasted the longest but, from 1913 onwards, produced commercial vehicles. In contrast, the Argyll Company did attempt to meet the new mass consumer demand for cars. It opened a new factory in Alexandria in 1906 which had been specially designed to exploit economics of scale and thus reap the benefits of mass production.

5. Ibid., p. 259.

However, the early death of its founder led to the company folding in 1914. Even when the new consumer industries did become established in Scotland, they typically had a lower rate of growth than in the rest of the country so that 'the effect of an unfavourable structure was thus compounded by poor performance'.[6] This limited success in diversification of the Scottish economy has been generally attributed, then and since, to a lack of vision and enterprise on the part of Scottish industrialists. Significantly, efforts to reverse these trends then became focused upon the attraction of industry from elsewhere.

However, Scotland's problems were not entirely structural. The transport and housing infrastructures were poor, especially when compared with southern England. There was limited mobility of labour within Scotland, not helped by poor housing provision. It was possibly easier for Scots to migrate to England, as movement of people to Corby following the relocation of the Stewarts and Lloyds steel company showed.[7] Migration from Scotland reached very high levels in the 1920s, amounting to nearly 400,000 people over the decade.[8] Migration was of course both a manifestation of lack of alternative job opportunities and, in the short term, a safety valve which prevented unemployment rates from increasing more than they did.

Unemployment in the 1930s was highest in west central Scotland, where the dependence on engineering, metalworking and coal-mining was greatest, but unemployment rates in most of eastern and southern Scotland, with the notable exception of Dundee, were below the Scottish average. In and around Edinburgh, unemployment rates were as low as anywhere in the UK. Unemployment could still be a major problem in these parts of Scotland, but it tended to be localised, often concentrated in specific industries. Examples included the jute industry in Dundee, the linen industry in Dunfermline, fishing and granite in Aberdeen and the herring industry in the towns on the Moray Firth.

Some industries emerged or expanded significantly in the 1930s, many of them in the Edinburgh area. These included papermaking in Aberdeenshire, printing and publishing in Edinburgh and Dundee, the production of various foods in Perthshire and Edinburgh, and the generation of hydro-electricity in the Highlands.

Several attempts were made to devise what would now be called local economic development strategies, although they had limited success in attracting new industry. A Development Board for Glasgow and District

6. Lee, *Scotland and the United Kingdom*, p. 59.
7. Lenman, *Economic History of Scotland*, p. 222.
8. Lee, *Scotland and the United Kingdom*, p. 69.

was formed in 1930. The crisis in the jute industry in Dundee in the early 1930s led to the creation of a Development Committee, with local government, business and trade-union representation, which produced a substantial volume promoting Dundee, *Industrialists at Home and Abroad*. In the Highlands, the North of Scotland Hydro-Electric Board, established in 1943, became a quasi-development agency.

Clydeside was one of the four areas made eligible for regional assistance under the 1934 Special Areas Act. This had some modest benefits. It led to the creation of the large industrial estate at Hillington in Glasgow and three smaller estates. By 1939, Hillington accommodated some seventy-five firms employing about 1,500 people. These firms were mostly in light industries which had already become established in eastern Scotland but represented the beginnings of diversification for Clydeside. Valuable as these developments were, employment at Hillington only accounted for some 3 per cent of local unemployment and many of the jobs were for women while the unemployed were predominantly men.

STRUCTURAL CHANGE AND THE SCOTTISH REGIONS, 1945–75

During the Second World War, there were a number of major discoveries or developments of new products. These included magnetron valves, radar, jet engines, nuclear power, electronic computing and antibiotics. In some parts of the UK, notably the south-east of England, new profitable industries appeared to exploit these commercial opportunities. Very few of these industries became established in Scotland. Only thirty-two government factories were built in Scotland during the course of the war and most of these, including factories manufacturing motor vehicles and aircraft, were closed soon after. One of the few which survived was the Rolls-Royce engine works at Hillington.[9]

The most important development during wartime in terms of its implications for the future of the Scottish economy concerned Ferranti. Ferranti, then based in Manchester, gained the government contract for gyroscopic gunsights, but a shortage of labour in Manchester led to its relocation to Edinburgh. This became the basis of the Scottish electronics industry, although far from immediately. Indeed, once the war ended, there was a period of severe retrenchment. Employment in the industry fell at one point to 300. Ferranti itself only survived because

9. Lenman, *Economic History of Scotland*, p. 237.

the government placed contracts with it and because it was chosen as a nursery for the training of electronic engineers.

The immediate chance to achieve some diversification having been lost, the short-term trend after 1945 was reversion to Scotland's traditional heavy industries. Thus, in the middle of the twentieth century, the industrial distribution of Scotland still showed the strong imprint of the pattern which developed in the Victorian period. The major part of industry and population was in the central belt of the Lowlands and of this the greatest concentration was in the Clyde valley centred on Glasgow. The industrial specialisation in shipbuilding and marine engineering remained prominent. Shipbuilding, with its ancillary trades, was much the biggest manufacturing industry in Scotland.

The Ayrshire plain was effectively an extension of the central belt, sharing the industrial development of the Glasgow area. Agriculture and coal-mining were important and the area also had a wide range of manufacturing, particularly textiles and engineering. The Borders were largely agricultural, although there was some manufacturing. Woollen cloth was particularly important in the south-east. In the south-west, manufacturing was more various, including chemicals, food processing, textiles and engineering. Aberdeen and the coastal areas of the north-east had a variety of manufacturing industry, particularly engineering, but were also very dependent on agriculture and fishing. The Highlands and Islands depended mainly on agriculture, forestry, fishing and tourism. The chief manufacturing industry in the Highlands and Islands was woollen textiles.

While textile industries producing cotton, wool, linen and jute remained important to a number of Scottish regions, they had all ceased to be expanding sectors. Industrial adjustment was particularly traumatic in Dundee with the decline of jute, but the gap was filled in due course by the expansion of new light engineering industries producing cash registers, batteries, watches, toys and sound equipment. A number of the incoming firms were American, attracted by cheap female labour, among them Timex, which established a large factory to manufacture clocks and watches. In this regard, Dundee was typical of much of Scotland. Between 1950 and 1975, over a quarter of the 230,000 jobs created in firms opening in Scotland were in foreign-owned concerns.

Changes to Scotland's industrial structure accelerated from the 1950s onwards. For example, Grangemouth grew rapidly in the 1950s and 1960s on the back of a number of large petrochemical complexes which are important local employers to this day. The chemicals industry in turn stimulated the growth of the port. By the end of the 1960s, there were container terminals at Grangemouth and also Greenock and Leith. However, while containerisation aided large ports like Leith, it helped kill off smaller harbours like Alloa and Bo'ness.

Many of the new industrial developments of this period were due in part to the development of government regional policy or at least an increased government role in industrial location decisions. In 1958 a new semi-continuous steel-strip mill was allocated to Ravenscraig in Lanarkshire, the result of a government decision to divide a larger proposed plant in two and give half to Scotland and half to Wales, and a cold-strip mill to Gartcosh. The location of a British Motor Corporation factory at Bathgate in 1961, producing trucks and tractors, and a Rootes plant at Linwood in 1963, producing Hillman Imp cars, were further government responses to pressure to provide new jobs in the west of Scotland.

In the Highlands, the pulp mill at Corpach outside Fort William was established in 1962 with a combination of government and Wiggins Teape money. Then, in 1965, the government created the Highlands and Islands Development Board (HIDB). Partly as a result of the establishment of the HIDB, by the end of the 1960s, the Highlands was securing 10 per cent of government expenditure in Scotland, despite having only 5 per cent of the population. The HIDB helped persuade the government to locate a fast breeder nuclear reactor at Dounreay in Caithness and a large aluminium smelter at Invergordon on the Moray Firth.

Among older industries, shipbuilding underwent a period of turmoil in the late 1960s and early 1970s. Two large Clydeside consortia were formed in 1967–8 with an injection of government funds, the Scott-Lithgow group on the lower reaches of the river and the ill-fated Upper Clyde Shipbuilders (UCS). Yarrow's, the only profitable company in UCS, bought itself out in 1970. After the UCS work-in, when workers refused to leave the shipyard, staying at their work to prevent closure, yet another consortium was formed in 1972. Govan Shipbuilders comprised three of the UCS yards while the fourth, the Clydebank Yard, was taken over by an American firm, although again with substantial support from public funds. Employment in shipbuilding on the Clyde was 98,000 in 1945. Thirty years later it was one-quarter of that figure. Nor was this painful process of contraction confined to the Clyde. In 1969 the Burntisland Shipping Company on the Forth went bankrupt, leaving Robb Caledon of Dundee and Leith and Hall Russell of Aberdeen as the only significant shipbuilders on the east coast.

Income and employment levels reflected the regional distribution of industry and the relative health or otherwise of different industries.

Scottish unemployment in 1960 was one-third higher than it had been in 1948. The lowest rates of unemployment in the 1950s were in the Borders, Edinburgh and the Lothians. The highest rate was in the Highlands and Islands. Unemployment rates were also above the Scottish average in Glasgow and the adjacent counties of Lanarkshire, Renfrewshire and Dunbartonshire – these areas together had slightly more than half the total unemployment in Scotland – Kilmarnock and north Ayrshire, and the north-east (outside Aberdeen). The familiar response was that many emigrated. In the 1950s, over three-quarters of the natural increase in population left Scotland, mainly to jobs in England.

There were also important population shifts within Scotland in response to changes in industrial structure. The concentration of Scotland's population in the central belt, which had been a marked feature of the early twentieth century, continued in the 1930s, 1940s and 1950s. Between 1931 and 1961, the population of all the counties in the central belt increased with the sole exception of Kinross. Dumfriesshire, Moray and Kincardineshire also grew. The largest increases were in Lanarkshire (over 50,000), Renfrewshire and Ayrshire (both over 40,000), and Midlothian and Fife (both over 20,000). The counties with the largest decreases in population were Banffshire (over 8,000), Aberdeenshire (over 7,000) and Ross and Cromarty (over 5,000). Six of the seven crofter counties suffered losses while Caithness lost 3,000 between 1931 and 1951 but gained nearly 5,000 between 1951 and 1961, principally because of the development of Dounreay.

Thus, by the middle of the twentieth century, the Clydeside conurbation accounted for about one-third of the population of Scotland and the central industrial belt about three-quarters. While, in 1801, nearly half the Scottish population lived in the northern and Highland counties, by the 1950s fewer than 20 per cent did. The long process of urbanisation was slowing by the mid-twentieth century, by which time Scotland was a largely urban society. In 1951, 83 per cent of Scots lived in urban areas. Three of the four Scottish cities grew in size between 1931 and 1961, Edinburgh by 29,000, Aberdeen by 12,000 and Dundee by 6,000. Most Scottish burghs also expanded in size, with the largest increases in Dunfermline (12,100), Coatbridge (10,400), Kilmarnock (8,800), Kirkcaldy (7,600) and Paisley (7,400). The glaring exception to this pattern of continued urban growth was Glasgow. Between 1931 and 1961, its population fell by 39,000, the bulk of this loss occurring in the 1950s.

Not surprisingly, the new towns expanded very rapidly. East Kilbride rose from 5,000 to 32,000 between 1951 and 1961, Glenrothes from

2,000 to 13,000 and Cumbernauld from 3,000 to 5,000. The growth of the new towns was of course bound up with the introduction of overspill policies, particularly from Glasgow. The necessity for population overspill from Glasgow was recognised from the very beginning of postwar reconstruction. The Clyde Valley Regional Advisory Plan of 1946 recommended that population which could not be properly accommodated within Glasgow and other overcrowded areas of the region should be relocated. The government adopted overspill as a national policy with the designation of the new towns of East Kilbride and Cumbernauld. Then, in the late 1950s, the government enabled local authorities to promote their own growth through the reception of people from Glasgow and provided financial assistance for them to do so.

The contemporary argument for overspill from Glasgow was that a shortage of suitable sites was a deterrent to the attraction of new industry and the expansion of existing industry. As the Toothill Report noted in 1961: 'Glasgow needs more employment for its existing population – as is recognised by its inclusion among the development districts – but in the long run conditions favourable to growth can be secured only by reducing congestion.'[10] As for the towns to which population and industry was to be decentralised from Glasgow, it was believed that overspill would provide wider job opportunities, enhance growth prospects and permit the diversification of industry.

Parallel to the development of overspill policy, Glasgow, grappling with unsatisfactory planning procedures and inadequate resources, sought to deal with housing problems in the city by creating a number of peripheral working-class estates such as Drumchapel, Easterhouse and Castlemilk. However, lacking social amenities and local employment opportunities, they soon became as bad as the inner-city areas they were supposed to replace. The role of housing in the postwar economic development of Scotland and its constituent regions received much attention. In some areas, there was an absolute shortage of housing and in other areas an unsatisfactory quality of housing. The effect was to limit the geographical mobility of labour and the overall flexibility of the Scottish economy. There were familiar criticisms of the housing system, particularly council housing. Low rents and complex points systems for the allocation of local-authority housing meant that in many areas the existing stock of housing was not used effectively and waiting lists remained long despite heavy postwar building programmes. Most local

---

10. Scottish Council (Development and Industry), *Inquiry into the Scottish Economy, 1960–1961: Report of a Committee under the Chairmanship of J. N. Toothill* (1961), p. 140.

authorities' allocation schemes required a residential qualification, as much as seven years in some areas, thus discouraging people both from moving within Scotland and to Scotland to get a job or a better job. Housing scarcities were made worse by rent controls, which applied to the majority of unfurnished private lettings. These problems were encountered throughout the UK but were particularly severe in Scotland because the number of owner-occupied houses and new houses built for sale was distinctly smaller than in England.

Ravenscraig, Gartcosh, Bathgate, Linwood, Corpach, Dounreay, Invergordon and UCS were all to varying degrees the result of nakedly political decisions on the part of successive governments. Simultaneously, however, a less explicitly political and rather more systematic regional policy was emerging although equally driven by a concern with unemployment. For example, under the 1960 Local Employment Act, the rate of local unemployment was the sole criterion for designation of development districts and the relief of unemployment the test for whether a particular project be given public support. Even at the time, there was an awareness of the possible drawbacks of giving such prominence to the immediate provision of employment: that effectively resources were devoted to the propping up of dying industries and that potential growth areas were denied support. As the Toothill Report remarked: 'The build-up of industrial complexes and centres which offer prospects of becoming zones of growth cannot be the only aim but it should be one of the principal aims of policy.'[11]

There was a serious contemporary debate about the role of inward investment in improving the performance of the Scottish economy and in tackling regional disparities in unemployment within Scotland, but again some recognition of the risks of overdependence on inward investment, particularly of subsidiaries which had limited strategic and operational independence from their foreign-owned parent companies.

There was a flurry of government plans relating to parts of Scotland beginning with the *Central Scotland Plan* in 1963. The *Grangemouth–Falkirk Plan* appeared in 1968 and *Tayside: Potential for Development* in 1970. In 1966 the government published *Plan for Expansion*, a white paper detailing plans for the future development of the Scottish economy. This argued that old declining industries should be slimmed down and modernised and that resources and employment should be shifted into new growing industries such as cars and electronics. Declining regional economies such as the north-east and the Borders

11. Ibid., p. 154.

would require specific assistance to achieve such changes. In the end, the whole of Scotland, except the Edinburgh–Leith area, was proposed as a development area. Despite this denial of development-area status to Edinburgh and Leith, the concentration of industry and population in the central belt meant that it remained the principal political and planning focus within Scotland, although there was also an effective Highland lobby, especially after the creation of the HIDB.

For all these regional policy developments, government had a much greater impact on the reduction of disparities between Scotland and the rest of UK and between different regions within Scotland in other ways. The expansion of the welfare state and its myriad effects on health, education, housing and social security was a very strong equalising factor. The growth of the public sector and employment legislation in the private sector led to the spread of national agreements regulating, and standardising, wages and conditions of employment.

THE REGIONAL ECONOMIES OF SCOTLAND, 1975–2000

By the end of the twentieth century, the Scottish economy had become ever more closely integrated into the UK economy, with the consequence that many economic developments in Scotland closely follow the UK trend. Gross Domestic Product per head in Scotland towards the end of the twentieth century hovered about 92–96 per cent of the UK average.[12] The only major gap in terms of income is between Scotland and the south-east of England. Compared to the other regions of England, and indeed compared to many other countries in western Europe, Scotland is a middle-income region. Unemployment in Scotland was higher than the UK as a whole for most of the twentieth century, distinctly higher than the southern regions of England and comparable with the northern regions. In recent years, however, the gap between Scotland and the UK average has closed somewhat and, while unemployment is still higher than in the south, it is significantly lower than in the north of England.

This relative stability of Scottish economic performance compared to other parts of the UK disguises the dramatic changes which have taken place. The last twenty-five years have seen a massive restructuring of the Scottish economy. In particular, the traditional metal and metal-using industries of steel, shipbuilding, transport equipment and mechanical

---

12.   G. Storie and J. Home, 'Economic review', *Scottish Economic Bulletin*, 58 (1999), pp. 5–22.

engineering have all experienced sharp decline. Another notable trend of recent decades is the increase in external ownership of Scottish industry, partly as a consequence of merger and takeover activity, partly as a result of the attraction of foreign direct investment from North America and East Asia. While most small- and medium-sized firms are still Scottish owned, only 33 per cent of Scottish businesses in the employment size band 250–499 in 1998 had Scottish headquarters. For the largest businesses of all, with employment of 500 or more, the figure was a mere 19 per cent.[13]

By the end of the twentieth century the Scottish economy, like that of the UK and other developed countries, was dominated by the service sector. In 1995 services accounted for 63 per cent of output, or gross value added (and an even higher proportion, 75 per cent, of employment). Of the non-service industries, the production and construction sector, agriculture, forestry and fishing accounted for just 3.0 per cent, mining and quarrying, and electricity, gas and water supply for 4.7 per cent and construction for 6.4 per cent. Manufacturing, once the mainstay of the Scottish economy and a major determinant of the fortunes of Scottish regions, made up 22.6 per cent of Scottish output.[14]

While agriculture, forestry and fishing now form a very small part of the Scottish economy, and there are areas with almost no representation in these sectors, the primary industries remain important in some parts of Scotland. The local authority areas with most jobs in agriculture, forestry and fishing are Aberdeen, Dumfries and Galloway, Shetland and Orkney (each around 11 per cent of employment).

Manufacturing also has distinct regional patterns of location. By the end of the twentieth century, the three largest manufacturing sectors in Scotland were food and drink (3.5 per cent of total Scottish output), metalworking, mechanical engineering and transport equipment (4.7 per cent) and electrical and instrument engineering (6.0 per cent). Food and drink employed 58,000 people in 2,000, of whom about a quarter were employed in the whisky industry. However, whisky accounted for about one-fifth of all manufacturing exports. The largest whisky company was still Distillers, as it had been at the beginning of the twentieth century, operating a large number of distilleries and bottling plants throughout Scotland. Elsewhere in the drinks industry, Scottish and Newcastle and Tennent Caledonian were major brewing concerns, concentrated in Edinburgh and Glasgow respectively. The bulk of the remainder of the

13. A. Campbell and D. MacDonald, 'Small and medium sized enterprises in Scotland', *Scottish Economic Bulletin*, 58 (1999), pp. 33–41
14. Scottish Executive, *Scottish Economic Statistics* (Edinburgh: Scottish Executive, 2003).

food and drink sector was accounted for by meat and fish processing and the manufacture of bread, biscuits and confectionery. This sector was particularly important to the regional economies of Orkney, Shetland, Grampian and Strathclyde.

Metalworking, mechanical engineering and transport equipment was the sector which drove the whole Scottish economy a hundred years ago. Although now a rump of what it was, it still employed 73,000 people in 2000. There are some companies in this sector all round Scotland, but, apart from Fife and the Highlands (mainly the oil platform construction yards), it remains concentrated on Clydeside, with the surviving ship-building and repair yards and engineering firms such as Anderson Strathclyde (mining equipment) and Weirs (pumps and valves).

Electrical and instrument engineering employed 61,000 people in 2000. This sector is concentrated in central Scotland with Silicon Glen stretching from Fife through Edinburgh and West Lothian to Inverclyde, west of Glasgow. Production covers electronic data-processing equipment, including computers, electronic components and, latterly, mobile phones. There are some indigenous companies, notably Ferranti (now part of the BAE group), but a striking feature of the electronics industry has always been the number and importance of inward investors including IBM, Honeywell, NCR, Digital Equipment, Motorola, National Semiconductors, NEC and Mitsubishi.[15] This has raised concerns about Silicon Glen being a branch plant economy, and certainly comparison with other concentrations of electronics in the UK, such as Silicon Fen in the Cambridge area, suggests that the Scottish cluster is weaker. Employment within Scotland is skewed towards partly skilled employment such as assembly work while other clusters have higher concentrations in management and research and development.

By the end of the twentieth century, most Scots worked in the service sector. In terms of their contribution to Scottish output in 1995, the main service sectors were hotels and restaurants (3.0 per cent), financial services (4.1 per cent), transport and communications (7.6 per cent), wholesale and retail trade (10.4 per cent), property and business services (15.3 per cent) and public services (21.2 per cent).

An important distinction can be drawn between dependent or local services and autonomous or exporting services. Dependent or local services include the pub, the supermarket, the garage, the post office, the primary school, the GP practice and the bus service. The scale and range

15. Scottish Office, *Scotland: An Economic Profile* (Edinburgh: HMSO, 1988).

of these services depend upon the amount of local spending or in some cases, such as education and health care, the size of the local population. Autonomous or exporting services are ones which serve a national or international market. Banks and insurance companies in Edinburgh are engaged in global financial transactions. Oil-supply businesses in Aberdeen support oil exploration and production in new provinces in Africa and Asia and elsewhere across the world. The distinction between dependent and autonomous services is not always easily drawn. In practice, many services have both local and national or international markets. French tourists as well as locals will have a drink in a pub in Inverness. Aberdeen University has students from Aberdeen but also from elsewhere in Scotland, from England and from around the world. The Royal Bank of Scotland has become one of the largest banking groups in the world but also still maintains branches in just about every town in Scotland. Nevertheless, the distinction is of great significance, not least for the pattern of economic activity in different areas. Dependent or local services are, almost by definition, found everywhere in Scotland and to that extent the increased importance of the service sector has been a force for the greater uniformity of the regional economies of Scotland. In contrast, autonomous or exporting services can be as or more geographically concentrated than coal-mining, ship-building and mechanical engineering were in Scotland a hundred years ago. The continued existence of regional economic disparities within Scotland is largely attributable to the appearance of new specialisations in these types of service industries.

New clusters of service industries were emerging as the twentieth century ended, such as one in biomedical sciences in Dundee, but over the preceding thirty years the two significant clusters which accounted for much of Scotland's economic growth, as well as the eastward shift in the balance of the economy, were financial and business services and oil-related services. The financial and business services sector provides employment for about 150,000 people, more than twice the number employed in metalworking and mechanical engineering, although its importance is not reflected in the availability of data or analysis or indeed public recognition.[16] The sector covers an enormous range, including banking, finance, insurance, property, accountancy, commercial law, advertising, consultancy and IT. Financial services in particular account for some of the most profitable, innovative and fastest-growing com-

---

16. R. Perman, 'Living in the past: why is Scotland's financial services sector ignored?', *Scottish Economic Report* (June 2001), pp. 91–5.

panies in Scotland. Ten of the largest twenty companies located in Scotland are in financial services. They account for 62 per cent of the turnover, 70 per cent of the profits and 33 per cent of the employment of the top twenty firms. Scotland is the sixth largest fund management centre in Europe (by institutional equity holdings) while in the banking sector alone Scotland again ranks sixth in Europe.[17]

Edinburgh is Scotland's financial centre, helping explain why by the end of the twentieth century it had become the most dynamic regional economy in Scotland. Edinburgh is the headquarters of the Royal Bank of Scotland, the Bank of Scotland, merchant banks, insurance companies, investment managers and numerous other financial institutions. However, Glasgow is also an important base for a range of financial services. Just over half, 51 per cent, of all financial services employment is located in Edinburgh and 16 per cent in Glasgow although, for data reasons, these figures probably understate the dominance of the two cities. A few other areas also have a significant concentration in parts of the financial-services sector, generally because of the presence of one or two companies with large offices there. These include Fife (in building societies), Tayside (in insurance and fund management) and Grampian (again in fund management).[18]

Aberdeen is Edinburgh's closest rival in terms of a prosperous regional economy. Aberdeen is the main onshore base for the North Sea oil industry, although there are smaller bases on Shetland and Orkney. Aberdeen's economy has been transformed since the first commercially viable discoveries of oil were made in 1969. Prior to that, the Aberdeen economy was relatively depressed with low wages and large-scale emigration of people from Aberdeen in search of better employment prospects elsewhere. The arrival of the oil industry radically changed Aberdeen's economic circumstances with significant growth of employment and a reversal of the trend of population movements. The population of the city rose by 15 per cent, to quarter of a million. The oil industry now dominates the Aberdeen economy.[19] The jobs created by oil are relatively well paid. As a result, average earnings in Aberdeen for men have risen markedly compared to the rest of the country, and are distinctly higher than the national average. The same is not true, however, for women, only a comparatively small number of whom are

17. S. Dunlop, 'Financial services and the Scottish economy', Fraser of Allander Institute *Quarterly Economic Commentary*, vol. 26, no. 1 (2001), pp. 31–8.
18. Ibid.
19. D. Newlands, 'The oil economy', in W. H. Fraser and C. H. Lee, (eds), *Aberdeen, 1800–2000: A New History* (East Linton: Tuckwell Press, 2000), pp. 126–52.

employed in the oil industry. The oil industry is the biggest single individual employer in Aberdeen, with some 50,000 people working for the oil companies and numerous oil supply firms. Relatively small numbers are now employed in Aberdeen's traditional industries, only a few thousand in fishing, only some 15,000 in total in manufacturing. Most of the oil businesses in Aberdeen are foreign companies. The Wood Group is one of the few examples of a local business exploiting the opportunities offered by oil.

Shifts in the relative fortunes of different industries within Scotland has had important implications for the distribution of population, income and employment. Strathclyde region accounted for 49 per cent of the total Scottish population in 1971. By 2001, the corresponding local authority areas made up only 44 per cent of the Scottish total. The former Lothian, Grampian, Tayside, Fife and Central regions come next in population size, in that order. All these regions have experienced an increase in their share of the Scottish population. For Grampian, the increase was substantial, a rise of nearly 20 per cent between 1971 and 2001. Overlaying the general shift in population distribution from west to east, Glasgow and Dundee have experienced major declines due in part to people moving out of the cities to surrounding areas. The increased extent of commuting, particularly in the central belt, has been partly a response to increasing disparities in house prices between different parts of Scotland with prices rising particularly sharply in Edinburgh from the 1980s onwards. Even with commuting, differentials in house prices risk becoming as much an impediment to the movement of labour around the country as were council housing allocation procedures forty or fifty years ago.

Again employing the former regional authorities, Grampian had the highest Gross Domestic Product per capita in 1995, followed by Lothian. The lowest GDP per capita was in the Highlands and Islands with Strathclyde only marginally higher. Comparison with 1977 shows some changes in rankings.[20] In 1977 GDP per capita was again highest in Grampian but followed closely by Central, Fife, the Highlands and Islands and then Lothian. The poorest regions were, in ascending order, Strathclyde, Tayside, and Dumfries and Galloway. More significantly, the comparison between 1977 and 1995 shows an increasing disparity between richest and poorest regions. In 1977 the difference in GDP per capita between richest (Grampian) and poorest (Strathclyde) was 18 per cent. By 1995, the gap between richest (Grampian) and poorest

20. J. Peat and S. Boyle, *An Illustrated Guide to the Scottish Economy* (London: Duckworth, 1999).

(Highlands and Islands) had increased substantially, to 62 per cent. Similar inequalities can now be observed for earnings from employment. In 2002 average gross weekly full-time earnings in Aberdeen city were 46 per cent higher than in the Scottish Borders and in Moray, and 42 per cent higher than in Inverclyde.[21]

The growth in regional economic disparities within Scotland over the last twenty-five years, after a long period in which they were declining, partly reflects specific factors, such as the rapid expansion of certain highly profitable and well-paid industries including finance and oil. However, to a greater extent it is simply a Scottish manifestation of wider phenomena. The play of market forces has been given greater scope through privatisation, deregulation and restrictions over the power of trade unions. Conversely, the redistributive role of the state has been curtailed through the reduced progressivity of income and other taxation, a contraction of the welfare state, a devaluation of the importance of full employment and a cultural shift which has led to greater tolerance of very high and very low incomes.

Unemployment in Scotland rose sharply in the late 1970s and early 1980s. It then fell significantly from the mid-1980s onwards, apart from a blip in the early 1990s. Similar cyclical movements applied across all regions, with Grampian a partial exception because of developments within the oil industry, such that rankings by unemployment rate have not changed significantly over the last twenty-five years. Rankings by unemployment, or indeed by other measures of job opportunities such as economic activity rates, are much as would be expected. In the late 1970s or early 1980s, the lowest unemployment rates were in Grampian and Shetland and the highest in Strathclyde and the Western Isles. Twenty years later the lowest unemployment rates were in Aberdeen city and Shetland and the highest in Glasgow city, North Lanarkshire, East Ayrshire and Dundee city.

Similar patterns are evident with regard to poverty. Bramley et al.[22] employ data on the take up of social security benefits, specifically Income Support (IS) and Housing Benefit (HB), to describe the geography of poverty in Scotland (in 1996). The average for the whole of Scotland was 32 per cent of households (for IS alone) or 33 per cent (for IS and HB together). The lowest poverty figures were for Aberdeen (16 per cent for IS and 17 per cent for IS/HB) and then relatively affluent commuter areas, such as Aberdeenshire and East Renfrewshire, and two of the

21. Scottish Executive, *Scottish Economic Statistics* (Edinburgh: Scottish Executive, 2003).
22. G. Bramley, S. Lancaster and D. Gordon, 'Benefit take-up and the geography of poverty in Scotland', *Regional Studies*, vol. 34, no. 6 (2000), pp. 507–20.

island groups, Shetland and the Western Isles. By far the highest figures were for Glasgow (52 per cent for both measures), which puts the much-touted economic renaissance of the city firmly in perspective. Other high poverty areas were Dundee, north Lanarkshire, South Ayrshire and west Dunbartonshire (all in the range 36–40 per cent). The figures for Edinburgh were 27 per cent (IS) and 32 per cent (IS/HB), close to the Scottish average.

The principal vehicles of regional and industrial policy within Scotland over the last quarter of a century have been the development agency networks. To the Highlands and Islands Development Board (HIDB), created in 1965, was added the Scottish Development Agency (SDA) in 1975, with responsibilities for the economic development of Lowland Scotland. The records of both the HIDB and the SDA in the 1970s and 1980s were generally reckoned to be in credit. In some ways, the subsequent reconstitution of the HIDB and SDA in 1991 as Highlands and Islands Enterprise (HIE) and Scottish Enterprise (SE) could have been expected to increase their effectiveness, both in raising the growth rate of the Scottish economy as a whole and in addressing the scale of regional economic disparities. HIE and SE took over the training functions previously exercised in Scotland by the Training Agency while there was a further decentralisation of economic development and train- ing responsibilities to Local Enterprise Companies (LECs) throughout Scotland. However, the creation of the LECs may have been a de- centralisation measure too far, with the loss of a central strategic overview of the problems of the Scottish economy and a multiplication of the problems of co-ordination, between the various LECs, between HIE and SE and the LECs, and between the whole HIE and SE structures and the economic development efforts of Scottish local authorities.

There were a variety of other policy initiatives in the late twentieth century. A number of areas of Scotland benefited from European Union regional aid, notably the Highlands and Islands, which was a so-called Objective One region. The government created four Enterprise Zones in Scotland in the 1980s and 1990s. The Tayside Enterprise Zone covered a number of sites, in Dundee and Arbroath, but the other three were all intended to attract business to areas which had experienced the closure of a single major employer: the Singer sewing machine factory at Clydebank, the aluminium smelter at Invergordon and the steelworks at Ravenscraig. The latter two were of course symbols of the failure of earlier regional policy measures.

The final policy development of the twentieth century was possibly the most important of them all, namely the creation of the Scottish Parliament in 1999. Since then, there has been renewed interest in regional economic inequalities within Scotland. Seeking to ensure that all regions of Scotland contribute to, and benefit from, economic growth is one of the four principal objectives of the Scottish Executive's economic strategy.[23] Whether, for all the economic powers that the Parliament possesses, it will be able to achieve this objective is a question for the future. Meanwhile, and somewhat ironically, the very establishment of the Parliament has fuelled Edinburgh's economic boom and widened the contrast between the capital's economic fortunes and those of many other parts of Scotland.

CONCLUSIONS

Scotland is not just one economy but a fairly large number of regional economies of different sizes. The central belt accounts for the largest part of Scottish population, income, output and employment. However, while there are similarities in economic structure and performance between the more industrially based economies of west central Scotland, there are also major differences between Strathclyde and Lothian. Moreover, the economy of the central belt is in turn very different to that of the Borders or the north east or the Highlands and Islands (and indeed Orkney, Shetland and the Western Isles are all quite distinct from each other).

To some extent, the continued existence of very distinctive regional economies in Scotland is surprising. Scotland is a relatively small place. Even at the beginning of the twentieth century, the Scottish economy was fairly well economically integrated and the extent of that integration increased as the century progressed with improved transport and communication networks and greater migration and commuting. It has been suggested that, while regional economic differences pose a number of problems, regional diversity also brings strength to the economy as a whole.[24] The argument is that diversity provides protection against adverse events within one or a small number of industries. This is perhaps true but only if the period of dominance of prosperous, growing sectors is used to good effect, to open up opportunities for their

23. Scottish Executive, *The Way Forward: Framework for Economic Development in Scotland* (Edinburgh: Scottish Executive, 2000).
24. Peat and Boyle, *Illustrated Guide*, p. 71.

successors. It would be hard to argue that this process was well managed during the twentieth century in Scotland. At the beginning of the twentieth century, the Clydeside shipbuilding and engineering complex was the most dynamic sector of the Scottish economy. At the end of the century, the financial-services sector based in Edinburgh was the driving force. However, it took almost the entire hundred years in between to achieve the transition from one to the other.

FURTHER READING

Campbell, R. H., *Scotland since 1707: The Rise of an Industrial Society*, 2nd edn (Edinburgh: John Donald, 1985).

Johnston, T., Buxton, N. and Mair, D., *Structure and Growth of the Scottish Economy* (Glasgow: Collins, 1971).

Lee, C. H., *Scotland and the United Kingdom: The Economy and the Union in the Twentieth Century* (Manchester: Manchester University Press, 1995).

Lenman, B., *An Economic History of Modern Scotland, 1660–1976* (London: Batsford, 1977).

Peat, J. and Boyle, S., *An Illustrated Guide to the Scottish Economy* (London: Duckworth, 1999).

Randall, J. N., 'Scotland', in P. Damesick and P. Wood (eds), *Regional Problems, Problem Regions, and Public Policy in the United Kingdom* (Oxford: Oxford University Press, 1987).

Scottish Council (Development and Industry), *Inquiry into the Scottish Economy, 1960–1961: Report of a Committee under the Chairmanship of J. N. Toothill* (1961).

CHAPTER SEVEN

The Modernisation of Scottish Agriculture

Ewen A. Cameron

INTRODUCTION

Scottish agriculture in the twentieth century has been characterised by considerable change and modernisation. The most basic point is the decline of the contribution of agriculture to Scottish Gross Domestic Profit, a trend which has accelerated in recent years. As late as the mid-1970s the gross product of agriculture was equivalent to 4 per cent of Scottish GDP; this has declined steadily since then until 2001, when the figure stood at 1.1 per cent.[1] The relatively labour-intensive system of the early twentieth century has given way to a much more highly capitalised system. Communal labouring has also declined markedly and in recent years, as margins for farmers have become very tight, part-time labour has increased in importance. Mechanisation has had a considerable impact with the increasing use of tractors and combined harvesters from the 1950s. The political economy of farming has also been subject to massive change as the British government and subsequently the European political structures, through the Common Agricultural Policy, have become increasingly interventionist. This intervention encouraged production of agricultural commodities with farmers being rewarded for intensive production. More recently, however, subsidy has increasingly taken the form of direct payments to farmers with additional measures designed to encourage more extensive forms of farming. This has involved a profound shift in the culture and mentality of the farming

1. These figures have been calculated from data on agriculture published annually in the *Economic Report on Scottish Agriculture* (Edinburgh: Department of Agriculture and Fisheries for Scotland) from 1930 to 2002 – hereafter referred to as *ERSA* – and those relating to Scottish GDP published annually in the *Scottish Economic Bulletin* (Edinburgh: HMSO) over the same period.

community: after nearly fifty years of being paid to produce, they were now faced with a situation where the opposite was required: 'Farmers were previously used to having the nation dependent on them for supplies of food, now they find themselves dependant on the public for their support.'[2]

TRENDS

Under these influences holdings have become larger and fewer, the number of farmers has dropped and their position in rural society has been dramatically altered. Part-time farming has increased, and farmers and their families have had to become adept at maximising their income from an increasingly diverse range of activities. These important changes form a crucial component of any overview of agricultural change in twentieth-century Scotland. Furthermore, they tie the Scottish experience into a wider British and, since the early 1970s, European framework.

The economic history of farming is governed by the largely immutable characteristics of geographical conditions and the ungovernable variations of the weather. The weather can have dramatic effects on the agricultural economy and there have been a number of crisis seasons in the twentieth century in this regard: the two most obvious examples are the winter of 1946/7, which devastated the livestock of Scottish hill farms, and the exceptionally wet harvest season of 1985. Farming is also an unusual area of the economy in that 'income elasticity of demand' is low in the food sector and it grows at a much slower rate than the economy as a whole. This helps to explain its diminishing share in the economy, a diminution which affects agriculture as one, although not the only, part of that sector.[3] This has profound effects on land use as primary food production becomes less important and the premium on intensive farming is reduced.[4]

Nevertheless, the drive since the 1930s to intensify farming methods has had a massive impact on the yields for most of the major crops. Over that period the yields (tonne per hectare) of wheat has risen by a factor

2. H. L. McHenry, 'Understanding the farmer's view: perceptions of changing agriculture and the move to agri-environmental policies in southern Scotland' (University of Aberdeen Ph.D., 1994), p. 80.
3. J. McInerney, 'Agriculture at the crossroads', *Journal of the Royal Agricultural Society of England*, 160 (1999), pp. 8–27, at 11 and 17.
4. T. G. Maxwell and M. G. R. Connell, 'The environment and land use of the future', in G. Holmes and R. Crofts (eds), *Scotland's Environment: The Future* (East Linton: Tuckwell Press, 2000), p. 41.

of nearly three, barley by a factor of nearly 2.5, that of oats by 2.7. A similar story can be told for potatoes and crops for fodder such as turnips and swedes. The impact of fertilisers, improved seed strains and more sophisticated methods of cultivation have all contributed to this increase. A similar picture can be seen in the livestock sector, where, for example, lambing percentages have increased from 76 per cent in the early 1950s to levels of between 95 per cent and 105 per cent in the last ten years.[5] The impact of improved veterinary medicine and better education of sheep farmers in matters of husbandry have been the obvious contributory factors. This has taken place despite the fact that there have been worries about the impact of intensive sheep grazing on fragile hill land.[6]

THE NATIONAL FARM AND REGIONAL DIVERSITY

It is important to consider the characteristics of what an earlier author has called the 'national farm',[7] the principal distinguishing characteristic of which is the concentration on livestock, as opposed to arable farming and the production of cereals. Whether one examines the extent of land devoted to different agricultural activities, or the contribution of these activities to Scottish agricultural output, it is clear that livestock dominates the Scottish agrarian economy and this has remained so throughout the century. In the inter-war years livestock contributed between 77 per cent and 83 per cent of Scottish agricultural output.[8] This figure has fallen in recent years but remains at around 60 per cent. In the 1950s the average contribution of livestock to total output was 77 per cent; this fell only slightly in the 1960s to 76 per cent, was down to 72 per cent in the 1970s, 70 per cent in the 1980s, but the average since 1990 is only 64 per cent and the 1995 figure of 58.5 per cent was the lowest since 1950.[9] This change has been due to the falling prices for livestock in recent years as well as the increasing contribution of cereals as prices and yields have risen.

This picture is confirmed if the agricultural area of Scotland is examined. It is clear that grass and crops associated with livestock

5. *Agricultural Statistics (Scotland)* (Edinburgh: HMSO, 1935–1979); *ERSA*, 1980–2002.
6. A. S. Mather, 'The alleged deterioration of hill grazings in the Scottish Highlands', *Biological Conservation*, 14 (1978), pp. 181–95.
7. G. F. B. Houston, 'Agriculture', in A. K. Cairncross (ed.), *The Scottish Economy: A Statistical Account of Scottish Life* (Cambridge: Cambridge University Press, 1954), pp. 84–108, at 85.
8. R. Anthony, *Herds and Hinds: Farm Labour in Lowland Scotland, 1900–1939* (East Linton: Tuckwell Press, 1997), p. 24.
9. *Scottish Agricultural Economics*, 1–30, 1950–80, *ERSA*, 1980–2002.

dominate, and that cereals, with the exception of barley, have a minor role to play. The most recent figures show that around two-thirds of the agricultural area of Scotland is composed of rough grazing compared to 28 per cent in Wales, 17 per cent in Northern Ireland and only 11 per cent in England.[10] This has a marked effect on the kind of agricultural activities which can be undertaken in the different regions.[11] Changes in the way statistics have been collected makes comparison over the course of the century somewhat difficult, but certain characteristics can be identified. The Highland region, for example, contained around 55 to 60 per cent of all the rough grazing in Scotland, but typically less than 5 per cent of the wheat and barley areas, and less than 10 per cent of the area devoted to the production of oats. The clearest contrast is with the South-East region, which provided only around 6 per cent of the rough grazing, but over 40 per cent of the barley acreage and 30 per cent of the wheat acreage. East central Scotland showed similar characteristics in many ways, with over 50 per cent of the wheat acreage and nearly 30 per cent of the barley acreage. This region also provided the vast bulk of the acres devoted to the more specialised crops of fruit and sugar beet. Around 5,000 hectares were devoted to the production of sugar beet, which was processed at Cupar in Fife, until the factory there closed in 1971.[12] The North-East was the most diverse of all the regions with a regime of mixed farming. Substantial areas were devoted to barley and oats, but the importance of livestock to the area is clear from the high numbers of cattle and sheep as well as the fact that around 40 per cent of the land used for the production of turnips and swedes for stockfeeding could be found in this area. Livestock, especially dairy cattle, were more important in the South-West, which had a smaller area of land devoted to cereal production, but around half of Scotland's permanent grass could be found in this area. The picture which emerges is of an agrarian economy devoted to the production of livestock with a substantial amount of land taken up with the growth of forage crops.[13] A recent change has been the increasing contribution of cereals, even wheat, to

10. *Economic Report on Scottish Agriculture* (2002), chart C1.
11. Prior to 1970 for statistical purposes Scotland was divided into five regions based on county boundaries: Highland, North-East, East Central, South-East and South-West. After 1970 this was refined to include only four regions: North-West (which includes the local government areas of Highland, Western Isles, and Orkney and Shetland), North-East, South-East (which includes Tayside, Fife, Lothian and the Borders), and South-West (Argyll and Bute, East Central, Clyde Valley, Ayrshire, and Dumfries and Galloway).
12. J. Bryden, 'Scottish agriculture, 1950–1980', in R. Saville (ed.), *The Economic Development of Modern Scotland, 1950–1980* (Edinburgh: John Donald, 1985), pp. 141–62, at 149; W. Harley, 'The "beet" generation: sugar beet and Fife', *History Scotland*, vol. 3, no. 1 (2003), pp. 50–5.
13. *Agricultural Statistics (Scotland)*, 1935–1979; *ERSA*, 1980–2002.

Scottish agricultural output since the entry to Europe. This has been part of a move to greater specialisation in farming, especially a concentration on arable production in the east of Scotland.[14] The days when, as one farmer put it, 'we all grew some grain and, you know, had a bit of this and a bit of that', were gone.[15]

A further issue worthy of consideration here is the position of the Highlands in the Scottish agrarian economy. As will be discussed below, the seven crofting counties from Argyll to Shetland had, from 1886, a different system of land tenure which gave tenants a considerable degree of legal security, in contrast to the historical experience of this group. Further, the development of institutions to service this new legal code was among the earliest forms of government intervention in agriculture and rural society. Although the social and demographic impact of these reforms has been massive, their agricultural impact is limited. Throughout the twentieth century there has been a paradox at the heart of the agrarian history of the Highlands. On the one hand, there is no denying the importance of agriculture to the Highlands, as has been noted: 'The Highlands was an extensive area where agriculture retained its ancient dominance long after industrialisation had transformed other districts.'[16] On the other hand, the contribution of the Highlands to the output of Scottish agriculture was minimal. Agricultural activity was driven by the fact that most of the land in the crofting counties was rough grazing and resulted in sheep farming being the dominant land use. The Highlands had very low areas of land under crop, only around 2.5 per cent in the period from 1877 to 1960 in the case of Sutherland; around 5 per cent in the case of Argyll; only just over 6 per cent in the case of Ross-shire. Only Caithness with values of just over 20 per cent approached the Scottish average over this period. This data has been used to 'confirm the unimportance of Highland experience in the general history of Scottish agriculture'.[17] It would perhaps be fairer to say that the evidence confirms the distinctiveness of the region. Crofting, its defenders would argue, although it is only a part of the overall Highland experience, is not to be seen in terms of agricultural output, which is slight, but in social terms.[18]

14. G. Sprott, 'Lowland country life', in T. M. Devine and R. J. Finlay (eds), *Scotland in the Twentieth Century* (Edinburgh: Edinburgh University Press, 1996), pp. 170–87, at 183.
15. McHenry, 'Understanding the farmer's view', p. 70.
16. R. H. Campbell, 'Too much on the Highlands? A plea for change', *Scottish Economic and Social History*, 14 (1994), pp. 58–75, at 60.
17. Ibid., pp. 62–3.
18. J. Hunter, *The Claim of Crofting: The Scottish Highlands, 1930–90* (Edinburgh: Mainstream, 1991).

FARM LABOUR AND MECHANISATION

The principal point to note in the history of farm labour in the twentieth century is the overall decline in numbers, which has reduced agricultural labour to a tiny element within the Scottish labour force. Figures from the decennial census show the numbers of persons employed in agriculture in 1901 to be around 210,000, 11 per cent of the total workforce, but this includes farmers and their families as well as hired workers.[19] This number had declined to less than 30,000 by 1991 and amounted to no more than 1.4 per cent of the workforce.[20] It is more difficult to analyse the number of hired workers at the beginning of the century, but recent research has concluded 'that there were about 100,000 farm workers in Scotland prior to the First World War, of whom roughly 85,000 were regular workers'.[21] The period between the wars was one of decline in the size of the agricultural labour force and at the beginning of the Second World War there were around 83,000 workers, of whom about 72,000 were regular workers. Although the Second World War saw an increase in the full-time labour force to around 96,000, as strenuous efforts were made to increase the domestic production of food, the years since the war have seen a continual decline in the overall size of the agricultural labour force, to around 16,000. The structure of the labour force has also changed markedly with a much greater reliance on the labour of farmers, their families and part-time workers. In 1955 there were around 7,000 part-time workers, amounting to 8 per cent of the total number of workers; the most recent figures show that the 6,986 part-time employees amounted to 26 per cent of a much reduced total number of employees. This has been a profound change over the last ten years as the number of part-time workers has risen from 5,600 in 1991, whilst the number of full-time workers has slumped. The labour of occupiers, spouses and other family members appears to have increased in importance in recent years, but, as Richard Anthony has argued, this may well be the result of more sophisticated collection of statistics.[22] Ethnological and sociological work has emphasised the importance of the family in the Scottish agricultural labour force throughout the twentieth century.[23]

19. Anthony, *Herds and Hinds*, p. 59.
20. C. H. Lee, *Scotland and the United Kingdom: The Economy and the Union in the Twentieth Century* (Manchester: Manchester University Press, 1995), p. 65.
21. Anthony, *Herds and Hinds*, p. 62.
22. *Agricultural Statistics (Scotland)*, 1935–79; *ERSA*, 1980–2002; R. Anthony, '"What hope for farmers?" Agriculture in southern Scotland', *Scottish Affairs*, no. 3 (1993), pp. 55–63, at 59.
23. G. J. West, 'Working the heartland. Farm, family and neighbourhood in post-Improvement

The principal reason which has been advanced for the overall decline in farm labour in the postwar period is mechanisation.[24] The use of tractors, for example, expanded in the 1950s: in 1948 there were around 30,000 tractors on Scottish farms, this had risen to 60,000 by 1961. In the 1930s an Ulsterman, Harry Ferguson, had begun to develop a tractor which could readily perform a number of tasks, from ploughing and harrowing to mowing, but the depression put such expensive machines beyond the pockets of most farmers and it was not until the postwar years that the 'Fergie' became popular among crofters and farmers throughout Scotland.[25] Tractors not only became more numerous but also more sophisticated and powerful, capable of carrying out a greater range of tasks ever more quickly. Combined harvesters also became more popular, replacing older more limited machines such as binders, in the years from the end of the Second World War to the 1970s, but especially during the 1960s. There were only 100 such machines on Scottish farms in 1944, the majority of which were tractor drawn; but by the mid-1970s there were over 7,500, of which all but 200 were self-propelled.[26] These, influences, however, were most evident on arable farms and additional reasons must be sought for the decline in the agricultural labour force. Two other factors can be pointed to: the first is the increasing importance of specialised cereal production in Scottish arable farming; the labour requirements for such an agrarian regime are lower and more concentrated at harvest time than in a system predicated on rotations of crops. Second, the decreasing number of farm units and the concomitant rise in the average size of units has resulted in shedding of labour as farms have been amalgamated and land has been sold out of farming.[27] Changes in farming practice have also resulted in the shedding of labour, for example the considerable amount of effort which went into the making of hay in the early part of this period was reduced when silage began to become more prominent in the 1950s and 1960s.[28]

The dominance of livestock farming in Scotland meant that the labour force was highly skilled, with a lower proportion of general labourers than the English labour force, which was engaged in arable work to a

Perthshire: an historical ethnography' (University of Edinburgh Ph.D., 1999), pp. 99–140; L. Jamieson and C. Toynbee, *Country Bairns: Growing Up, 1900–1930* (Edinburgh: Birlinn, 2000).

24. Bryden, 'Scottish agriculture', p. 159.
25. Sprott, 'Lowland country life', pp. 180–1.
26. *Agricultural Statistics (Scotland)*, 1944–75.
27. Bryden, 'Scottish agriculture', in Saville (ed.), *Economic Development*, pp. 159–60.
28. *Agricultural Statistics (Scotland)*, 1950–79; *ERSA*, 1980–2002; P. Brassley, 'Silage in Britain, 1880–1990: the delayed adoption of an innovation', *Agricultural History Review*, 44 (1996), pp. 63–87, at 77.

greater extent. In a Board of Trade survey of around 20,000 labourers in 1907 this pattern can be seen very clearly: 62 per cent were horsemen and only 11 per cent were 'orramen', or ordinary labourers, in England the latter class of labourer formed 43 per cent of the labour force.[29]

The speed of Scottish industrialisation and the high levels of emigration from Scotland in the nineteenth century considerably reduced the agricultural labour supply, by about a third over the period from 1861 to 1891, and placed the labour force in a fairly strong bargaining position in relation to their employers.[30] Although the years immediately prior to the Great War saw the formation of both the Scottish Farm Servants' Union (SFSU) and the National Farmers' Union of Scotland, there was considerable resistance to institutional intervention to govern wage rates. The SFSU had been formed by an Aberdeen political activist, Joseph Duncan, who had been the organiser for the Independent Labour Party in the east of Scotland in the aftermath of the general election of 1906, so it was not lacking in political awareness.[31] His union's liking for voluntary agreements was purely pragmatic in that he recognised that the introduction of a formal structure could represent a gain for the employers. Although state intervention in agriculture was slow during the Great War, minimum wage rates were introduced in 1917, but they were largely irrelevant in high-wage areas such as the Scottish Lowlands. The depression of 1921 and the associated reductions in public expenditure meant the end of minimum wages in agriculture, a move which brought 'howls of protest' from unions in England and Wales but which was 'happily accepted in Scotland'.[32]

The worst effects of the depression in Scotland in the 1920s were mitigated by emigration as farmers took advantage of the Empire Settlement Act 1922 to emigrate to the Dominions, with the promise of larger holdings and a better agricultural environment. For example, in the years 1924–6 a total of 8,300 members of the farm labour force emigrated.[33] The 1930s saw a very different situation with rising unemployment and world-wide economic depression limiting the oppor-

---

29. R. Anthony, 'The Scottish agricultural labour market, 1900–1939: a case of institutional intervention', *Economic History Review*, 2nd series, 46 (1993), pp. 558–74, at 559.
30. T. M. Devine, 'Scottish farm labour in the era of agricultural depression, 1875–1900', in T. M. Devine (ed.), *Farm Servants and Labour in Lowland Scotland, 1770–1914* (Edinburgh: John Donald, 1984), pp. 243–55, at 251.
31. J. H. Smith, *Joe Duncan, the Scottish Farm Servants and British Agriculture* (Edinburgh: University of Edinburgh, Department of Politics, for the Scottish Labour History Society, c. 1973).
32. Anthony, 'Scottish agricultural labour market', p. 565.
33. M. Harper, *Emigration from Scotland between the Wars: Opportunity or Exile?* (Manchester: Manchester University Press, 1998), p. 120.

tunities for migration or emigration, and placing the farm workers in a much weaker position than hitherto. This was the context in which a minimum wage was accepted in 1937 and had a positive effect on the position of the Scottish agricultural labour force.[34]

In the postwar period the conditions faced by agricultural workers have improved dramatically. Housing conditions, for long a subject of controversy especially in Scotland, where tied houses are more common than in England,[35] and wage rates have increased, but, as has been noted, the size of the labour force has declined. In the inter-war years, although Scottish agricultural labour was well paid compared to other farm workers, their position relative to other workers was not strong. The position has changed markedly over the period since the beginning of institutional intervention in the 1930s. Nevertheless, even the best-paid farm workers, grieves, receive only around 90 per cent of average earnings; general workers remain badly off with approximately 70 per cent of average earnings.[36]

STATE INTERVENTION IN WAR AND DEPRESSION

Initial state intervention was in tendril matters: the Agricultural Holdings Acts of the 1870s and 1880s and the regionally specific crofters' legislation, which began in 1886, gave farmers and crofters greater security of tenure and the right to compensation for improvement.[37] The Great War saw important steps being taken by the government to increase food production. The first two years of the war, however, saw very little change in the structure of Scottish farming and it was only after 1917 that minimum prices were introduced.[38] In England and Wales dramatic increases in cereal production were evident over the years from 1914 to 1918: 44 per cent in wheat, 50 per cent in oats, and 42 per cent in potatoes. In Scotland the change in production of these commodities was of a lesser magnitude: 26 per cent, 40 per cent and 7 per cent respectively. This was partly because the arable acreage had not declined to the same extent during the years of depression and there was not the

34. Anthony, 'Scottish agricultural labour market', p. 572.
35. Houston, 'Agriculture', in Cairncross (ed.), *The Scottish Economy*, p. 107.
36. *ERSA*, 1980–2000.
37. E. A. Cameron, *Land for the People? The British Government and the Scottish Highlands, c. 1880–1925* (East Linton: Tuckwell Press, 1996); L. Leneman, *Fit for Heroes? Land Settlement in Scotland after World War One* (Aberdeen: Aberdeen University Press, 1989).
38. Anthony, *Herds and Hinds*, p. 21.

same slack to be taken up.[39] The impact of legislation to guarantee corn prices was minimal as the guaranteed prices were so much lower than the market price. More important was the work of the Board of Agriculture for Scotland, working through local agricultural executive committees to increase production. Despite strained relations with Lowland landowners and farmers it was quite successful in this task, increasing the corn acreage by 21 per cent over the 1916 to 1918 period. In addition to corn production elaborate procedures were introduced to control the sale of livestock. Potato prices were guaranteed and the acreage devoted to this crop was expanded from 1916. Prices of agricultural commodities, such as milk, cheese and butter (the making of which was discouraged), in demand by consumers were subject to maximum levels from late 1916 or early 1917; eggs were added to this list in December 1918. Although numbers of livestock fell modestly, this has to be set alongside the fact that there were nearly 180,000 fewer acres available for grazing in 1918 as compared with 1914, with a particularly steep decline of over 100,000 acres between 1917 and 1918.[40]

Alongside the intervention of central government and the local stimulation of the Board of Agriculture for Scotland, the third principal factor which induced these changes was the increased wartime prices for the majority of agricultural products. The all important oat crop was fetching an average price of 76s in 1918, compared to 34s 4d in 1914. The price of feeding stuffs also increased dramatically in the same period: linseed cake from £7 15s to £19; and bean meal from £8 to £27 15s. Nevertheless, farming was still carried out at a profit during the Great War.

Other difficulties during the First World War included the demands of the army for labour, horses and fodder, all of which placed the Board of Agriculture for Scotland in a difficult mediating position. In numerical terms Scottish agriculture faced labour problems of a lesser magnitude than England and Wales. A lower proportion of the labour force enlisted, and the effect of conscription from January 1916 was mitigated by the decision to make agriculture a completely reserved occupation in June 1917, a policy that remained in force until the demand for men became urgent in the spring of the following year.[41] Scottish agriculture, however, seems to have been able to find replacements for men who enlisted, through soldier, child and volunteer labour.

39. C. Douglas, 'Scottish agriculture during the war', *Transactions of the Highland and Agricultural Society of Scotland*, 31 (1919), pp. 1–66, at 3, 10–11, 49.
40. Ibid., pp. 46–7.
41. P. E. Dewey, *British Agriculture in the First World War* (London: Routledge, 1989), pp. 99–102.

Even so, problems did ensue because, as we have seen, specialist labour for the care of livestock was prominent in Scotland and was difficult to replace at the same level of skill.[42] It has also been suggested that qualitative labour problems were acute in Scotland because of the 'preponderance of small farms which are more vulnerable to labour shortage at key points in the year'.[43]

At the end of the Great War the complex structures of food price control were withdrawn, but the government made an initial commitment, through the Agriculture Act of 1920, to guarantee the price of corn.[44] This was suddenly withdrawn in 1921 as the government became chary of the potentially massive costs of guaranteeing prices which were now falling rapidly, in contrast to the position during the war. For political reasons the government could not justify the expenditure of up to £20 million on support to agriculture when other industries were being left to cope with difficult economic conditions without intervention.[45] The traditional view of this policy change, based partly on interviews with English farmers, is of a 'betrayal'.[46] More recent research emphasises debates within government on the wisdom of a long-term commitment to price guarantee and notes the extent to which farmers resented government interference in their activities.[47] Scottish farmers seemed not to be discomfited by the withdrawal of support in 1921, a situation partly realised by fairly generous compensation for the 1921 crop of oats and wheat. Elements of the farming press demonstrated an uneasiness about subsidy, which would not be replicated in later generations, noting that it was 'inimical to enterprise and initiative'.[48] The situation had changed markedly by the middle of the 1930s, however, and there were frequent demands for intervention, especially restriction on imports from the Dominions. The Blackface Sheep Breeders' Association was a case in point, writing to the Secretary of State for Scotland in 1935, demanding protection of home produce and

42. Anthony, *Herds and Hinds*, pp. 95–9.
43. Douglas, 'Scottish agriculture', p. 36.
44. C. Douglas, 'The policy of the Agriculture Act', *Transactions of the Highland and Agricultural Society of Scotland*, 33 (1921), pp. 1–20.
45. R. Perren, *Agriculture in Depression, 1870–1940* (Cambridge: Cambridge University Press, 1995), p. 39.
46. E. H. Whetham, 'The Agriculture Act, 1920, and its repeal – the 'great betrayal', *Agricultural History Review*, 22 (1974), pp. 36–49.
47. A. Cooper, *British Agricultural Policy, 1912–1936: A Study in Conservative Politics* (Manchester: Manchester University Press, 1989), pp. 42–60; E. C. Penning-Roswell, 'Who "betrayed" whom? Power and politics in the 1920/1 agricultural crisis', *Agricultural History Review*, 45 (1997), pp. 176–94.
48. *Scottish Farmer*, 3 September 1921, quoted by Anthony, *Herds and Hinds*, p. 40.

fair dealing from butchers.[49] Farmers felt that their interests were being sacrificed on the altar of cheap food.[50]

The principal factor which had produced this change in the outlook of farmers and landowners was the prolonged agricultural depression which afflicted British agriculture between 1921 and the outbreak of the Second World War. Unlike the depression of the late nineteenth century it is difficult to argue that the structure of Scottish farming exempted it from the worst effects of the downturn. There are a number of indicators which can be used to measure the extent of the depression, but the most obvious one is to look at the index of agricultural prices kept by the Department of Agriculture for Scotland from the late 1920s to 1961, with averages of prices in the years from 1927 to 1929 used as the base; indispensable work by Anthony has extended this series back to 1922, providing us with evidence from the entire depression period and beyond.[51] These data demonstrate clearly that there was a 'continual downward trend' in the prices of the products of both the arable and livestock sectors.[52] In the period before 1934 when government inter-vention became a factor, the strategy of farmers was to reduce costs. In Scotland the absence of wage regulation meant that one way to do this was to reduce the wages paid to farm labourers; in England wage regulation meant that this was impossible and the overall size of the agricultural labour force fell during the depression. There were, of course, significant regional variations within Scotland: in the early 1930s, the worst years of the depression, while dairy farmers in the south-west of Scotland saw a return on their capital of between 10 and 20 per cent, the sheep farmers of the Borders saw losses, up to 14 per cent in 1931–2.[53] This evidence shows that it was still possible for farmers to make a profit during the depression, but this view was drowned out at the time by the welter of rhetoric and anecdotal evidence which emphasised the woes facing the farming community.[54]

49. Alex Cowan, Penicuik, Blackface Sheep Breeders' Association, to John Colville, 14 December 1935, AF43/123/6, National Archives of Scotland (NAS).
50. John McMorran, Tynehead, Midlothian, to Godfrey Collins, 9 May 1936, AF43/123/12, NAS. Landowners were broadly in agreement with these sentiments: see Lord Stonehaven to Collins, 2 July 1936, AF43/123/13; and Earl of Caithness, convenor of the County of Aberdeenshire, to John Colville, 20 December 1938, AF43/123/48c.
51. I have been reluctant to employ this index for analysis of the postwar period due to published uncertainties about its values, eventually leading to its cessation in 1961 and its replacement by a UK-wide index. See 'New Agricultural price indices for the United Kingdom', *Economic Trends*, no. 100 (February 1962).
52. Anthony, *Herds and Hinds*, pp. 40–1.
53. Ibid., pp. 42–4.
54. Frederick B. Jamieson, North Braco, Hatton, Aberdeenshire, to Stanley Baldwin, 8 February 1936, AF43/123/7, NAS; Perren, *Agriculture in Depression*, p. 42.

The combination of political and economic pressure compelled the government to act, and the response was an about-turn in agricultural policy. One element of this was the protection demanded by farmers, although imperial preference and agreements with countries such as Denmark and Argentina were part of the scheme. This was part of the wider move away from free trade initiated by the National Government in 1931. The government, of course, had to balance the interests of the farmers with the more politically powerful interests of the consumer, which could not be sacrificed on the altar of dear food. The second element of the new policy was the support given to the prices of particular commodities; this began with wheat in 1932 and was expanded to include barley and oats in 1937 (although sugar beet had been supported since the mid-1920s).[55] A wheat subsidy was no great comfort to Scottish farmers outside the Lothians, although it did stimulate an expansion in the wheat acreage, and was worth nearly £1.4 million over the period 1932 to 1938. The support for oats and barley was much more modest and provided Scottish farmers with only around £170,000 in the period 1937 to 1939. Scottish farming received a lower share of subsidy than its share of UK output would appear to indicate because of the relative prominence of wheat in the regime. Subsidy was also directed towards livestock, especially cattle, which attracted £3.9 million in support from 1934 to 1938. Sheep, however, were only belatedly (1939) and modestly supported, despite the index of sheep-related products plummeting to below 70 in 1932 and 1938 in the case of fat sheep, and 34 in 1932 in the case of wool.[56] This policy of support did not appease Scottish farmers and this was communicated to politicians when they dared to venture out among the farming community. When the Secretary of State toured the north-east in January 1939 he encountered one farmer who, 'speaking with unrestrained vehemence … referred to the wheat subsidy as "giving money for growing hen's food"'.[57]

With the outbreak of the Second World War, agriculture was faced with a daunting task: to increase food supply and thus reduce the dependence on imports and save money. This had to be achieved, however, with a smaller workforce and the government recognised that unprecedented levels of intervention were necessary. Such intervention involved control of agricultural production and the labour force as well

55. Ibid., p. 53.
56. Anthony, *Herds and Hinds*, pp. 42, 53.
57. Note by R. E. C. Johnson on the visit of the Secretary of State to agricultural areas of Aberdeenshire and Banffshire, 26 January 1939, AF43/124/70a, NAS.

as payment of subsidies to provide incentives to farmers. The amount of land devoted to the production of crops was increased considerably. The grain acreage rose from 960,000 at the start of the war to a peak of 1.4 million in 1942, a level which was largely sustained until the end of the war. The bulk of this land was devoted to the growing of oats, nearly 1.2 million acres in 1942. Similar rises can be seen for potatoes, from 134,000 acres in 1939 to a peak of 239,000 by 1944, and turnips (largely used for the feeding of stock). There was a concomitant reduction in the extent of permanent grass, from 1.6 million acres in 1939 to only 1.1 million acres at the end of the war. Low prices during the inter-war years had seen an increase in permanent grass, but the 1945 extent of permanent grass was well below that of 1918. This increased acreage meant massive increases in production; for example, the 213,000 tons of barley produced in 1945 compared to an average of only 81,000 for the years 1936–8. The general index, which had been languishing around 85 in 1939 had risen to over 150 in the later years of the war as prices for important commodities rose markedly; barley, for example, doubled in price to 24s per hundredweight by 1945.[58] These changes, allied with price increases, meant that the arable farmer's experience of war was a positive one, so much so according to one as to 'look like a direct intervention of providence'.[59] The same could not be said for the livestock farmer, especially in the store sector, as land was turned over to crops. Sheep numbers, for example, fell by over a million over the course of the war.

Agricultural labour during the war was not pressed to enlist to the same extent as during the early years of the First World War, and it has been estimated that only 6,500 men were withdrawn to serve in the forces. Nevertheless, this was a serious depletion given the increase in labour-intensive cultivation during the war. The numbers were made up from a variety of sources, including the Women's Land Army (numbering 7,000–8,000) and prisoners of war, especially Italians, numbering nearly 20,000 by 1945.[60] Whilst the numbers were impressive, there were criticisms of the skill levels of the replacement labour. Wages for agricultural workers, regulated since 1937, were increased markedly during the war years, but the free movement of labour, a central

58. D. Marshall, 'Scottish agriculture during the war', *Transactions of the Highland and Agricultural Society of Scotland*, 58 (1946), pp. 1–77, at 58–62; J. H. Milne-Home, 'The war and the agriculturalist: I, the landowner', *Scottish Journal of Agriculture*, 25 (1944–6), pp. 188–92.
59. J. Keith, 'The war and the agriculturalist: II, the farmer', *Scottish Journal of Agriculture*, 25 (1944–6), pp. 193–8, at 194–5.
60. Marshall, 'Scottish agriculture', pp. 37–47.

characteristic of the Scottish agricultural labour force, was severely curtailed from 1941 onwards.[61]

THE 1947 REGIME

The end of the Second World War represents another important turning point for agriculture and, particularly, for the relationship between the government and agriculture. The policies which flowed from the Agriculture Act of 1947 built on experience gained during the war. The sudden withdrawal of state support from agriculture in 1921 was not to be repeated. The Agriculture Act 1947 made an unambiguously supportive statement, declaring that the aim of the Act was to promote:

> a stable and efficient industry capable of producing such part
> of the nation's food as in the national interest it is desirable to
> produce in the United Kingdom, and to produce it at minimum
> prices consistently with proper remuneration and living
> conditions for farmers and workers in agriculture and with
> an adequate return on capital invested in the industry.[62]

This bold statement masked a considerable degree of uncertainty about the future in the Department of Agriculture for Scotland in the immediate aftermath of the war. Policy makers were largely agreed on the need to maximise home production, thereby reducing imports and saving national resources. It was obvious that the future had to be planned for, but Matthew Campbell, a senior official in the Department of Agriculture for Scotland, made the salient point that there was a danger in precipitate action which would be based on an appreciation of the past, and the depression of the 1930s in particular, rather than the future.[63] Campbell argued for a four-year plan for increased output which would allow for a compromise between the need to look ahead and the need to retain sufficient flexibility to take account of changing conditions. He also foresaw some of the dangers of a subsidy approach, remarking that there could be 'a political difficulty of ending them when their purpose has been served'. Further, there would be no value in

61. J. F. Duncan, 'Agricultural labour under war conditions', *Scottish Journal of Agriculture*, 23 (1940–2), pp. 246–52.
62. B. A. Holderness, *British Agriculture since 1945* (Manchester: Manchester University Press, 1985), pp. 13–14.
63. Minute by Mr Campbell on postwar agricultural policy, AF45/454/1, NAS.

bolstering uneconomic activities or creating international animosity through protective measures for domestic agriculture.[64] The latter point was especially relevant as Britain had relied to such a great extent on imports of agricultural commodities.

The 1947 Act and the Agriculture (Scotland) Act 1948 both contained important provisions designed to try and increase the efficiency and output of Scottish agriculture. An Agricultural Expansion Programme was initiated in August 1947 calling for a 20 per cent increase in the agricultural output of the UK to be achieved by 1951/2. In a Scottish context it was recognised that while crop acreages had to be maintained, the real effort would be in the livestock sector. The objective was to increase the production of beef by 15 per cent, mutton by 18 per cent, pig meat by 85 per cent, eggs by 90 per cent and milk by 15 per cent. This was not a simple matter, however, as for a long period much of the feeding stuff for Scottish livestock had been imported and a concerted effort was made to improve the quality of Scottish grassland through reseeding, increased fertilisation and better management of grazing. Optimism was generated from inter-war experiments in Orkney, where both cattle and sheep numbers had been increased after reseeding. The Scottish agricultural colleges also had a role to play in research and dissemination of knowledge.[65] As hill farmers played such an important part in Scottish agriculture, and as they had largely missed out on the prosperity engendered by intensive production during the war, much Lowland grazing which had been used for fattening purposes by purchasers of store livestock had been turned over to arable production – special measures, including subsidies, improvement schemes and efforts to provide high-quality sires, were introduced. Although modest improvements in production were expected from the arable sector, this was expected to arise from more efficient use of existing acreage leading to increased yields, rather than extension of arable land use.

At a UK level the disparities in results from these plans have been described as affording 'some embarrassment' to the government in the middle of the planning cycle.[66] Although the Scottish objectives were different, there was a similar difficulty in progressing evenly towards all the objectives. The National Farmers' Union of Scotland felt that insufficient certainty about continuing government support for farming was the central problem, but that this was exacerbated by technical

---

64. Ibid.
65. 'Scottish Economic Conference: Plans for increasing agricultural output in Scotland' (Report by the Department of Agriculture for Scotland), 6 July 1948, AF 45/22, NAS.
66. Holderness, *British Agriculture*, p. 17.

difficulties with such things as mechanisation and fertiliser supply.[67] By the early 1950s the expansion programme had run into the sand and, although a new programme was initiated in 1952, government policy changed and the production and marketing of food was freed from government control, as world food supply was no longer in crisis, although subsidies remained.

Alongside control and the expansion programme was a structure of subsidy which had its origins in the Second World War. The way that subsidy levels were arrived at represented an example of corporatism involving the agricultural ministries and the farmers' organisations. Guaranteed prices were set at an Annual Price Review, which began in wartime but was given official status by the 1947 Act.[68] In the 1940s and 1950s about 90 per cent of the agricultural produce of Scotland was covered by this arrangement. The system worked well in the immediate postwar years, but as competition and free marketing increased in the mid-1950s, the system was deemed to provide insufficient stability for farmers. Consequently, limits outwith which annual price changes could not take place were introduced.

THE EUROPEAN DIMENSION

Britain's entry to the European Community (EC) in 1973 was the next major turning point for Scottish farming. The abortive attempts to join and the protracted negotiations leading up to entry meant the European dimension was a factor in thinking about agriculture in government for most of the 1960s. The Common Agricultural Policy (CAP) presented a quite different method of supporting agriculture than had been the case in Britain since 1947. Each year the Council of Ministers set minimum prices for a variety of agricultural commodities: if market prices fell below these prices intervention was triggered and the EC purchased the commodity in question. The notion was that commodities were taken off the market and stored during time of surplus and returned to the market in times of shortage. The intensity of production in European farming meant that surpluses were the norm and a steadily increasing proportion of the EC budget was been taken up with these intervention purchases. The prevention of imports at less than the minimum price and the

67 'Food production, limiting factors as described by National Farmers' Union at Meeting on 23 November (1948)', AF45/22, NAS.
68. D. Milne, *The Scottish Office and Other Scottish Government Departments* (London: George Allen and Unwin, 1957), p. 61.

charging of import levies ensure that consumers pay a relatively high price for their food. Thus the consumer, rather than the taxpayer, foots the bill for the CAP. A further important point is that a relatively small amount of money from the CAP went directly to the producer, most of it, around 70 per cent prior to the reforms of 1992, went to the traders from whom the EC made its purchases. The CAP has been least successful in its objective of protecting farmers' incomes, especially those of small farmers.[69]

As the United Kingdom approached entry to the EC there was a mixture of confidence and trepidation about the fate of Scottish agriculture. It was noted that the intervention price system gave 'less assurance' to farmers than the guarantee price system. More specifically the expectation was that arable farmers in the east of Scotland would benefit from higher cereal prices as would those involved in the production of milk and fat cattle. There was no regime for sheep products but the increased export opportunities were expected to benefit fatstock producers.[70] There was less confidence over hill farming in the European regime. In the late 1960s there was a widely held view in the Scottish Office that the future of subsidy to hill farmers was uncertain and that alternative ways of supporting hill farmers, necessary for social as much as economic reasons, would have to be found. In the event when the UK did enter Europe, a compromise was reached on this point.[71] In economic terms the 1970s have been presented as one of increasing output in Scottish agriculture, although the price of inputs, especially feed for livestock, increased as well, something which had worried civil servants contemplating entry, although they remained confident about the efficiency of the intensive livestock sector.[72]

The growth of the CAP to dominate the budget of the EC, the drive towards liberalisation in world trade talks and the potential enlargement of the European Union (as the EC became in 1992) were major forces towards the reforms of that year. These had a number of objectives: the first was to shift the burden of paying for agricultural support away from the consumer, introduce more direct payments to farmers and reduce the overall level of support by reducing the intervention prices which lay at the heart of the CAP. The intervention price for cereals was to be

69. B. Gardner, *European Agriculture: Policies, Production and Trade* (London: Routledge, 1996), pp. 30–61.
70. 'EEC – Scottish Office Composite Picture of Developments: Agriculture', by D. M. Rowand, Department of Agriculture and Fisheries for Scotland, 4 May 1971, AF71/100, NAS.
71. See the contents of the following files in NAS: AF71/100, 152; AF45/489, 634.
72. 'EEC – Scottish Office Composite Picture of Developments: Agriculture', by D. M. Rowand, Department of Agriculture and Fisheries for Scotland, 4 May 1971, AF71/100, NAS.

reduced by 29 per cent and that for beef by 15 per cent. Compensation came through the introduction of the Arable Areas Payment Scheme and headage payments for livestock, such as the Sheep Annual Premium, with similar structures for beef and dairy production. Production was to be controlled, as it had been in the dairy sector since the 1980s, through the introduction of quotas in an attempt to limit surpluses.[73] These changes were phased in over the period from 1993 to 1996 and despite the tortuous process from which they emerged the farming press criticised them for their precipitate introduction and the level of central control and bureaucracy which they involved. One agricultural economist reported that a Polish colleague had remarked 'we have just given up a centrally planned economy and you are just starting one!'[74] The economic effects of these changes were most evident in the arable areas of Scotland: in the first year of the new regime agricultural output in Tayside was reduced by 9 per cent, in Fife by 6 per cent and in the Lothians by just over 4 per cent. This reflected the drive towards reducing production on large intensive units found in disproportionate numbers in these areas.[75] One regional study of farmers' attitudes towards these changes found that, in Grampian, smaller farmers were more positive towards the new regime than larger farmers.[76] The MacSharry reforms also shifted the pattern of support for agriculture in Scotland, reducing the upland/lowland distinction in this regard and increasing the level of direct support.[77] The £124 million of direct CAP support received in Scotland in 1990 amounted to only 26 per cent of overall support; the shift can be seen when one considers the £473 million in direct support in 1999 and the fact that it amounted to 62 per cent of total support.[78] A greater proportion and absolute amount of this money was directed towards Lowland arable farming: Fife, for example, experienced an increase in total direct subsidy to agriculture of over

73. A. K. Copus and N. Tzamarias, 'The consequences of the MacSharry reform proposals in Scotland', *Scottish Agricultural Economics Review*, 6 (1991), pp. 165–89; A. Skea, 'The effects of CAP reform on Scottish farming', *Scottish Agricultural Economics Review*, 7 (1993), pp. 1–14.

74. P. Cook, 'Coping with the complexities of beef and sheep CAP reform', *Scottish Farmer*, 3 April 1993, pp. 36–7.

75. A. K. Copus, 'Monitoring the initial impact of CAP at the sub-regional level in Scotland', *Scottish Agricultural Economics Review*, 8 (1995), pp. 1–14, at p. 5.

76. R. S. Stewart, 'The impact of the 1992 MacSharry CAP reforms on agriculture in the Grampian region' (Robert Gordon University Ph.D., 2000), p. 227.

77. D. Patel and M. O'Neill, 'The Common Agricultural Policy and measuring support to the Scottish agricultural sector', *Scottish Economic Bulletin*, 53 (1996), pp. 21–30.

78. U. K. Khan, 'Levels of agricultural support in Scotland, 1990–1999', *Scottish Economic Report*, January 2001, pp. 78–83.

1,000 per cent between 1991 and 1995, and increases in the order of 300–400 per cent were seen in areas such as Tayside and Lothian.[79]

The second strand of change involved trying to encourage arable producers to farm in a less intensive way by encouraging the setting aside of land. Cereal farmers could qualify for direct support if they set aside, initially, 15 per cent of their land. This was a profound change in direction for the farming community, which had been paid to produce and indulge in intensive farming by the 1947 Agriculture Act and the CAP. The MacSharry reforms, however, were part of a wider movement which saw the increasing involvement of conservation agencies in farming and an ever more diverse range of schemes which paid farmers to produce environmental goods.[80] This produced a number of difficulties for farmers: the bureaucracy associated with the new regime was disliked, although some farmers resigned themselves to it with the thought that it was linked to income, as one remarked: 'it's quite an easy way to make money, filling out forms and that'.[81] Farmers also found it difficult to accept the change involved in the move away from their role as food producers: a practising farmer with a newspaper column had the following to say about the set-aside scheme:

> Farmers hate it for obvious reasons. Not only does it fly in the face of what we've tried to do since the onset of time – making the most of our land – but it also smacks of big brother not only watching what you do but controlling it as well.[82]

Environmental policies were not a new development in the early 1990s. The EC took 'halting steps' in the mid-1980s with the creation of 'Environmentally Sensitive Areas' (ESAs) – of which five were located in Scotland – where less intensive farming was supported by subsidy.[83] It should be pointed out that the bulk of land in the Scottish ESAs is not farmed intensively and the favoured subsidy schemes have been those, such as for the construction of dry-stone dykes, which have a minimal impact on farming practice.[84]

79. Stewart, 'Impact of the 1992 MacSharry CAP reforms', p. 139.
80. M. Winter, 'Strong policy or weak policy? The environmental impact of the 1992 reforms to the CAP arable regime in Great Britain', *Journal of Rural Studies*, 16 (2000), pp. 47–59.
81. McHenry, 'Understanding the Farmer's view', p. 72.
82. B. Henderson, 'CAP – it's not common and there's no agricultural policy in it', *Scottish Farmer*, 10 October 1992, p. 16.
83. D. G. Mackay, 'Rural land-use in Scotland: a review of the 1980s', *Scottish Geographical Magazine*, 106 (1990), pp. 12–19.
84. D. Gourlay and B. Slee, 'Public preferences for landscape features: a case study of two Scottish Environmentally Sensitive Areas', *Journal of Rural Studies*, 14 (1998), pp. 249–63.

In the mid-1990s the government expressed a degree of cautious optimism in the Scottish agricultural sector. The Scottish Office, in evidence to the Scottish Affairs Committee of the House of Commons in 1996, noted: 'Increased farm incomes and direct payments to farmers in recent years have put Scottish agriculture in a good position to face the challenges and opportunities of a more competitive market place in the future.'[85] Following devolution, a more pessimistic perspective has emerged. A recent Scottish Executive publication has noted that 'the days of the mid 1990s are unlikely to return'.[86] There are a range of causes for this more pessimistic outlook, ranging from the strong pound and the weak euro, which work against an export-orientated industry, to the CAP reforms discussed above. Scottish livestock agriculture has also had to cope with the results of two disease-related crises which were particularly damaging to export markets.

In March 1996, when the notion of a possible link between BSE and human health was announced, a 'significant short-run fall in consumer confidence was compounded in the UK by the EU ban on British exports of beef'.[87] Large numbers of cattle over the age of thirty months were removed from the food chain and a selective cull was introduced. These policies did not prevent the market for beef and other meats experiencing considerable difficulties, and knock-on effects being experienced by suppliers to the livestock industry as well as food processors in this highly interdependent area of the agricultural economy. Perhaps more significant, however, was the outbreak of foot and mouth disease in February 2001, the first epidemic since 1967. Scottish agriculture, dominated by livestock enterprises, was seriously affected, with confirmed cases on 187 farms. The UK adopted a stamping-out policy to deal with the epidemic and culled animals from infected farms, together with animals deemed to have had dangerous contact with them and, in the cases of sheep and pigs, animals within 3km of an infected farm.[88] This meant that 735,500 animals, 643,900 of

---

85. Scottish Affairs Committee, third report, *The Future for Scottish Agriculture*, July 1996, vol. II, p. 1, Memorandum submitted by the Scottish Office, HC 629-II.
86. Agricultural Strategy Steering Group, *A Forward Strategy for Scottish Agriculture* (Edinburgh: Scottish Executive, 2001), p. 5.
87. S. McDonald and D. Roberts, 'The economy-wide effects of the BSE crisis: a GCE analysis', *Journal of Agricultural Economics*, 49 (1998), pp. 458–71.
88. An attempt was made to control the disease by disinfection at farm gates, on principal thoroughfares in rural areas and other sites; for example, while conducting research for this chapter at the library of the Edinburgh School of Agriculture, the author had to disinfect his shoes before entering the building.

them sheep, were culled between February and June 2001. A further 440,000 animals were slaughtered under the Livestock Welfare Disposal Scheme and the Light Lamb Scheme, due to problems arising from restrictions on movements and loss of markets.[89] Although the outbreak in Scotland was confined to Dumfries and Galloway and the Borders, the extent of movement of livestock in the modern agrarian economy meant that the cull affected a wider area and the economic impact was felt much more widely. Indeed, it has been argued that the economic impact was felt most profoundly in sectors other than agriculture, especially tourism; although the localised effect in Dumfries and Galloway and the Borders, where agriculture is a particularly important part of the local economy, should not be underestimated. Around £170 million was paid in compensation to farmers whose livestock was culled.[90] This was intended to cover loss of capital rather than loss of income, and the latter has been estimated at around £60 million. The estimates for agricultural output in 2001 showed significant downturns compared to 2000: finished cattle and calves down from £504.4 million to £448.9 million, and finished sheep and lambs down from £205.5 million to £159.6 million. Perhaps most significant of all is the fall in output from the store sheep sector, which was particularly affected by the restrictions on movement, down from £11.7 million to only £6.3 million. Foot and mouth disease is not the only factor here, of course; the falling prices for store livestock over the last five years have also reduced output from a recent peak of £18.5 million in 1996.[91] The effect on tourism is difficult to quantify, but in evidence to a Royal Society of Edinburgh enquiry, VisitScotland estimated that spending by tourists in 2001 fell by around 3 per cent compared to 2000 and visitor numbers were down by around 7 per cent in the first nine months of the year, and a loss of over £200 million in gross revenue from tourism has been estimated.[92]

CONCLUSION

Over the course of the period reviewed here, farming has declined as an element of the output of the Scottish economy, as an employer of labour and as a user of land. Farming has also drifted out of the national

89. Royal Society of Edinburgh (RSE), *Inquiry into Foot and Mouth Disease in Scotland* (Edinburgh: Royal Society of Edinburgh, 2002). See http://wwwma.hw.ac.uk/RSE
90. This money came from the Department of the Environment, Food and Rural Affairs (DEFRA) and the UK Treasury and not from the funds of the Scottish Executive.
91. *ERSA*, 2001–2.
92. RSE, *Inquiry into Foot and Mouth*, pp. 7–8.

consciousness in the second half of the century. Prior to the 1950s several themes had ensured relatively high status for farmers in the public mind: sympathy for political grievances relating to perceived landlord exploitation and the fact that the Liberal and Labour parties attempted to make political capital on these points; the role of the farming community in feeding the nation during the global conflicts of 1914–1918 and 1939–45, and in the period of austerity following the latter; the role of family memory in the history of migration in Scottish rural society meant that quite a large section of the urban population had a link with the farming community, were aware of the key issues facing farmers, and their role in the production of food; a perception that farmers were the protectors of the natural order in the countryside also contributed to this sense of integration between rural and urban Scotland. These factors have all been overturned in the second half of the twentieth century. Rural issues are no longer central to a political agenda dominated by taxation, employment and welfare. As the urban population is increasingly conditioned by convenience foods and the ubiquity of the supermarket there is comparatively little thought given to the processes relating to the production of food prior to its deposit in the supermarket trolley. Urban and rural populations have become more dislocated and even the recent trend towards counter-urbanisation and the re-population of some areas of the countryside has been driven by lifestyle considerations rather than a migration of those desirous of economic participation in agriculture in a serious way. The perception of farmers as protectors of the natural order has been disrupted by the recent scares associated with the products of livestock farming and the debate over genetically modified crops in arable farming. Very recent changes have, perhaps, provided some interruption to these trends as the niche popularity of organic foods and the direct selling of agricultural produce in farmers' markets has raised consciousness among a minority. Nevertheless, although there have been great practical and political changes in the way farmers have gone about their business, there are also considerable continuities governed by the soil and the climate: despite changes at the margins the Scottish agricultural economy is still engaged in a struggle with difficult land; livestock remains the most important product in terms of volume; and arable farming, although valuable, is a minority pursuit.

FURTHER READING

Anthony, R., *Herds and Hinds: Farm Labour in Lowland Scotland, 1900–1939* (East Linton: Tuckwell Press, 1997).

Bryden, J., 'Scottish agriculture, 1950–1980', in R. Saville (ed.), *The Economic Development of Modern Scotland, 1950–1980* (Edinburgh: John Donald, 1985).

Cameron, E. A., *Land for the People? The British Government and the Scottish Highlands, c. 1880–1925* (East Linton: Tuckwell Press, 1996).

Campbell, D., 'The real crisis of Scottish agriculture', *Scottish Government Yearbook* (1985), pp. 107–33.

Campbell, R. H., 'Too much on the Highlands? A plea for change', *Scottish Economic and Social History*, 14 (1994), pp. 58–75.

Douglas, C., 'Scottish agriculture during the war', *Transactions of the Highland and Agricultural Society of Scotland*, 31 (1919), pp. 1–66.

Douglas, C., 'The policy of the Agriculture Act', *Transactions of the Highland and Agricultural Society of Scotland*, 33 (1921), pp. 1–20.

Holderness, B. A., *British Agriculture since 1945* (Manchester: Manchester University Press, 1985).

Houston, G. F. B., 'Agriculture', in A. K. Cairncross (ed.), *The Scottish Economy: A Statistical Account of Scottish Life* (Cambridge: Cambridge University Press, 1954).

Leneman, L., *Fit for Heroes? Land Settlement in Scotland after World War One* (Aberdeen: Aberdeen University Press, 1989).

McHenry, H. L., 'Understanding the farmer's view: perceptions of changing agriculture and the move to agri-environmental policies in southern Scotland' (University of Aberdeen Ph.D., 1994).

Marshall, D., 'Scottish agriculture during the war', *Transactions of the Highland and Agricultural Society of Scotland*, 58 (1946), pp. 1–77.

Maxwell, T. G., and Connell, M. G. R., 'The environment and land use of the future', in G. Holmes and R. Crofts (eds), *Scotland's Environment: The Future* (East Linton: Tuckwell Press, 2000).

Perren, R., *Agriculture in Depression, 1870–1940* (Cambridge: Cambridge University Press, 1995).

Sprott, G., 'Lowland country life', in T. M. Devine and R. Finlay (eds), *Scotland in the Twentieth Century* (Edinburgh: Edinburgh University Press, 1996).

Stewart, R. S., 'The impact of the 1992 MacSharry CAP reforms on agriculture in the Grampian region', Robert Gordon University Ph.D., 2000).

Whetham, E. H., *The Agrarian History of England and Wales*, vol. VII: *1914–1939* (Cambridge: Cambridge University Press, 1978).

CHAPTER EIGHT

Unbalanced Growth: Prosperity and Deprivation

C. H. Lee

THE DIMENSIONS OF ECONOMIC CHANGE: NATIONAL INCOME

The outstanding characteristic of Scottish economic performance prior to 1914 was the combination of economic progress and the creation of wealth juxtaposed against extremes of poverty and deprivation. The same diversity of performance and outcome was also the prime characteristic of Scotland's experience in the twentieth century. By the beginning of the twenty-first century, Scotland possessed great diversity in affluence and quality of life that divided social and economic groups as well as different regions of the country. But those differences were modified in the second half of the twentieth century, primarily as the result of government intervention.

By the twentieth century the availability and quality of statistical evidence makes it much easier to measure progress. The critical indicator used to determine progress in general is national income. From the Second World War onwards government statistics provide a clear and credible series of data. For the inter-war period, we have Campbell's estimates, which express Scottish GDP per head as a share of the United Kingdom aggregate. This is slightly misleading since the aggregate figure is biased by inclusion of the data for Scotland. Since Scotland has been below the national average in most years, this comparison tends to underestimate slightly the gap between them. Campbell's estimates show Scottish per capita income declining from 96 per cent of the United Kingdom average in 1924 to a minimum of 87 per cent in the early 1930s, before recovering with fluctuations to reach 92 per cent by 1949. Campbell further disaggregated his income data into three subgroups, namely property income, wages and salaries. The Scottish figures showed a strong performance in property income, a reflection of the strong *rentier* strand of development that was also manifest in the previous century. The relatively weak overall performance of the Scottish economy was due to performance in the other two sectors, that is in wages and salaries, which were both relatively low. Campbell explained these data as indicating the concentration of Scottish manufactures in industries that paid poorly, to a greater reliance on female employment that was also poorly paid, to a higher level of unemployment, and lower productivity than was found in other parts of the United Kingdom.[1]

Information for the second half of the twentieth century is both more abundant and of more certain accuracy. Compared against the United Kingdom average, Scotland fared poorly in per capita GDP terms through the 1950s and early 1960s, dipping to about 87 per cent of the national average. But from the mid-1960s Scotland's performance improved markedly so that per capita GDP converged towards the national average, reaching 98 per cent by 1980. Thereafter performance has been erratic. Scotland was hit severely by the deflation of the early 1980s, recovered to be hit by the oil industry crisis in the second half of the decade, before recovering in the early 1990s.[2]

POPULATION, MIGRATION AND THE LABOUR MARKET

Population growth, and the migration that it stimulated, was a prime determinant of the pattern of economic development recorded by Scotland during the two centuries before the Great War of 1914. In sharp contrast to the great population increase experienced in the nineteenth century, the twentieth century was a period of slow population increase leading, by the close of the century, to fears of actual decline.

With regard to natural increase, births and deaths, Scotland's experience was determined by a similar combination of causal changes found widely in western Europe. Both the birth rate and the death rate continued to decline in the twentieth century, at a faster rate than before 1914 so that they converged in the last quarter of the century. At the point of convergence there is no natural increase as births and deaths are in balance with each other and the population, without other changes,

1. A. D. Campbell, 'Changes in Scottish income, 1924–49', *Economic Journal*, 65 (1955), pp. 233–4.
2. C. H. Lee, *Scotland and the United Kingdom: The Economy and the Union in the Twentieth Century* (Manchester: Manchester University Press, 1995), p. 53.

remains static. In some years towards the end of the century the death rate in Scotland was higher than the birth rate, indicating a net fall in natural increase. The principal forces behind these changes are well understood. The accelerated fall in the death rate reflected both improved living conditions, leading to the curtailment of infectious diseases that took such a heavy toll of premature death on the young before 1914, and advances in medicine. Both effects enabled many more people to survive into old age than had been the case in earlier periods. There is, of course, a limit below which the death rate cannot be pushed, and the decline in the second half of the twentieth century was very modest from 12.9 per 1,000 in 1951 to 11.3 in 2001, suggesting that Scotland was not far from this limit.

Birth rates have always been managed by social preference, and control increased in the twentieth century with the increasing efficiency of contraceptive protection against unwanted pregnancy, and supported by the knowledge that infants and children had a much better chance of survival than hitherto. A family hoping to have three children did not, therefore, have to produce six children in order to allow for some premature deaths, as had been common practice among the more affluent families in the nineteenth century. But that does not really explain the near-collapse of the birth rate in the final quarter of the century, to a level so close to the death rate as to allow little natural increase in most years. Furthermore, in the six consecutive years 1996–2001 the natural rate decreased as deaths exceeded births in each year. The loss of many potential parents through migration over the previous centuries must have contributed significantly to this particular trend.

As in the nineteenth century, outward migration continued to exert a powerful influence over the pattern of Scottish population change. The outward flow of population continued throughout the years from the conclusion of the First World War until the 1980s, broken only by the return of the armed forces after 1945. By the final decade of the twentieth century migration had become a relatively small-scale effect, with erratic periods of inward migration, determined by the current health of the oil industry, and the long-established tradition of seeking better opportunities elsewhere. Inter-regional migration within the United Kingdom involved significantly more people than international migration by this time. In 1997 and 1998, for example, Scotland gained 108,000 people from other regions of the United Kingdom, in exchange for 107,000 moving to other parts of the country. The respective figures for international migration were 35,000 inward migrants and 44,000 emigrants.[3] It may be that the long drain of human resources from Scotland, which cast a large shadow over its economic progress for two centuries, is now coming to a conclusion, although fears of actual decline are real in view of recent trends in natural increase.

Changes in population had significance for the economy in two particular ways, in the changing distribution of the population between age groups and between regions. Pre-industrial populations with relatively low life expectancy tended to have a high proportion of their citizens in the lower age ranges. Webster's estimates for the population of Scotland in 1755 indicated that 44.1 per cent of the population were aged less than 20 years, while only 7.3 per cent were aged 60 or above.[4] The nineteenth-century population filled by those aged up to 14 years reached a peak in 1911, falling thereafter and sharply declining in the final three decades of the twentieth century. The number of children aged up to 14 years of age in Scotland in 2001 was only 67 per cent of the number in 1971. By comparison the cohort of adults of working age, between the ages 15 and 64, remained relatively stable and, in the second half of the twentieth century, was virtually static. The decline in the young coincided with a substantial increase in those aged 65 or over. Through the second half of the nineteenth century, this group had comprised 4 to 5 per cent of the total population. By 1951 this share had risen to 9.9 per cent and by 2001 to 15.0 per cent. The increase in absolute numbers in the twentieth century showed an increase from 216,000 to 807,000. These changes are, of course, consistent with the changes in natural increase, in increased longevity and in the collapsing birth rate.

These changes were also reflected in significant regional readjustments in population in the twentieth century. Three regions remained largely static through the century, and these were the rural extremities of Scotland, in Dumfries and Galloway, the Borders and the Highlands and Islands. Two of the established industrial regions, Strathclyde and Tayside experienced population decline after 1961 and 1971 respectively, while the other three regions grew in population. The reasons for these changes are apparent when the pattern of employment structure is examined. The economic expansion of Victorian Britain was based heavily on the creation of new jobs within a labour-intensive structure of production. Productivity improvements, requiring less labour per unit

---

3. National Statistics, *Regional Trends*, 35 (2000), p. 60.
4. J. G. Kyd (ed.), *Scottish Population Statistics, including Webster's Analysis of Population, 1755* (Edinburgh: Scottish Academic Press, 1975).

of output, or a loss of competitive advantage would place such employment at risk. Both factors were persistently influential throughout the twentieth century with the result that many of the jobs created in the previous century were lost. Thus the mining industries, principally coal production, employed 26,000 workers in Scotland in 1841. This had increased to a peak in 1921 when 181,000 workers were employed. By 1971 employment had fallen to 36,000.[5] This pattern of growth and decline was the characteristic experience of heavy industry and of the complex of related manufactures in Strathclyde. The exhaustion of natural resources, increased international competition, technological difficulties and the replacement of labour by capital were all contributory factors. The outcome was sustained decline in the industrial heartland of Scotland in the final quarter of the twentieth century.

At face value there appears to have been little change in Scottish employment in the course of the twentieth century, since the aggregate changed little. But this conceals change as fundamental and extensive as that characterising the nineteenth century. But twentieth-century change was different. Many new jobs were created, but just as many were lost. In fact only three of the nine major employment divisions grew in the course of the century, distributive trades, financial services and public administration. The latter was especially important, becoming the largest single category by 1921 and accounting for 35 per cent of all employment by the 1990s. Every other category of employment, including all the manufacturing sectors, lost workers. These changes brought a fundamental change to the structure of employment, and brought an equally profound additional change. Those who lost jobs were not always the ones who secured alternative employment. Much of the decline focused upon heavy industry, which had been the preserve of skilled, male, manual workers. But many of the new jobs were semi-skilled or unskilled, often part-time, and suitable for women balancing the care of a family with the need to earn. The labour force in 2001 was, therefore, substantially different from that which had existed in Scotland a hundred years earlier. The consequence of these changes was to shift the balance of work away from male manual work to white-collar work generally and to women's employment in particular. The number of men in work in Scotland reached a peak in 1921 at 1.57 million. By the end of the century this number had fallen to 1.329 million, almost the same number as in 1901. In 1901 the female labour force in Scotland

5. C. H. Lee, *British Regional Employment Statistics, 1841–1971* (Cambridge: Cambridge University Press, 1979).

numbered some 580,000 women. By 1951 this had increased to 670,000 and exceeded one million by the end of the century.[6]

The process of restructuring was also reflected in unemployment rates, an indicator that provided fuller and more accurate information in the twentieth century than it had earlier. In 1931, in the depth of the inter-war recession, Scotland's unemployment rate has been estimated at 16.1 per cent of the labour force, similar to the other regions of Britain that were home to heavy engineering, coal-mining, shipbuilding and associated trades. Through the second half of the century, unemployment rates were generally lower and the activity rate, that is the proportion of those of working age who offer themselves for employment, was substantially higher than between the wars. In that context Scottish unemployment remained at levels similar to those in industrial England. Nevertheless, unemployment was both persistent and significant in Scotland, falling below 3 per cent only in the 'full employment' years of 1954–63, and reaching 11.6 per cent in the 1980s. Between the wars unemployment reflected a reduced level of demand that was induced by extensive depression in international trade. It was, therefore, a universal problem facing manufacturers of capital equipment and engineering products. After 1945, however, world markets improved and the next two decades represented a massive boom in trade and manufactures. Scottish difficulties in this later period stemmed from competitive weakness as new producers, such as Japanese shipbuilders, entered the market with new designs and low prices. In Scotland, Clydeside was the principal location for the engineering-related industries that struggled under the new market conditions. Employment in the Clydeside conurbation fell by 200,000 jobs between 1952 and 1984, a loss of almost a quarter of the total employment. Glasgow was particularly severely affected, where male unemployment increased from an annual average of 19,000 in the 1960s to 54,000 two decades later.[7] By the 1980s a substantial number of long-term unemployed men, who had not worked in the previous five years, had accumulated, the number in Glasgow alone being estimated at 5,000.

Before 1914 the abundance of available labour in Scotland helped to keep wages down to levels that helped competitiveness but stifled material improvement in the lives of many citizens. The changes that occurred in the twentieth century in population, migration and adjust-

---

6. Ibid.; *Regional Trends*, 35, p. 78.
7. W. Lever and C. More, 'The city in transition: policies and agencies for the regeneration of Clydeside', in V. A. Hausner (ed.), *Economic Change in British Cities* (Oxford: Oxford University Press, 1986), pp. 2–4.

ments in the employment structure did little to ameliorate this situation until after 1945, the continuation of outward migration throughout the century, albeit offset by immigration induced by the oil industry in the final quarter of the century, together with persistent and significantly high unemployment, especially among men, prevented any lasting shortage of labour to push up wage levels. The rapidly changing labour market of the late twentieth century exacerbated rather than eroded the weaknesses of labour oversupply that had been endemic in the Scottish economy throughout the era of industrialisation. Only the intervention of government made substantial improvement possible in the second half of the century.

INCOME DISTRIBUTION AND SPENDING POWER

Modern economies rely heavily on the spending power of consumers to provide effective demand for goods and services. The scale, distribution and growth of income provide, therefore, both a highly significant indicator of prosperity and an essential vehicle for the generation of economic growth. Information of this kind is scarce in historical records, as relatively few individuals were liable to income tax, the main source of information, until after the Second World War. In the late 1930s only about four million citizens in the United Kingdom were liable to pay income tax. By 1949/50 the number had risen to almost 18 million, and only 9.2 per cent of the employed in England and Wales, and 11.1 per cent of the employed in Scotland, received incomes that left them below the then threshold income of £135 per annum at which liability to pay income tax commenced. By the end of the century the minimum threshold for taxation had become £4,195 and the median income had risen from a little over £300 per annum in 1949/50 to about £10,000. In the analysis that follows the total number of incomes have been divided into four groups with approximately 30 per cent of the total incomes (in A, B, and C) and 10 per cent (in D, the highest income band), to offset the difficulty caused by the changing monetary values of the income ranges.

In 1949/50 the two lowest income groups comprised many activities dominated by women such as shop assistants, domestic servants, laundry and dry cleaning. Women in manufacturing were also included, including weaving and clothing, and boot and shoe manufacture. At the upper levels of these income ranges came typists and clerks. There was some overlap with the middle-income ranges, as represented by category

C that encompassed a very wide range of activities by the 1950s. In the lower reaches came unskilled manual workers, labourers and dock porters, unskilled building workers, postmen and nurses. In the middle range, around £500 per annum, came carpenters and bricklayers, bakers, women teachers, clerks and railway guards. In the highest level, over £600, were assistant principals and executive officers in the Civil Service, male teachers, army officers and draughtsmen, together with professional workers such as barristers and solicitors, doctors and dentists, accountants and architects, engineers, chemists and the higher ranks of the Civil Service with salaries ranging between £1,500 and £5,000 per year. By the close of the century, all categories of income had increased substantially, although proportionately the four categories were similar in size. By 1998/9 the highest group, category D, comprised incomes of £30,000 and over, approximately identifying those workers who paid some income tax at the highest rate. By 1978 the two lowest categories included employment up to £2,500 per annum and were very largely confined to women's manual work. The next category, to £4,000, included semi-skilled and unskilled male workers, clerks of both sexes and females in managerial and lower professional employment. The highest group, as in other categorisations, included skilled male manual workers, managers and those in professional occupations.[8]

Using these categories to compare Scottish income distribution with that of England and Wales shows that Scottish incomes and taxable income have been more heavily clustered in the lower parts of the distribution while those for England and Wales were more prominent in the higher ranges. As a result, taxable income per head in Scotland was substantially lower than it was in England and Wales, 82.3 per cent of the other jurisdiction in 1949/50 but improving to 89.2 per cent per capita by 1998/9. At the two lowest income levels, Scotland showed little difference from the equivalent figures for England and Wales, but in the two higher categories Scottish income was substantially less in 1949/50. By 1998/9 the gap had almost closed in category C, but Scotland had fallen further behind in category D. There are two possible explanations for this, both of which may well have contributed to the observed outcome. It might be that Scotland had the same employment structure as its southern neighbour but lower rates of pay, or it might be that Scotland was relatively deficient in employment that generated the highest incomes. In either event, the effect was effective in restricting

8. G. Routh, *Occupation and Pay in Great Britain, 1906–79* (London: Macmillan, 1980), pp. 63–73, 90, 101–21, 131.

the Scots to a lower per capita return from work. This diminished potential consumer spending power, and with it the capacity to generate further economic activity and employment. The results of this survey are consistent with the continued outward migration and relatively high interest rates in Scotland. These phenomena would be obviously consistent with an income structure that was relatively weak in the middle and higher levels.

In addition to the relative weakness of the Scottish income distribution, there were considerable variations between Scottish regions. Lothian had by far the highest rate of income per head of population in 1949/50 at £153, while four regions rated above £130, with the rural periphery following: Dumfries and Galloway and Grampian at £120, and the perpetually impoverished Highlands at £84. In each case the reason for the relatively weak performance lay in the low level of income generated within the upper ranges of the distribution. With regard to the lowest incomes only the Highlands performed significantly poorly. But in the higher income groups, five of the eight Scottish regions performed very poorly and even the best, Strathclyde, Lothian and Central/Fife, were significantly below the average for England and Wales. At the level of the highest income in category D, only Lothian, Borders and Tayside performed well. In sum, Scotland generated £29 per head of population in taxable income less than its southern neighbour, and £27 of that deficit occurred in the two higher income groups. In the process of economic development, income and prosperity is supposed to trickle down the income distribution as a self-sustaining process. This happened to a limited extent only in modern Scotland, with a severely deleterious effect on growth and prosperity.

While convergence to the per capita income level of the United Kingdom average in the second half of the twentieth century represented significant progress, the aggregate performance continued to mask great variations. By the mid-1990s, when the Scottish average was approximately equal to the United Kingdom average, denoted by 100 as a per capita index, the regions of Scotland ranged far above and far below that level. Edinburgh recorded the highest income at an index of 148, followed by West Lothian at 126 and the North-East at 135. At the lower end of the distribution were included the Highlands and Islands recording an index of 78, North Lanarkshire at 74, and Clackmannan and Fife at 81. In 1994 the Highlands was awarded Objective One status by the European Union as a 'lagging region', thus joining Ulster and Merseyside as officially disadvantaged. The two outstanding characteristics of Scottish economic performance since 1950 are, apparently, contradictory. One the one hand there was a marked improvement in performance since the mid-1960s, eventually achieving convergence with the United Kingdom average, while maintaining, indeed increasing, the wide gulf in prosperity between constituent regions of Scotland.

These data may be compared to the first published estimate of the distribution of wealth in Scotland, relating to 1973. This information is consistent with the above income estimates in showing greater inequality in Scotland than in England and Wales. The top 5 per cent of wealth holders in Scotland owned 30.6 per cent of the national total, and the top 10 per cent enjoyed 79.3 per cent. Comparable figures for England and Wales were 22.8 per cent and 66.1 per cent respectively. Only one-third of adult Scots were identified as wealth holders, compared to half the adults in the south.[9] There is no evidence to suggest that Scotland had been moving towards greater inequality during the previous century. There may have been some modest trend in the opposite direction. Nevertheless, the principal cause of declining inequality in wealth distributions has been the growth of owner-occupied property. That increased in Scotland but relatively modestly. But it is a factor that might have contributed to the difference in wealth distribution with England and Wales, where owner-occupied property was more widespread in the 1970s.

ECONOMIC CHANGE: MARKET FORCES

Two principal influences determined the performance of the Scottish economy in the twentieth century, market conditions and government policy. Market forces were overwhelmingly powerful between the wars and entirely negative in their effects. The collapse of international trade severely affected the export-oriented industries of the west of Scotland and caused prolonged and extensive unemployment. Only rearmament in the second half of the 1930s stirred these industries into revival. The inter-war years may, thus, be legitimately regarded as a continuation of the economic structure that applied before the Great War and that relied entirely on market forces. The economy obviously revived during the two world wars, both of which had a positive impact on economic activity in the greater Glasgow area. But the postwar period, after 1945, witnessed a substantial change in the economic environment and introduced a period of sustained growth that lasted until the 1970s and was

---

9. *Royal Commission on the Distribution of Income and Wealth*, Report No. 1 (1975), p. 123.

without precedent. Thereafter, more troubled economic times returned.

Several elements of the post-1945 economic revival were particularly helpful to the Scottish economy. The revival of international trade stimulated shipbuilding and the range of heavy industry that supported it. The Clyde yards enjoyed considerable success in the 1950s but suffered from increasingly effective Japanese competition in the following decade, and lost orders accordingly. If the revival of heavy industry was a temporary phenomenon, there were other changes in the structure of the economy that promised both greater stability and prosperity. The structure of work changed considerably in the second half of the twentieth century. Manual work for men, which had previously been the basis of most work, began to be replaced by white-collar jobs and service-sector jobs began to expand as manufacture contracted. Much of this work was generated by prosperity itself. As consumers were presented with a much wider range of goods and services, so the distribution networks greatly increased, offering semi-skilled and unskilled work. Many of the new jobs were suitable for women looking for part-time employment. Prior to 1900 most women's work had been confined to domestic service, textiles and clothing manufacture, or agriculture. From the beginning of the century, women increasingly found employment in other work, both manual and white collar, and unskilled or skilled. But the big change came after 1945, continuing the liberating effect of wartime employment and taking advantage of the increasing demand for labour, so that the proportion of women in employment increased substantially.

The increase in work for women had a profound effect on standards of living as families were now often able to draw on several family incomes. Between the wars, the problems of unemployment were exacerbated by the fact that most households had a single earner and that unemployment for the male breadwinner often meant little income was available given poor social welfare provision. By the spring of 2000, over 56 per cent of Scottish households had all members in employment and only 20 per cent had no person in work.[10] Other influences made work more secure. One of the major changes in the labour market after 1945, and possibly the most influential, lay in the growth of the public sector to balance the decline of the heavy industry. In terms of employment this represented a significant improvement since the volatile and cyclical industries subject to wild and unpredictable fluctuations in demand were replaced by stable and secure employment. These services, including

10. *Regional Trends*, 35, p. 93.

education, health and social work, did not fluctuate with market demand but by political decision. They offered reliable and for the most part expanding employment opportunities in the second half of the twentieth century.

The higher level of economic activity after 1945 provided a much more favourable work environment for the majority of Scots. The levels of pay and prosperity before 1914 were determined by a labour market that was biased against employees because of the abundance of potential workers. Between the two great wars of the twentieth century, this state of affairs continued with high and sustained unemployment, and Scottish wages fell to 5–10 per cent below the United Kingdom average in the 1930s.[11] Organised labour continued to have the worst of industrial disputes. In 1922 the Amalgamated Engineers Union was defeated by an employers' lock-out that pushed it to the verge of bankruptcy. Its membership in Scotland fell by 38 per cent and its reserves of £3.25 million were almost totally exhausted. The General Strike of 1926 similarly ended in defeat for the trade unions. But after 1945 national rates of pay were increasingly applied. The change in employment structure changed trade-union representation. Characteristic of the Victorian and inter-war years had been small Scottish-only trade unions devoted to plant-level collective bargaining. As unions became larger, the Scottish unions were absorbed into larger organisations operating throughout the United Kingdom. But this gave greater bargaining strength, and national pay rates helped the Scots to catch up with their neighbours. It also enabled them to close the gap in trade-union membership. In 1924, it was estimated that 11 per cent of the adult population of Scotland were trade-union members, a rate that increased to 17.7 per cent by 1947. This was lower than the equivalent proportions for England and Wales, 12.8 per cent and 18.2 per cent at the two dates respectively.[12] By the 1980s the gap was even smaller, and the Scottish share of union membership stood at 19.7 per cent.[13] By the end of the century, white-collar unions were in the ascendant, representing local government, health and education workers. Scottish rate of unionisation has passed that of England and Wales.[14]

11. J. Foster, 'A proletarian nation? Occupation and class since 1914', in Tony Dickson and James H. Treble (eds), *People and Society in Scotland*, vol. III: *1914–1990* (Edinburgh: John Donald, 1992), p. 210.
12. W. W. Knox, 'Class, work and trade unionism in Scotland', in Dickson and Treble (eds), *People and Society in Scotland*, p. 122.
13. Foster, 'Proletarian nation', p. 211.
14. *Regional Trends*, 35, p. 94.

THE GROWTH OF THE STATE AND ECONOMIC POLICY

While there is no doubt that changes in the international economy and the Scottish labour market in particular were helpful to widening the benefits of economic advance, the main change after 1945 was brought about primarily by other means, by the growth of the state and the expansion of economic policy. Intervention by government to alleviate the greatest deprivation of the inter-war years had been brought to bear on a very modest scale through reluctance to commit large-scale resources to the problem. First, and probably most significantly, was a radical change in attitude towards policy that took the form of a commitment of all political parties to place the maintenance of full employment at the heart of the policy to avoid the problems and deprivations of the inter-war years. This consensus lasted until the mid-1970s when a new set of economic problems shifted popular anxiety away from unemployment to inflation as the greatest threat to prosperity and social order. The curtailment of inflation became the principal economic policy objective for the final quarter of the century. The means by which unemployment was to be contained was primarily through the management of the demand side of the economy, by creating conditions conducive to spending by consumers and investment by companies. In the event, little management was required for most of the twenty-five years after 1945 as pent-up demand from wartime earnings and the process of postwar recovery contributed to a period of sustained growth and high employment that affected all parts of the United Kingdom. Even though Scotland continued to suffer outward migration and a relatively high level of unemployment compared to other parts of the country, the labour-market situation benefited the workers more than at any time in the previous century.

There were additional policy introductions that helped raise and sustain standards of living. After 1945 greatly improved social-security provision ameliorated the effects of unemployment and thereby reduced one of the principal causes of deprivation that had prevailed before the war. Families faced less immediate threats from unemployment after 1945 as a result of greater work opportunities and lower unemployment, female employment and welfare provision. Social-security payments increased in availability and value. The number of Scots receiving supplementary benefit increased from 190,000 in 1961 to 535,000 by 1987. The category of claimants defined as 'unemployed without contributory benefits' accounted for much of the increase. By the close of the century, needy citizens were entitled to a wide range of benefits from the state: income support, housing benefit, jobseeker's allowance, incapacity or disability benefit, child benefit and the retirement pension. By 1998/9 some 71 per cent of Scottish households were in receipt of one or more of these benefits, the highest proportions being for pensions, 39 per cent, council tax benefit, 29 per cent, child benefit, 26 per cent, and housing benefit, 24 per cent.[15]

The increased availability of work was supported by government policy. The commitment to full employment took the form in the 1960s and 1970s of attempts to relocate employment from areas with labour shortages to locations with surplus labour. Central Scotland offered a number of locations suffering from the decline of heavy industry. Incentives to establish the motor industry at Linwood, near Paisley, were typically expensive and relatively short-lived. But the period of time in which these employment transfers were effective, between the mid-1960s and 1980, was exactly the period during which Scottish GDP per head made significant progress in catching up with the United Kingdom average. It was estimated that between 1966 and 1978 Scotland secured inward factor transfers worth 39,000 new jobs.[16] With indirect multiplier effects added, the final net gain may have been as many as 70–80,000 new jobs. Since the Scotland labour force in 1971 comprised approximately 2.2 million persons, such an addition would have accounted for about 3.5 per cent of that labour force. Assuming the alternative for those employed by this means would have been unemployment, this represents a significant reduction to the unemployment rate that was actually about 4.7 per cent at the time. But the cost to the Exchequer was considerable at an estimated £42,000 per job. Nevertheless, it is difficult to avoid the conclusion that these transfers played a major part in upgrading Scottish per capita incomes to the national average.

There was a further element to the benefit gained by Scotland from interventionist policies. The relative poverty of Scotland carried an entitlement to greater support through public expenditure than some other regions of the United Kingdom. By the same token, Scotland's relative poverty meant that the tax contribution of Scots to the Exchequer was less than was paid by more prosperous regions. The scale of the transfer effect comprised both a gain in services and support compared to some other parts of the United Kingdom and a lower tax burden to meet that cost. The only comprehensive analysis of regional tax and expenditure covered the four financial years from 1974/5 to

15. Ibid., p. 123.
16. Lever and Moore, 'City in transition', pp. 10–11.

1977/8. These estimates showed large losses sustained by some regions and large gains obtained by others. In absolute terms Scotland was the greatest beneficiary of these transfers with a net surplus of spending over taxation of £913 million, equivalent to 9 per cent of Scottish GDP. In per capita terms, Scotland came second to Northern Ireland.[17] David Heald's estimates extended this analysis into the 1980s and showed Scotland benefiting from public expenditure at the rate of 20 per cent above the average. Related data for revenue suggested that Scotland paid about 5 per cent less tax than the United Kingdom average. It seems likely, therefore, that towards the end of the twentieth century Scotland was spending five pounds from the public purse for every four pounds raised in revenue. The balance represented a subsidy from the rest of the United Kingdom.[18]

The recognition that the intervention of the state had played a significant role in raising the standard of living in Scotland and closing the gap with England underpinned the strong response against government cutbacks in public spending. What was less widely recognised was the fact that some of the costs of these transfer payments represented subsidies from the rest of the United Kingdom, or at least from some of its more prosperous regions. The existence of the Scottish Office gave Scotland an advantage in the decades after 1945 when the annual grant from Whitehall had to be negotiated. A combination of special pleading and a familiarity with the workings of government generated favourable settlements. The adoption of the Barnett formula in 1978 proved to be even more beneficial. This determined that expenditure in any of the component parts of Great Britain had to be replicated in all jurisdictions according to a funding formula that gave England, Wales and Scotland, respective shares of 85/5/10 per cent of the total outlay. Since the population of Scotland was closer to 8 per cent of the British total, this proved to be a highly beneficial formula. It was somewhat ironic, in view of this favourable dispensation, that the Scottish National Party made political progress in the 1970s on the basis of the slogan that 'England expects Scotland's oil'. Identifiable public expenditure in 1989/90 showed that Scotland enjoyed 21.8 per cent more than the United Kingdom average, or £531 per head. This 'excess' payment was allocated principally to education and science, £134, to health and personal social services, £129, to social security, £74, and to housing £49.

---

17. J. Short, *Public Expenditure and Taxation in UK Regions* (Farnborough: Gower, 1981), pp. 44–51, 64–71.
18. D. Heald, *Financing a Scottish Parliament: Options for Debate* (Edinburgh: Scottish Foundation for Economic Research, 1990), p. 56.

ROLLING BACK THE STATE: THATCHERISM AND SCOTLAND

The stability of the new employment structure helped reduce the income gap. It was estimated that Scottish average incomes lagged only 5 per cent behind the national average by the 1960s. A substantial part of that stability rested on a considerably extended public sector that offered employment in major sectors such as education, health and local government and ensure the maintenance of the provision for consumers. Fundamental elements of social life thus became controlled and guaranteed by the state. But the consensus that underpinned the full employment regime that had supported and sustained the growth of the public sector was fractured in the later years of the century. The difficulties initially appeared in the 1970s, although there had been warning signals before then in wage inflation, but the accelerating inflation in that decade was accompanied by rising unemployment and government debt. This brought a major shift in public perceptions as inflation came to be regarded as a greater threat than unemployment. As part of the same popular diagnosis, heavy expenditure on 'wasteful' public goods paid for by 'excessive' taxation imposed on the hard-pressed citizen compounded the effect of inflation as it eroded savings and punished the virtuous and thrifty.

The Conservative administration, headed by Mrs Thatcher, was elected in 1979 with a clear mandate to give priority to curbing inflation, and did so without regard to any consequences that policy might have for the level of unemployment. The government also had a related agenda of rolling back the state, as it blamed the growth of the public sector for unsatisfactory competitiveness in absorbing resources and directing them to unproductive ends in an expanded welfare programme. The government view was also that there existed a substantial lack of competitiveness within industry itself. The severe deflationary policy adopted by the government was intended to 'shake out' resources from inefficient companies and so reaped a harvest of bankruptcies in the early years of the administration. The principal policy strategy was to free industry from the shackles of red tape and to offer incentives for business, and especially inducements to start new enterprises. This policy met a poor response in Scotland, although Scotland had suffered more than any other part of the United Kingdom in loss of manufacturing capacity. In the 1980s new firm formations recorded a weak response to incentives offered.[19] One study of new firm formation, taking

19. D. J. Storey and S. Johnson, 'Regional variations in entrepreneurship in the UK', *Scottish Journal of Political Economy*, 34 (1987), pp. 162–6.

a longer perspective and looking back to the 1950s, concluded that new firm formation was greatest when unemployment was high but falling, so that individuals were pushed into striking out alone. A study of firm formation and failure in Scotland in the second half of the 1970s found that there was a link between high fertility and mortality, notably in Grampian and the Highlands, and probably linked to opportunities in the oil industry.[20] But several regions of Scotland recorded extremely low rates of new firm creation, notably Strathclyde, Central and Tayside. Other investigations found a close and inverse relationship between firm formation and public-sector housing, since owner-occupied housing has frequently been identified as a significant indicator for economic independence and collateral for loans. Scotland compared poorly with much of the rest of Britain because it had low levels of wealth as proxied by home-ownership, a sociological structure in which managerial and professional skills were under-represented, and a plant structure which to some extent militated against workers gaining experience of small firms.[21]

In addition to the weakness of new firm formation, there was widespread opposition in Scotland to attempts to cut public spending and dislike for the government's disregard for unemployment. The new regime marked an explicit rejection of the consensus that had endured since 1945 and that had been so helpful to Scotland. Not surprisingly, the performance and achievements of successive Conservative administrations, which remained in office until 1997, were regarded without enthusiasm by many in Scotland. The size of the Conservative vote in general elections had been in steady decline from a postwar high point of 41.5 per cent in 1955, and finally collapsed in 2001 when it failed to yield a single parliamentary seat. The enthusiasm for free markets and low taxation appealed to the prosperous regions of southern England, but traditional Conservatism in Scotland seemed to fade with the passing of the lairds.

COMPENSATING FOR MARKET FAILURE: SCOTTISH HOUSING

Perhaps the most distinctive element of Scottish life in the twentieth century, and the one that most clearly distinguished its experience from

---

20   M. E. Beesley and R. T. Hamilton, 'Births and deaths of manufacturing firms in the Scottish regions', *Regional Studies*, 20 (1986), pp. 281–8.
21   B. K. Ashcroft, J. H. Love and E. Malloy (1991), 'Firm formation in the British counties with special reference to Scotland', *Regional Studies*, 25 (1991), pp. 395–409, at 404.

that of its southern neighbour and reflected the strong support for social provision in Scotland, lay in the development of housing. The roots of the problem lay in the previous century but were fully recognised and analysed by the 1917 Royal Commission on the Housing of the Industrial Population of Scotland. It identified an existing housing stock of desperately poor quality, often lacking basic water and sanitation, made worse by extensive overcrowding. By the end of the First World War, the Royal Commission estimated that 236,000 new houses were needed. If the lack of wartime construction was included, it has been estimated that the true deficit was probably 300,000.[22] There was wide-spread recognition that an effective response to this task was beyond normal market forces. Compensation for market failure, therefore, had to come from the state through a programme of subsidies. The first of many schemes was introduced immediately after the First World War. These schemes applied throughout Britain, but it was in Scotland that greatest advantage was taken to them and where, relatively, the construction of public-sector housing was greatest. By 1980, 64 per cent of Scottish homes were publicly provided, as compared to England and Wales, where the proportions were approximately reversed. Thereafter a marked change in government policy curtailed the expansion of public-sector housing.

The clear difference in housing strategy between Scotland and England was obvious between the wars when the rate of housing construction was similar in each jurisdiction, but the proportion provided by the public-sector was, respectively, 67 per cent and 25 per cent.[23] The great period of public-sector housing construction in Scotland came in the quarter-century following 1945 when 650,000 new houses were built. The scale of public-sector housing reflected the need to compensate for neglect in the past. By the inter-war period it was recognised that overcrowding was closely allied to poor health as it provided an excellent environment for the spread of infections. A survey taken in 1935 con-cluded that 25 per cent of Scottish houses were overcrowded compared to less than 4 per cent in England. In some parts of the greater Clydeside area, including Port Glasgow, Coatbridge, Clydebank and Motherwell, overcrowding characterised over 40 per cent of the housing stock in the 1930s.[24] By the end of the Second World War, Scotland was still short of

22. T. Begg, *50 Special Years: A Study in Scottish Housing* (London: Melland Press, 1987), pp. 7–8; *Royal Commission on the Housing of the Industrial Population of Scotland, Rural and Urban*, Cmd 8731 (1917), p. 292.
23. R. Baird, 'Housing', in A. K. Cairncross (ed), *The Scottish Economy: A Statistical Account of Scottish Life* (Cambridge: Cambridge University Press, 1954), p. 205.
24. I. H. Adams, *The Making of Urban Scotland* (London: Croom Helm, 1978), p. 176.

half a million houses, with almost the same number of existing houses needing improvements in sanitation and water supply.[25] There was also a political problem regarding Glasgow City Council, which was proving slow to respond to the need for new housing and unsupportive of the government's policy of seeking to disperse population from its crowded inner suburbs. In the event the process of population dispersal was undertaken, based on new towns like East Kilbride, Cumbernauld, Livingston, Irvine and Glenrothes, and new peripheral estates on the fringes of Glasgow, such as Easterhouse and Drumchapel. Glasgow City Council embarked on a major building programme in the 1950s and demolished 268,000 dwellings within two decades. Private housing construction increased steadily but, until the 1980s, was heavily over-shadowed by the public sector.

Throughout the great boom period of public-sector housing, between 1920 and 1980, the financial contribution of central government was an essential component of the cost, possibly as much as 40 per cent of the total required, and amounting to the full cost of 20 per cent of Scottish housing built in the twentieth century.[26] Central government contributed to the cost of public-sector housing, undertaken primarily by local authorities, through a series of subsidies that underwent modification over the sixty years of the policy. The basis for the programme from the early 1920s until 1957 took the form of a subsidy on each house built to be claimed back by the local authority when construction had been completed. Subsidies were higher in rural areas, and were supplemented by payment to rehouse slum dwellers and to reduce overcrowding. By the 1930s there were additional subsidies to encourage the construction of larger houses, and in the 1940s for the inclusion of lifts and for other improvements. There was a change introduced in 1957, an attempt by the Treasury to exert some control over an escalating programme, in that the subsidy became a flat-rate payment. But even then there remained additional payments for overspill or incoming workers. Initially the house-building subsidy was offered for a period of twenty years per property, but this was subsequently extended to forty and then to sixty years.

Housing policy changed direction sharply under the Thatcher administration. But public-sector housing policy was already experiencing difficulties in Scotland. The rush to build in the postwar years

25. A. Gibb, 'Policy and politics in Scottish housing since 1945', in R. Rodger (ed.), *Scottish Housing in the Twentieth Century* (Leicester: Leicester University Press, 1989), p. 157.
26. Lee, *Scotland and the United Kingdom*, p. 194.

had overlooked the provision of social amenities, and a lack of quality control or concern for the preferences of potential tenants, so that many of the new estates combined different forms of social deprivation in new locations. In the 1970s public policy adjusted from construction to renovation of the existing housing stock. In the 1980s policy made a more radical shift to the sale of the housing stock by an administration committed to privatisation in all forms. Public-sector tenants gained the right to purchase their homes or to transfer their tenancies to new owners such as housing associations, co-operatives or private landlords. Accordingly, the scale of the public sector declined. In Scotland 310,000 public-sector houses were sold between 1979 and 1999. As a consequence the balance of ownership changed sharply, owner occupation increasing from 43.1 per cent to the housing stock in 1986 to 59.2 per cent in 1996, while local authority housing fell, by almost the same proportion, from 46.9 per cent to 29.7 per cent during the same period.[27]

The public-sector housing programme played a major part in the rehousing of many Scots in the sixty years after the First World War. Much of the initiative as well as the funding came from central government. In Scotland this was especially influential since the existence of the Scottish Office provided an effective mechanism for the implementation of policy. It used agencies such as the Scottish Special Housing Association (SSHA) to implement policy, as in the provision of contracts to build houses in the new towns until a change of government persuaded Glasgow City Council that it could no longer resist the Scottish Office policy of dispersing population from the inner city to peripheral estates and the new towns. SSHA building in the new towns represented 'an attempt by the Scottish Office ... to intervene in the heartlands of Scottish Labour in housing politics by reducing the influence of Glasgow, by boosting the power of adjacent burghs, and by obtaining a say in the redevelopment programme'.[28] In sum the SSHA built over 110,000 houses in the half-century following its foundation in 1938. It provided an alternative source of public housing to local authorities, and undermined their control of rents by leading the pressure to increase rents in the late 1950s.

The public-sector housing programmes undertaken by local authorities were not simply the provision of an alternative to the unsatisfactory private market, nor simply an attempt to ameliorate the living conditions

---

27. National Statistics, *Scottish Abstract of Statistics*, 26 (1998), p. 82; *Regional Trends*, 35, p. 98.
28. R. Rodger and H. Al-Qaddo, 'The Scottish Special Housing Association and the implementation of housing policy, 1937–87', in Rodger (ed.), *Scottish Housing in the Twentieth Century*, p. 199.

of the poorest citizens, although these aims were partly sought and realised. But the public-sector housing programmes developed a significant political aspect in that they were closely linked to the political advance of the Labour Party in local government. From the 1930s the party strongly supported the provision of council houses and, by the 1950s, the control of rents had become a major part of that policy. This represented another compensation for the failings of the labour market, establishing rents at below-market prices to make up for the deficiencies of prevailing low wages. The scale of this transfer is illustrated in an example relating to 1956. The annual loan and maintenance charges on a four-roomed house were £100. The subsidy from the Treasury was worth £42.25p, and the subsidy from the rates covered a further £14.25p. This left a balance of £43.50p that should have been met by rent payments. But the average annual rent was £18, leaving a substantial deficit.[29] Most authorities run by the Labour Party, and that was the great majority in central Scotland, preferred to avoid rent increases, relying on increased payments by ratepayers or an accumulating debt to meet the deficit. There emerged, therefore, a politico-fiscal solution to the problem of market failure, a series of subsidies from central government, ratepayers or local authority debt. This proved hard to unravel. After a decade of cutting government subsidies and following the abolition of agencies like SSHA, a survey found in 1991 that in Glasgow rents were still set at only 50 per cent of the value of a realistic market rent, which meant that each tenant was subsidised to the value of £1,174, far greater than was found to be the case in any of the English cities examined.[30]

THE DEPENDENCY CULTURE

Given the severity of its social and economic problems, and the long experience of market failure, it is perhaps not surprising that Scotland should develop a strong dependence on government intervention as the twentieth century passed. The structure of government itself made this easier than in other parts of the United Kingdom. Scotland had enjoyed particular representation at Westminster since the formation of the Scotch Office in 1885. Its successor, the Scottish Office, moved its centre

---

29. R. D. Cramond, *Housing Policy in Scotland, 1919–1964: A Study in State Assistance* (Edinburgh: Oliver and Boyd, 1996), p. 39.
30. D. Maclennan, K. Gibb and A. Moore, *Fairer Subsidies, Faster Growth: Housing Government and the Economy* (York: Joseph Rowntree Foundation/London: National Federation of Housing Associations, 1991), pp. 24–9, 44.

of operations to Edinburgh in 1935, and following the Second World War became increasingly proactive in its operations. It also had the advantage of direct access to Whitehall and familiarity with the functioning of government, neither of which were available to most other regions. Characteristically the Scottish Office worked through agencies like SSHA and sought to induce economic growth and improved welfare.

Typical of this kind of intervention was the policy of the Scottish Office towards the Highlands, manifestly one of the poorest areas within the United Kingdom. The establishment of the North of Scotland Hydro-Electric Board (Hydro) immediately after the Second World War was intended both to harness the potential energy resources of the northern counties, and to regenerate their economies with a view to stemming the outward flow of migrants. The profits of the company were to be used 'for the economic development and social improvement of the North of Scotland district', while Lord Airlie, who became the first chairman of the Hydro, argued that the public sector should provide a cheap and widely available source of electricity in the north of Scotland since the private sector would never find such an enterprise sufficiently rewarding, providing yet another recognition of market failure. Thus the Hydro was obliged to provide electricity throughout the Highland counties, an undertaking that required massive capital investment. This included the construction or improvement of 400 roads by the Hydro. By the 1960s the level of provision had increased considerably but at massive cost. By the end of that decade, Peter Payne estimated, over 25 per cent of consumers were being supplied on an uneconomic basis at an annual cost of £1.75 million.[31] Since the Hydro refused to adjust tariffs or apply differential tariffs, the customers on the east coast subsidised those in the rural west.

In the same spirit and with similar disregard to cost, the Highlands and Islands Development Board (HIDB) was founded in 1965. Its remit was to stem the continuing decline of the Highlands in spite of the efforts of the Hydro, the Crofters' Commission established in 1954 to address the perpetual and complex issues of land tenure, together with afforestation schemes. The HIDB set out its aims in an introductory statement:

---

31. P. L. Payne, *The Hydro: A Study of the Development of the Major Hydro-Electric Schemes undertaken by the North of Scotland Hydro-Electric Board* (Aberdeen: Aberdeen University Press, 1988), pp. 190, 208.

First, a policy of concentration on objectives worth investing in, on the points identified as centres of the main labour catchments areas ... secondly, the development of forestry and forestry-based industries to give in the long-term a core of employment in much of the region; thirdly, the complementary development of tourism both to assist consolidation in some of the main centres and give a supplementary income to the dispersed population engaged in primary and service industries.[32]

Two decades later, the Scottish Affairs Committee reiterated its commitment to the work of the HIDB and endorsed its original policy.

In our view it was Parliament's intention in 1965 that the newly created Board should endeavour not merely to retain the population base of the Highlands and Islands area taken as a whole but also to retain, as far as sensible and practicable, the existing settlement pattern; and we believe that this objective still commands general political support.[33]

In the event a variety of conflicting interests sought to use the HIDB to achieve their specific goals, whether that be to create an idealised crofting community irrespective of cost, or to use the spending power of the agency to develop tourism.

By the 1980s Scotland had a plethora of state-sponsored agencies seeking to offset the effects of decline and to foster regeneration, and the Scottish Office had a staff well in excess of 10,000. Important policy changes were introduced in the last two decades of the century under the Conservative administration, and government agencies were among the casualties. SSHA became Scottish Homes with a remit to dispense with its existing stock of properties, while the HIDB was replaced by Highlands and Islands Enterprise. Another casualty was the Scottish Development Agency (SDA) founded in 1975 to further economic development, to promote and protect employment, to promote efficiency and to protect the environment. It was replaced in 1991 by Scottish Enterprise and new agencies called Local Enterprise Companies were established. These changes marked the response of the new government to curb the independence of the SDA and to transfer its

32. Highlands and Islands Development Board, *Annual Report* (1965), p. 1.
33. Report from the Scottish Affairs Committee, *Highlands and Islands Development Board* (1985), p. ix.

resources and powers to business interests. The new agencies were no more successful than the old ones they replaced in generating recovery in the declining parts of the Scottish economy. The slow rate of new business start-ups in Scotland, the poorest in the United Kingdom, reflected the lack of enthusiasm in many sections of the community for the excitement and opportunities of the market. The extent of the state intervention in so many economic activities, reflected in the pervasive influence of employment in national or local government controlled activities, from education and health to housing and social welfare created in Scotland some elements of what became termed the 'dependency culture'. Thatcherism, however radical and insistent, made little impact on Scotland other than inciting virulent hostility.

The Scottish economy has undergone extensive change in the past half-century, and has made progress in increasing prosperity. Nevertheless, the unevenness that characterised past development still remains, in centres of considerable prosperity and areas of manifest deprivation. The latter remain as evident testimony both to the severity of Scotland's economic problems and to the long-recognised effects of market failure. The growth, virtually all recorded since 1945, has been due in substantial part to government intervention, both in stimulating economic change and providing social-welfare support through the transfer of resources from central government. There has been extensive debate among historians about the benefits, if any, that Scotland derived from the Act of Union. In the eighteenth century these benefits concerned access to the English market and to England's colonial markets. Whatever the verdict in these issues, which remain contentious, it seems safe to conclude that for the next 250 years the effect of the Union, in economic terms, was largely, even completely, neutral in that Scotland was an integral and equal part of the United Kingdom and British Empire but without specific or peculiar advantages. But in the second half of the twentieth century, with the introduction of interventionist economic and social policy, there can be little doubt that Scotland as one of the weaker economies within the United Kingdom gained very considerably from the union. The popular support within Scotland for the new Parliament and for a formal structure of devolutions at the end of the twentieth century might indicate a growing preference for some degree of self-rule. But it was also at least a partial affirmation of the benefits of the state management of an economy faced with variegated and serious economic weaknesses. The early years of the Scottish Parliament have affirmed the greater enthusiasm for state involvement in Scotland than in the rest of the United Kingdom, manifest in distinctly different decisions about issues such as the charging students for their education and the elderly for their care.

FURTHER READING

Devine, T. M., *The Scottish Nation, 1700–2000* (London: Allen Lane/The Penguin Press, 1999).

Devine, T. M. and Finlay, R. J. (eds), *Scotland in the Twentieth Century* (Edinburgh: Edinburgh University Press, 1996).

Dickson, Tony and Treble, J. H. (eds), *People and Society in Scotland*, vol. 3: *1914–1990* (Edinburgh: John Donald, 1992).

Finlay, Richard, *Modern Scotland, 1914–2000* (London: Profile Books, 2004).

Knox, W. W., *Industrial Nation: Work, Culture and Society in Scotland, 1800–Present* (Edinburgh: Edinburgh University Press, 1999).

Lee, C. H., *Scotland and the United Kingdom: The Economy and the Union in the Twentieth Century* (Manchester: Manchester University Press, 1995).

Rodger, R. (ed.), *Scottish Housing in the Twentieth Century* (Leicester: Leicester University Press, 1989).

CHAPTER NINE

The Managed Economy: Scotland, 1919–2000[1]

G. C. Peden

The years 1919 to 2000 were marked by changes as dramatic as in any period of Scottish history. Agriculture, mining and many manufacturing industries shed labour on a massive scale. The slack was taken up by an expansion of employment in financial and public services, and tourism.[2] For most of the period unemployment was higher than in the UK as a whole, and would have been higher still had it not been for emigration down to the 1980s. Population growth since 1919 has been at best low, with actual decline between 1926 and 1930, 1941–5, and (very gradually) since 1980. Birth and death rates, and changes in migration, have been discussed in the previous chapter. The point to be made here is that the relative stagnation of the Scottish population, compared with that of England,[3] was both an effect and a cause of an industrial structure that reflected less innovation than in the UK as a whole. New industries, such as motor vehicles and telecommunications, tended to cater in the first instance for middle-class demand, and therefore located themselves in or near the region with the greatest concentration of such consumers – the south-east of England. If Scots often seemed more enterprising outside their country than in it, this characteristic reflected market opportunities. For much of the period Scots, on average, probably enjoyed an advantage in education relative to the rest of the UK, but an educated

1. I am grateful to the British Academy for funding the research for this chapter, and to Gavin McCrone for commenting on earlier drafts. Responsibility for remaining errors and omissions rests solely on the author.
2. C. H. Lee, *Scotland and the United Kingdom: The Economy and the Union in the Twentieth Century* (Manchester: Manchester University Press, 1995), pp. 62–5.
3. Between 1921 and 2001 the population of Scotland increased by 3.7 per cent to 5,064,000; over the same period the population of England increased by 40.2 per cent to 49,389,000 (National Statistics, *Annual Abstract of Statistics* (2004), Table 5.1).

labour force is mobile and need not remain in the country in which it was educated. A stable or declining population also affected economic growth in that there was less demand for the construction of housing, public buildings (such as schools) or roads and underground railways than in the south-east of England.

There have been excellent accounts of twentieth-century changes in the Scottish economy.[4] However, these economic histories tend to focus on what was happening in Scotland rather than in London. This chapter differs from them in that it looks at how Scotland was viewed from London, as well as how Scotland reacted to policies decided in London. Macroeconomic policy was conducted by the Treasury and the Bank of England, as was much microeconomic policy by the Board of Trade and its successor, the Department of Trade and Industry. However, in Scotland, weak economic performance for much of the period and substantial social problems led to a higher level of state intervention than for the UK as a whole, especially after the Second World War. The Secretary of State for Scotland represented Scottish interests in the Cabinet, and gradually acquired an influence on the Scottish economy as a result of political pressures to deal with unemployment and slums. The Scottish Office, agencies such as the Highlands and Islands Development Board or the Scottish Development Agency, local government and new-town corporations, all exerted some influence on the management of change in the Scottish economy. The development of the Scottish Office's capacity for dealing with economic planning from the 1960s led to Scotland being seen as an economic unit, notwithstanding considerable differences between regions within the country.[5]

From the early 1920s identifiable public expenditure per head in Scotland was higher than in England and Wales, and, apart from a period in the 1980s when tax revenues from North Sea oil were high, Scotland benefited from net fiscal transfers within the UK. In part this situation reflected greater than average UK needs, but it was also a measure of the success of successive Secretaries of State in presenting Scotland's case in the Cabinet. The Secretary of State's hand was strengthened by formulas used to allocate some forms of public expenditure to Scotland.

4. R. H. Campbell, *The Rise and Fall of Scottish Industry, 1707–1939* (Edinburgh: John Donald, 1980); Lee, *Scotland and the United Kingdom*; Richard Saville (ed.), *The Economic Development of Modern Scotland, 1950–1980* (Edinburgh: John Donald, 1985); Anthony Slaven, *The Development of the West of Scotland, 1750–1960* (London: Routledge and Kegan Paul, 1975).
5. John Gibson, *The Thistle and the Crown: A History of the Scottish Office* (Edinburgh: Her Majesty's Stationery Office, 1985); Ian Levitt, *The Scottish Office: Depression and Reconstruction, 1919–1959* (Edinburgh: Pillans and Wilson for Scottish History Society, 1992); Gavin McCrone, 'The role of government', in Saville (ed.), *Economic Development*, pp. 195–213.

The Goschen formula dated from 1888, when the Chancellor of the Exchequer, G. J. Goschen, used half of the revenue from probate duty to reduce the burden of local authorities' expenditure on ratepayers. The money was allocated to England and Wales, Scotland and Ireland in proportion to their then general contributions to the Exchequer, Scotland's share being 11/80s of that of England and Wales. The formula was used thereafter to share out Exchequer grants to local authorities, and from 1919 to 1920 it was applied to the expenditure of the Scottish Education Department. As Scotland's contribution to the Exchequer fell relative to England's, a net fiscal transfer occurred. The Treasury sought successfully to 'exorcise' the Goschen formula in 1958,[6] but identifiable public expenditure continued to be higher in Scotland than in England as governments attempted to deal with the consequences of the decline of the traditional Scottish economy. In 1978 a bill to give Scotland devolution led the Treasury, with Scottish Office participation, to establish a needs assessment study to provide a basis for allocating Exchequer funds without detailed discussions every year on each item of public expenditure. It was recognised that there were a number of reasons why public expenditure should be higher per head in Scotland than in England, including a relatively poor health record; greater dependence on local authority housing; proportionately more young people in education; and the cost of providing services in sparsely populated rural areas. In the event, nothing was done to follow up the needs assessment study. Instead, a new formula, named after the then Chief Secretary of the Treasury, Joel Barnett, was devised to increase the Scottish block vote in line with any change in comparable English public expenditure in accordance with the size of Scotland's population compared with England's. The formula survived the demise of the devolution bill and was applied to a wide range of identifiable public expenditure from 1979, although not to agriculture, which came from the European Community's Common Agricultural Policy following Britain's accession to the EC in 1973. Originally Scotland was allocated a ratio of 10: 85, or 11.79 per cent, of comparable English expenditure, a slightly generous figure as revised statistics subsequently showed that Scotland's population in 1979 had fallen to 11.1 per cent of England's. By 1992 the populations of the two countries had diverged further and

---

6. 'Goschen Formula for calculating the amount of Exchequer grants to be paid to Scotland', Treasury papers, series 227, file 533 (T 227/533), The National Archives of the UK: Public Record Office (TNA: PRO), at folio 44.

the formula was adjusted to 10.66 per cent of any change in comparable English expenditure.[7]

Despite the Scottish Office's increasing economic responsibilities, it only had professional economic advice at a junior level until 1970, when Gavin McCrone joined the staff; in 1972 he was appointed Chief Economic Adviser, a title he held in conjunction with other posts until he retired in 1992. Economists in Whitehall saw Scotland's problems from a UK, macroeconomic perspective, and allocation of funds tended to be decided by the hunch of administrative civil servants and the political concerns of ministers. The questions examined in this chapter are: what was the relationship between macroeconomic and microeconomic policies? Was there a coherent, overall, economic policy that was appropriate to Scottish problems, or was there simply a series of *ad hoc* measures? How successfully was economic change managed between 1919 and 2000?

Change there was bound to be. The shift in employment from agriculture and industry to services was a common feature of advanced western European economies from the 1970s. A decline in employment in manufacturing may occur even while industrial output is rising, if labour productivity increases more rapidly than output. On the other hand, employment in manufacturing may decline on account of a failure of industry in an economy to compete effectively with industry elsewhere, and may be associated with a decline in output. In the former case, de-industrialisation can be associated with increasing prosperity, provided that increased industrial incomes create effective demand for services. In the latter, de-industrialisation is likely to lead to reduced demand in the economy as a whole, leading to unemployment and emigration. Both kinds of de-industrialisation can, of course, be present in an economy. However, the inability to match international competition was particularly important for Scottish industry, for Scotland was, and is, a small, open economy.

Even when protective tariffs brought the era of Britain's free-trade policy to an end in 1931–2, Scotland remained much the smaller partner, compared with England, in the free-trade area and monetary union that was the UK. Moreover, Scotland's economic structure had been shaped in the era of free trade by specialisation in industries in which it then had a comparative advantage: shipbuilding, iron and steel, heavy engineering, coal, and cotton, jute and woollen textiles. The larger scale of

---

7. Gavin McCrone, 'Scotland's public finances from Goschen to Barnett', Fraser of Allander Institute, *Quarterly Economic Bulletin*, vol. 24, no. 2 (1999), pp. 30–46.

industrial development in west-central Scotland compared with the east coast partly reflected the distribution of coal and iron ore and partly the importance of Scotland's trade with North America and the British Empire via the Clyde. The First World War stimulated the expansion of industrial capacity abroad in shipbuilding, iron and steel and textiles, while Scottish firms were diverted from exports to meeting government orders. The war also accelerated the substitution of oil for coal. In the 1920s Scottish industry struggled in a world of excess capacity and high tariffs, as foreign countries sought to protect their industries. Over-valuation of sterling associated with the return to the gold standard between 1925 and 1931 was a further handicap for exporters. Then the world depression of the early 1930s further reduced demand for the products of Scottish industry. Government orders for armaments from 1935 and during the Second World War, followed by high demand for ships and engineering products in the period of postwar re-construction, revived the traditional Scottish economy. However, by the mid-1950s Scottish firms were facing intense competition from foreign rivals that had had better industrial relations and consequently higher productivity.

Moreover, Scottish entrepreneurs were less responsive than they might have been to the rise of a consumer society. Although the period 1951 to 1973 is remembered as the golden age of full employment and low inflation, unemployment in Scotland was persistently higher than the UK average, and was as low as it was only as a result of policies aimed at encouraging newer industries from outside of the country to set up branch factories. Economic development became less concentrated in west-central Scotland, especially as North Sea oil was developed from the 1970s, creating boom conditions in Aberdeen and the surrounding area. From 1973 to 1992 the Scottish economy was exposed to a series of external disturbances: two oil crises, in 1973 and 1981; a slowing down in the expansion of the international economy compared with 1951–73; and an overvalued exchange rate in 1980–1 and again in 1990–2. Finally, sterling depreciation in 1992, following the UK's departure from the exchange-rate mechanism of the European Monetary System, and a boom in the United States created more favourable conditions for the Scottish economy. This chapter is divided into periods corresponding to external influences on the economy.

DECLINE OF THE TRADITIONAL ECONOMY, 1919-34

Orders during the First World War for ships and munitions created much activity for Scottish industry, but the war was financed by government borrowing on a scale that was highly inflationary. Retail prices increased 2.4 times between 1914 and 1920. Banks and firms were flush with funds that were used to finance a brief restocking boom in 1919-20. However, prices fell sharply in the postwar slump of 1920-1, increasing the burden of debt in terms of current output needed to service loans, and discouraging investment so long as future prices seemed likely to be lower than current prices. The abrupt change was acutely felt by shipbuilders and their suppliers. Admiralty orders became very scarce in a period of naval disarmament, and demand for merchant ships was lower than expected, partly because of slower growth of world trade than before 1914, and partly because of increased foreign competition. Unemployment in the UK rose to an unprecedented level of 14.3 per cent of the insured labour force in 1922.

Some kind of postwar slump was doubtless inevitable, and similar dislocation occurred in other industrial countries moving from war to peacetime economies. However, most economic historians have argued that the policies of the Treasury and the Bank of England were unhelpful for the British economy as a whole, even if there is room for disagreement about how adverse the effects were. Sterling had been pegged to the dollar at $4.76 during the war, with the help of American loans. When these loans ceased, the gold standard was formally suspended in March 1919, and by February 1920 sterling had fallen to $3.40. Both the Treasury and the Bank intended to return to gold at the pre-war rate of $4.86 as soon as was practicable. The Treasury set about balancing the government's budget. The Bank of England raised its discount rate (bank rate) from 5 to 7 per cent in 1919-20, to help curb the postwar boom, but was slow to reduce it again in the ensuing slump, increasing the disincentive to investment caused by falling prices. Sterling's exchange rate rose sharply in 1921, and the gold standard was restored in 1925 at the pre-war parity. Estimates of the consequent extent of sterling's overvaluation vary, but there is no doubt that exporters found that their prices, principally wages, denominated in sterling, rose relative to the prices at which they could sell their goods in foreign currencies. Imposing the burden of adjustment on export industries, overvaluation adversely affected regions heavily dependent upon exports. It has been calculated, on the basis that sterling was overvalued by 10 per cent, that the effects would have been particularly marked in textiles, iron and steel, and coal in west-central Scotland, resulting in job losses equivalent to 1.9 per cent of the local workforce, compared with average job losses of 1.3 per cent of the workforce in Great Britain.[8] It is, perhaps, not surprising, therefore, that unemployment rose in 1925 and 1926, and was higher in Scotland than in the UK as a whole. On the other hand, most people in employment benefited from the revaluation of sterling, as money wages tended to stabilise after 1923, although retail prices continued to fall until 1934. Edinburgh, where relatively few people were engaged in export trades, and where there was a substantial middle class in secure employment or enjoying rentier incomes, prospered while Glasgow failed to flourish.

Scottish industry's response to the postwar challenge was more marked in terms of changes in output than in employment. Gross output of heavy industries (iron and steel, engineering, shipbuilding, mines and quarries) was 31 per cent by value of total gross output of Scottish industry in 1924, compared with 42 per cent in 1907. In contrast, the proportion of industrial employees in these industries hardly changed; 41 per cent in 1924 compared with 42 per cent in 1907. The failure of Scottish businessmen to recognise that Scottish industry was over-committed to the pre-1914 pattern of trade can easily be criticised in hindsight. However, the circumstances of the postwar period were so unusual that it is not surprising that they expected demand for the products of their firms to recover.[9] There was also an alternative to investment in new industries. Evidence of a tendency of capital in old industrial sectors to move into investment trusts and financial services can be traced back to the 1870s, and this tendency seems to have been particularly strong in the inter-war period.[10] Here perhaps we have another reason for the relative prosperity of Edinburgh compared with west-central Scotland.

The deflationary policies of the Treasury and the Bank of England were questioned by David Lloyd George, the Liberal prime minister heading the Conservative-dominated coalition of 1918–22. He raised the possibility of borrowing to pay for roads, trains, light railways and land settlement at a conference of Liberal ministers at Gairloch, where he happened to be on holiday in September 1921. However, the Treasury persuaded the Cabinet to restrict public works to what was just enough

8. M. E. F. Jones, 'The regional impact of an overvalued pound in the 1920s', *Economic History Review*, 2nd series, 38 (1985), pp. 393–401.
9. Campbell, *Rise and Fall*, pp. 146–61, 166–7, 197–8.
10. John Scott and Michael Hughes, *The Anatomy of Scottish Capital: Scottish Companies and Scottish Capital, 1900–1979* (London: Croom Helm, 1980), pp. 25, 70, 74–8, 107.

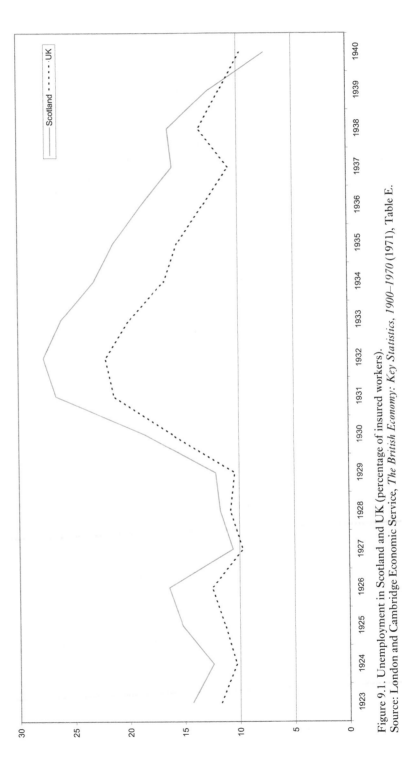

Figure 9.1. Unemployment in Scotland and UK (percentage of insured workers).
Source: London and Cambridge Economic Service, *The British Economy: Key Statistics, 1900–1970* (1971), Table E.

to prevent the unemployed from starving. Moreover, local authorities were responsible for most public works, and the poorer ones were the least able to undertake them, notwithstanding subsidies from central government. The principal form of public investment in Scotland was local authority housing. Scotland got more than its Goschen share for Exchequer funding for housing in 1925. Between 1926 and 1928 there was an experiment in building steel houses by a Scottish National Housing Company, which was funded by loans from the (UK) Public Works Loans Board and from the Scottish Board of Health. However, only 2,552 houses were built, mainly, it would seem, because Neville Chamberlain, the Minister of Health, who was responsible for housing in England and Wales, was determined that Scotland should not get more than what he considered to be its due share of Exchequer funding.[11] The government's preferred solution to the problem of unemployment in depressed areas was to assist migration through the Industrial Transference Board, which was set up in 1928. Lloyd George, as leader of the Liberal opposition, made unemployment a major issue in the election of 1929, advocating borrowing to double the current rate of expenditure on roads, housing, telephones and electrical development, with the support of the economist John Maynard Keynes. The election led to the defeat of the Conservatives and the formation of a Labour minority government, which had its own advocate of public works in Oswald Mosley. In the event Treasury opposition ensured that Labour's public works programme was more modest than what Lloyd George or Mosley had demanded, and the employment created by the programme was far less than the increase in unemployment in the post-1929 depression. The Treasury resisted public works on the grounds that borrowing by the government would tend to crowd out private enterprise – although there was little enough sign of private enterprise in Scotland after 1929. The Treasury likewise opposed tariffs down to 1931, on the grounds that they would provoke retaliation, ruining the industrial areas of Scotland and the north of England, with their dependence on exports.[12]

As exports collapsed in the world depression, unemployment more than doubled between 1929 and 1931, with the percentage unemployed being significantly higher in Scotland than in the UK as a whole (see Figure 9.1). The cost of unemployment benefits unbalanced the budget and undermined confidence in sterling. The Labour government

11. Tom Begg, *Housing Policy in Scotland* (Edinburgh: John Donald, 1996), pp. 32–4; Gibson, *Thistle and the Crown*, pp. 69–71.
12. G. C. Peden, *The Treasury and British Public Policy, 1906–1959* (Oxford: Oxford University Press, 2000), pp. 179–80, 219–33, 240.

split over the issue of cutting unemployment benefits and resigned. The Conservative-dominated National Government that followed found it had to suspend the gold standard in September 1931. Other things being equal, the fall in sterling's exchange rate would have helped exporters. However, the world depression – centred on the United States – was so deep that unemployment did not peak until 1932 – at 27.7 per cent of the insured labour force in Scotland, compared with 22.1 per cent in the UK as a whole. Free trade was abandoned at the end of 1931 and an imperial conference at Ottawa in 1932 agreed that tariffs on trade between Empire countries would be lower than tariffs on foreign goods. This system of imperial preference may have done something to maintain British exports as a whole, but at the same time it ruled out effective protection for Dundee jute against imports from India.

Suspension of the gold standard allowed the Bank of England to reduce bank rate. Both private and local authority housing benefited from a lowering of interest rates, but private housing was much less important in Scotland than in England, and the multiplier effect of demand for furnishings and household equipment was correspondingly less. Recovery in Scotland was slower than in the United Kingdom as a whole. Even in 1934 unemployment, at 23.1 per cent of the insured labour force, was still higher than the United Kingdom figure had been two years earlier. Scotland's traditional industries were deep in the doldrums and, as David Newlands in Chapter 6 above has noted above, new industries, like motor vehicles, had made little impact on the Scottish economy. Since 1929 the Bank of England had encouraged the rationalisation of firms in shipbuilding, steam-locomotive manufacture and steel, but, although the closure of surplus capacity might create leaner industries, it did not in itself lead management or labour to adopt more productive methods.[13] The Coal Mines Act of 1930 established a Coal Mines Reorganisation Commission, but succeeded only in arousing the hostility of colliery owners to the principle of compulsion. The Act also provided for the fixing of output and prices by district committees of colliery owners. Like all quota schemes, this tended to safeguard inefficient firms, although the Scottish district's performance in terms of mechanisation and labour productivity seems to have been better than average in the UK.[14]

13. Campbell, *Rise and Fall*, pp. 170–81.
14. Neil Buxton, 'Entrepreneurial efficiency in the British coal industry between the wars', *Economic History Review*, 2nd series, 23 (1970), pp. 476–97.

THE REVIVAL OF THE TRADITIONAL ECONOMY, 1934–51

By 1934, with an election in prospect, the National Government wished to be seen to be doing something about unemployment in the depressed areas. In that year subsidies were advanced to the Cunard Company, under the North Atlantic Shipping Act, to enable a liner, the future *Queen Mary*, to be completed at Clydebank. More wide-reaching, but also essentially a political gesture, was the Special Areas (Development and Improvement) Act of 1934. The government had commissioned studies of areas where average unemployment was around 40 per cent of the insured labour force, and the Clydeside and North Lanarkshire region was identified as one of four industrial areas in the UK for rehabilitation. However, the Scottish Special Area lacked any focus, because Glasgow was omitted, apparently on the grounds that unemployment was lower there than in surrounding communities. Moreover, the Act restricted finance to projects that could not be financed through some existing government grant, and profit-making enterprises were likewise excluded. As a result the commissioner for the Scottish Area spent no less than 90 per cent of his first year's budget on sewerage schemes. More promising from the point of view of stimulating enterprise was the establishment of a non-profit-making company to build an industrial estate at Hillington in 1937. Meanwhile the Special Areas Reconstruction Association had been set up by the Bank of England, with government backing, in 1936 to provide loan capital for small businesses in the special areas. However, such measures were not likely to help the large companies whose problems lay at the root of the area's difficulties. A step towards a more adequate regional policy was taken with the Special Areas Amendment Act of 1937. A Special Areas Loans Advisory Committee was set up to advise the Treasury on loans to firms in the special areas, and firms in the special areas could be given subsidies in respect of rent, rates and taxes. However, the combined effects of these measures and the continuing policy of industrial transference were small, either in terms of employment or in terms of attracting industrial development away from the booming Greater London area.[15] Scottish Office officials believed that there was a need for industrial diversification, but felt that Scotland's special problems were not understood in Whitehall.[16]

15. Carol E. Heim, 'Limits to intervention: the Bank of England and industrial diversification in the depressed areas', *Economic History Review*, 2nd series, 37 (1984), pp. 533–50; Gavin McCrone, *Regional Policy in Britain* (London: George Allen and Unwin, 1969), pp. 93–102.
16. R. H. Campbell, 'The Scottish Office and the Special Areas in the 1930s', *Historical Journal*, 22 (1979), pp. 167–83.

Meanwhile industrialists who had waited in hope for better times were rewarded with orders for ships, steel and heavy engineering products arising from the government's rearmament programme, which, so far as the navy was concerned, began in 1935. Rearmament had a greater multiplier effect on depressed regions than the contemporary housing boom did.[17] Nevertheless, it was not until 1940 that unemployment in Scotland fell below the UK average (see Figure 9.1). Even so, the gap between Scottish national income per head of population and the corresponding figure for the United Kingdom as a whole narrowed after 1935, and was negligible between 1940 and 1944.[18]

Rearmament and wartime demand for ships, heavy engineering products and jute sandbags tended to reinforce the traditional structure of Scottish industry. There was some diversification. Employment in motor vehicles, cycles and aircraft increased by 164 per cent to 30,000 between 1939 and 1946, compared with a 148 per cent increase to 56,180 in shipbuilding and ship repairing.[19] Motor-vehicle production did not include motor cars, but Rolls Royce set up a factory for aircraft engines at Hillington, and the Air Ministry put up the fixed capital for aircraft production at Prestwick, the factory being managed by Scottish Aviation Limited. Ferranti established production of advanced electronic equipment in Edinburgh during the war, providing a foundation for future growth of Scotland's electronics industry. Nevertheless the consensus among planners for the postwar Scottish economy was that diversification should be taken a good deal further. They were encouraged in this belief by the Royal Commission on the Distribution of the Industrial Population, which had reported in 1940 that inter-war experience showed that heavy industries no longer provided a suitable basis for regional development, besides being causes of unhealthy urban environments. Instead the report, known as the Barlow Report after the Royal Commission's chairman, looked to a future based on light industries located in new towns situated outside the old cities.[20] The wartime coalition government's white paper on *Employment Policy* in 1944 called for a balanced distribution of industry and labour to prevent any area being overdependent upon a single industry or a group of related industries (shipbuilding and heavy industries in Scotland being given

17. Mark Thomas, 'Rearmament and economic recovery in the late 1930s', *Economic History Review*, 2nd series, 36 (1983), pp. 552–73.
18. A. D. Campbell, 'Changes in Scottish incomes, 1924–49', *Economic Journal*, 65 (1955), p. 231.
19. Richard Saville, 'The industrial background to the postwar Scottish economy', in Saville (ed.), *Economic Development*, pp. 1–46, at p. 31.
20. *Royal Commission on the Distribution of the Industrial Population: Report* (Cmd 6153), Parliamentary Papers (PP) 1939–40, iv, pp. 263–592.

as an example).[21] The Clyde Valley Regional Plan of 1946 likewise identified shipbuilding as 'to some extent a source of weakness', as the industry had monopolised too much of the region's resources. Like the Barlow Report, it looked to a future based on lighter industry and town planning – unsurprisingly, given that Patrick Abercrombie, who was consultant for the Clyde Valley report, had been a member of the Royal Commission.

Another region for which a bright new future was planned was the north of Scotland. The Secretary of State for Scotland, Tom Johnston, promoted the Hydro-Electric (Scotland) Act of 1943 on the assumption that the building of dams would lead to the economic and social development of the Highlands. Hydro-electric works had been used since before the war for industrial purposes at Foyers, Kinlochleven and Fort William, but in the postwar period initial efforts to attract electro-chemical and electro-metallurgical industries failed. Even sustained efforts to attract light industries had disappointing results. The North of Scotland Hydro-Electric Board, chaired by Johnston himself from 1946, refused to subsidise heavy current users at the expense of other users, and distribution costs to remote communities were high. The Highland economy could not be transformed by hydro-electric power alone.[22]

The legislative framework for postwar regional policy was provided by the Distribution of Industry Act of 1945. In Scotland the pre-war special area, renamed a development area, was extended to include not only its regional focus, the city of Glasgow, but also the geographically separate city of Dundee. The intention was to identify districts that could act as focal centres for industrial development, and in 1948 Inverness and Dingwall, and their immediate hinterland, were also scheduled as the Scottish Highlands Development Area. Under the Act, the Board of Trade could build factories, buying land by compulsory purchase if necessary; make loans with the consent of the Treasury to industrial estate companies; make provision for basic public services; and reclaim derelict land. In addition, the Treasury was authorised to give grants or loans to commercially sound industrial projects, on the recommendation of the Development Areas Treasury Advisory Committee (DATAC), if finance could not be raised from another source. In contrast to pre-war regional policy, there were also controls over new factory construction outside the development areas, originally under the wartime building

21. *Employment Policy* (Cmd 6527), PP 1943–4, viii, pp. 119–50.
22. Peter Payne, *The Hydro: A Study of the Development of the Major Hydro-Electric Schemes undertaken by the North of Scotland Hydro-Electric Board* (Aberdeen: Aberdeen University Press, 1988), pp. 36–50, 190–209, 252–3.

licence system, and from 1947 by means of industrial development certificates. These negative controls were used with some vigour immediately after the war, but the proportion of industrial building going to development areas fell after 1947.[23] Despite the postwar Labour government's rhetoric of planning, the Board of Trade seems to have been guided almost solely by immediate employment creation, without consideration of what linkages there might be with the local economy. The Scottish Office advocated long-term, balanced development. In 1947 it objected to the use to which the Pressed Steel Company was to put a government-financed factory, pointing out that it appeared that the firm would not obtain its raw material in Scotland and that the product would be sent to England for assembly. The Joint Parliamentary Under-Secretary of State for Scotland, Tom Fraser, wanted an investigation into the possibility of large-scale development of the motor-car industry in Scotland. He also argued for research and development establishments to be located in Scotland, to enable Scotland to build on its scientific and technical heritage. However, there appears to have been no support in Whitehall for these ideas.[24] The Board of Trade lacked either the will or the know-how with which to persuade motor-car firms to invest in development areas, including Scotland.[25] The origins of Scotland's tendency to become a branch-factory economy, with heterogeneous assembly plants, can be traced in part to regional policy as pursued by the Board of Trade.

Postwar conditions were extremely favourable to traditional Scottish industries. The government gave priority to exports in the allocation of materials still under its control, to bring Britain's external payments into balance, and there was plenty of demand for ships, capital goods and coal as economies reconstructed after the war. The dislocation of industrial rivals, notably Germany and Japan, made it possible for Britain's share of world trade in manufactures to reach 25.4 per cent in 1951, compared with 21.3 per cent in 1937. Macroeconomic policy, informed by Keynesian analysis and buttressed by controls over investment, avoided the excesses of inflation and deflation that had marked the years immediately after the First World War. The Labour government took steps to encourage British industry to adopt best practice through various tripartite bodies, of which the best known was the Anglo-American

23. McCrone, *Regional Policy*, pp. 107–12, 115.
24. Peter Scott, 'British regional policy, 1945–51: a lost opportunity', *Twentieth Century British History*, 8 (1997), pp. 358–82.
25. Stephen Rosevear, 'Balancing business and the regions: British distribution of industry policy and the Board of Trade, 1945–51', *Business History*, vol. 40, no. 1 (1998), pp. 77–99.

Council on Productivity, which tried to make businessmen and trade-union leaders familiar with American methods. On the other hand, it has been argued that the postwar settlement between government, trade unions and industry precluded necessary reforms in industrial relations and anti-trust policy.[26] Nationalisation of the coal and steel industries, and rail and long-distance road services, created new monopolies. The continuation of wartime import controls had the effect of protecting British industry. It is not surprising if Scottish industrialists showed little inclination to take advantage of the sellers market to innovate and make their firms better prepared to meet competition in less favourable circumstances.

THE 'GOLDEN AGE', 1951–73

The industrial structure of Scotland in the early 1950s differed little in terms of industrial structure and distribution of population from the beginning of the century, but there were signs that that the Scottish economy was lagging behind the rest of the UK. Low unemployment concealed serious weaknesses: continuing dependence on heavy industries; an out-of-date transport infrastructure; and an appalling urban environment.[27] Unemployment in Scotland was higher than the UK average (see Figure 9.2), and by 1958 had come to be seen by the Prime Minister, Harold Macmillan, as a political problem. Economists in the Treasury's Economic Section shared the Scottish Office's belief that the higher Scottish figure reflected the fact that trade unions negotiated wage rates for the whole of the UK, but Scottish employers had higher transport costs than firms that were located closer to markets in England. Sir Robert Hall, who, as head of the Economic Section was the government's principal economic adviser, wrote in December 1958 that: 'if people live in an inaccessible place they must expect to pay for it'. He added that 'for political and social reasons' the government wanted to offset the disadvantages of industrial location in Scotland, 'and in the end the taxpayer has to do it'.[28] Regional policy, which had been largely in abeyance since the late 1940s, was reactivated by the Distribution of

26. S. N. Broadberry and N. F. R. Crafts, 'British economic policy and performance in the early postwar period', *Business History*, vol. 38, no. 4 (1996), pp. 65–91.
27. A. K. Cairncross (ed.), *The Scottish Economy: A Statistical Account of Scottish Life* (Cambridge: Cambridge University Press, 1954).
28. Sir Robert Hall to Sir Roger Makins (Permanent Secretary of the Treasury), 19 December 1958, T 234/343, TNA: PRO.

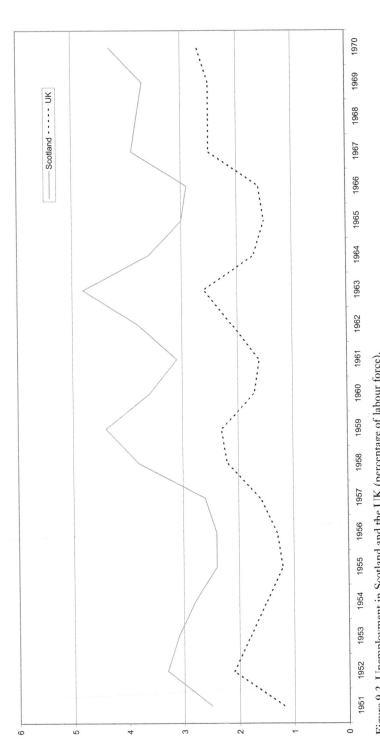

Figure 9.2. Unemployment in Scotland and the UK (percentage of labour force).
Source: London and Cambridge Economic Service, *The British Economy: Key Statistics, 1900–1970*, Table E.

Industry (Industrial Finance) Act of 1958. The Board of Trade was more willing to refuse industrial development certificates to firms that it believed could relocate in a development district. The Treasury's power to give loans or grants on the advice of DATAC was extended. Despite the title of the Act, this financial assistance could now be given to any form of trade, and not only industry, as hitherto – a sensible provision if the aim was to diversify the economies of industrial regions. On the other hand, regional policy was still tied to development areas that were defined by high rates of unemployment, and no thought was given to the development of the Scottish economy as a whole.

Scottish industry's problems in the late 1950s were not caused solely or even mainly by national wage rates and transport costs. There were also structural problems. In particular, the coal industry encountered geological difficulties, as well as competition from oil. Old seams in Lanarkshire were being worked out, and the attempt to develop central Fife foundered on the failure of the Rothes mine. Shipbuilding suffered from competition from Germany, the Netherlands, Sweden and Japan, where credit arrangements or subsidies encouraged investment in more modern techniques. The government was aware of the shipbuilding industry's problems and of their implications for Scotland, where one in eight of the employed population depended directly or indirectly on shipbuilding. However, the Cabinet's Economic Policy Committee took the view in 1959 that subsidies would serve no purpose unless both sides of the industry agreed on measures to improve industrial relations and reduce costs in line with their competitors. Such improvements could not be secured in time to enable the industry to compete at time when there was surplus building capacity in the world. By late 1961 the Conservative Secretary of State for Scotland, John Maclay, accepted that a contraction in the shipbuilding industry was 'almost inevitable'.[29] Many famous Clyde shipbuilders went out of business in the 1960s. The Labour government appointed the Geddes Committee to examine the industry and the subsequent report in 1966 was highly critical of management's short-term attitudes to markets and its failure to nego- tiate constructively on labour relations.[30] Following the Committee's recommendation that the industry should be rationalised into big and compact groups, Scott's and Lithgow's on the lower Clyde merged in 1967 and Fairfield's, John Brown's, Connell's, Yarrow's and Stephen's

29. Economic Policy Committee minutes, 4 February and 8 July 1959, Cabinet Office papers, series 134, volume 1681 (CAB 134/1681), and 'The Scottish Economy', memorandum by the Secretary of State for Scotland, 15 December 1961, CAB 134/1692, TNA: PRO.
30 *Shipbuilding Inquiry Committee, Report* (Cmnd 2937), PP 1965–66, vii, pp. 45–209.

were amalgamated into Upper Clyde Shipbuilders (UCS) in 1968. Fairfield's had already been rescued from bankruptcy by a Bank of England advance and made the subject of an experiment in tripartite management representing government, workers and private capital; improvements in industrial relations and productivity were achieved, but excess shipbuilding capacity in the world meant that survival also depended upon subsidies. The Conservative government withdrew support in 1971, leading to a famous 'work in' and the emergence of the wholly government-owned Govan Shipbuilders in 1972.[31]

The steel industry, comprising a number of small works in west-central Scotland, each using the open-hearth method, specialised in heavy steels, which were suitable for shipbuilding or the construction industry. By the late 1950s it was apparent that the cheapest way to produce steel was the basic oxygen process, which required larger works to maximise economies of scale; moreover the fastest-growing market was for lighter steels suitable for motor cars or consumer durables such as cookers or refrigerators. Expert opinion in the steel industry favoured a new strip mill at a coastal site in Lincolnshire, to minimise transport costs both for importing iron ore and for delivering steel to the Midlands, where the car industry was concentrated. In 1957 the Board of Trade pointed out that Grangemouth would be better from the point of view of dealing with unemployment, since the area around Grangemouth was affected by the decline of the shale-oil and iron-castings industries. Maclay strongly supported the case for Grangemouth, but added that the main argument was not the relief of local unemployment but the opportunity to establish a long-term balance of industry in Scotland.[32] However, as a result of the personal intervention of the Prime Minister in 1958, and the offer of government loans, the project was split, one strip mill being set up at Ravenscraig in Lanarkshire, and another at Llanwern in south Wales. The decision reflected social and political factors rather than economic ones. Neither of the new strip mills was large enough to enjoy the economies of scale of rivals abroad. Moreover, Ravenscraig, being inland, had higher transport costs for ore. Grangemouth would not have been much better, the Forth being too shallow for ore carriers above the rail bridge. Hunterston on the

31. Peter Payne, 'The decline of the Scottish heavy industries, 1945–1983', in Saville (ed.), *Economic Development*, pp. 79–113, at 105–7.
32. 'Steel: Location of Proposed New Strip Mill', memoranda by the President of the Board of Trade, 16 October 1957, and the Secretary of State for Scotland, 18 October 1957, CAB 134/1677; and 'Provision of a Fourth Strip Mill', memorandum by the Secretary of State for Scotland, 13 March 1958, CAB 134/1679, TNA: PRO.

Clyde was seen by many in the late 1960s and early 1970s as the best site for an integrated iron and steel works, but in the end only a new ore terminal was built there between 1973 and 1978 (to supply Ravenscraig), together with two direct reduction plants, which were never used. One problem that was foreseen by Sir Andrew McCance, the chairman of Colvilles, the firm responsible for choosing the Ravenscraig site, was that Scotland lacked the industries that would use strip steel, forcing the firm to send most of its output to England, incurring heavy freight charges. On the other hand, there was something of a chicken and egg problem: unless strip steel was produced in Scotland it would be harder to attract firms producing cars and consumer durables.[33]

Scottish industry's difficulties in the late 1950s were also related to the management of the national economy. In response to pressure on sterling, the Treasury used fiscal policy to deflate the economy from the autumn of 1955, and the Bank of England had raised bank rate from 5 per cent to 7 per cent in 1957. Deflationary policies acted with particular severity on areas, such as the west of Scotland, which specialised in the production of capital goods. Macmillan pressed the Chancellor of the Exchequer, Derick Heathcoat Amory, to reflate, which he did with his budget in April 1959. The Treasury also approved a large number of proposals from Maclay for expenditure in Scotland, including factory extensions in development areas, electricity undertakings, and roads, but the sum of these proposals, £4,284,000 was much less than the £50 million to be spent on Ravenscraig.[34] Reflation led to weakness in the balance of payments on current account, and deflationary measures followed in July 1961. Meanwhile, however, regional policy had been allocated a higher priority in economic management. The Distribution of Industry Acts of 1945 and 1958 were repealed and replaced with the Local Employment Act of 1960. The old areas qualifying for assistance were rescheduled by the Board of Trade in a way that increased the proportion of the insured population in Scotland in what were now called development districts from 55 per cent to 62 per cent. As before, the criterion for qualification for assistance was the level of unemployment – in practice about 4.5 per cent.[35]

This approach was challenged in the autumn of 1961 by a Committee of Inquiry into the Scottish Economy chaired by John Toothill, a

---

33. Payne, 'Decline', pp. 94–101.
34. P[eter] V[inter], 'Unemployment in Scotland', no date, but December 1958, T 234/343, TNA: PRO.
35. Neil Buxton, 'The Scottish economy, 1945–79: performance, structure and problems', in Saville (ed.), *Economic Development*, pp. 47–78, at p. 69; McCrone, *Regional Policy*, p. 122.

director of Ferranti Ltd, with Tom Wilson, the Adam Smith Professor of Political Economy at Glasgow University, as vice-chairman. The Toothill Committee had been appointed by the Scottish Council (Development and Industry), which represented the opinions of leading businessmen, but it enjoyed full support from the government. The Scottish controllers of the Board of Trade and the Ministry of Labour and senior officers from the Scottish Office representing the Scottish Home Department and the Department of Health for Scotland were appointed as assessors, and the secretariat was provided jointly by the Scottish Council and the Scottish Office. The Toothill Report recommended that policy should put greater emphasis on the promotion of sound economic growth, and less on palliatives for unemployment. In particular, it stated that policy should not aim to prop up inefficient or dying industries. It called for a widening and strengthening of the country's industrial structure through the development of science-based industries, the newer capital goods industries and engineering-based consumers' industries. It stressed the need to improve road and rail links, particularly with England, and air services. It identified the supply of skilled labour as a bottleneck and advocated more technical education in schools and colleges and training by the Ministry of Labour to supplement training by industry. It called for the co-ordination of regional development measures by a new department in the Scottish Office that would bring together its existing industrial and planning functions.[36]

As a result the Scottish Development Department was created with responsibilities for physical and economic planning and the development of infrastructure, including particularly housing, new towns and roads. The work of the Toothill Committee was carried forward by a group of officials drawn from the Scottish Development Department (which provided the chairman); the Scottish Office departments of Education, Home and Health, and Agriculture and Fisheries; and several Whitehall departments: the Board of Trade and the ministries of Labour, Aviation, Power, Public Buildings and Works, and Transport. The Scottish Development Group's study provided the basis of the Conservative government's white paper on central Scotland in 1963, which identified growth points centred on new towns and older areas where there was scope for rehabilitation or expansion. The white paper proposed improved social and economic infrastructure, including housing,

---

36. Scottish Council (Development and Industry), *Inquiry into the Scottish Economy, 1960–1961: Report of a Committee under the Chairmanship of J. N. Toothill* (1961).

schools, roads, airports and ports.[37] In May 1963 the Rootes car factory was opened at Linwood, following the starting of commercial vehicle assembly by the British Motor Corporation at Bathgate in 1961. Alas, linkages with local industry did not develop to the extent that had been hoped, and the Scottish factories found themselves at a disadvantage with English competitors, in that many parts for vehicles had to be brought from the south, where the major markets were also situated.

At the time, however, Scottish developments seemed to fit in with economic planning in London. The National Economic Development Council (NEDC) had been created in 1961 to bring together representatives of employers' organisations and the Trades Union Congress, together with ministers, to identify obstacles to economic growth. Imbalances between regions with labour shortages and regions with above average unemployment were one such obstacle, for macro-economic measures to increase demand tended to produce inflationary pressures before the economy reached what was then regarded as full employment.[38] In 1963 the Conservative Chancellor of the Exchequer, Reginald Maudling, decided to make a 'dash for growth' on the basis of an NEDC target for a rate of growth in national output of 4 per cent a year over the period 1961–6. He hoped that expanding macroeconomic demand and investment allowances would encourage sufficient improvements in productivity to enable the initial balance-of-payments problem to be overcome. The incoming Labour government in 1964 was no less committed to economic growth: it established a Department of Economic Affairs (DEA), which published a National Plan for a 25 per cent increase in GDP between 1964 and 1970. A plan for the expansion of the Scottish economy followed in January 1966.[39] The plan was drafted by the Scottish Economic Planning Board (the successor to the Scottish Development Group) in consultation with the DEA, the Treasury, the Board of Trade and the new Scottish Economic Planning Council, whose members were drawn from industry, commerce, trade unions, local authorities and universities. Unlike the earlier Conservative plan, Labour's Scottish Economic Plan covered the whole country, and broadened its scope to include tourism and the development of the

37   *Central Scotland: A Programme for Development and Growth* (Cmnd 2188), PP 1963–4, xxvi, pp. 251–99. The 'Central Scotland Study' can be found in CAB 134/1700 and in the Records of the Scottish Development Department, series 35, file 39 (DD 35/39), National Archives of Scotland, Edinburgh (NAS).

38.   *Conditions Favourable to Faster Growth* (London: National Economic Development Council, 1963).

39.   *The Scottish Economy, 1965–70: A Plan for Expansion* (Cmnd 2864), PP 1965–6, xiii, pp. 411–589.

Highlands and Islands. There was less emphasis on specific growth points in central Scotland and major development was to be encouraged at Galashiels to stimulate new growth in the Borders. In other respects there was considerable continuity with the Toothill Report and the central Scotland white paper. The 1966 Industrial Development Act made the whole of Scotland, except Edinburgh, a development area. The National Plan was in effect abandoned in July 1966 when a severe deflationary package was announced to prevent the devaluation of sterling (which nevertheless followed in November 1967). However, Scotland was shielded to some extent from the effects of deflation. The DEA and the Treasury agreed to encourage expansion in the development areas by introducing a regional employment premium (REP), which was in effect a subsidy to manufacturing employment there. The departments' economists argued that REP would involve no real economic cost. There was little danger of inflationary pressure in the development areas, which would benefit from a shift in demand away from the rest of Britain.[40] On the other hand, REP would tend to discourage efforts to raise labour productivity.

Scotland did well in comparison with the UK as a whole in the latter part of the 'golden age'. GDP per head, which had fallen from 92 per cent of the UK figure in 1951 to 87 per cent in 1962, climbed to over 94 per cent by 1973.[41] This relatively good performance partly reflected widespread growth in manufacturing, particularly in food, drink, tobacco, metal manufacturing, engineering and vehicles, and partly the fact that growth in construction in Scotland exceeded the UK average.[42] A stable level of employment was also maintained by an increase in jobs in services. Unemployment remained above the UK average, and was normally above the 3 per cent that was regarded as full employment at the time, but would have been much worse had steps not been taken to offset the decline in employment in agriculture, textiles and heavy industry.

Protection could not be used freely to support industry in the postwar period. Trade policy in the 1950s and 1960s aimed at mutual reductions in protection through the General Agreement on Trade and Tariffs (GATT). There were also pressures from Commonwealth countries that could not be ignored in the 1950s, when the Commonwealth was still seen as a source of British influence in the world. Dundee's jute industry,

40. Donald MacDougall, *Don and Mandarin: Memoirs of an Economist* (London: John Murray, 1987), p. 171; McCrone, *Regional Policy*, pp. 136–8.
41. Lee, *Scotland and the United Kingdom*, p. 53.
42. Buxton, 'Scottish economy', in Saville (ed.), *Economic Development*, p. 55.

which then employed 14,000 people, or 17 per cent of the city's insured population, directly, and many more indirectly, faced competition from Pakistan and India. A government Jute Control had been established during the war as a monopoly purchaser of raw jute and of imported jute goods, the latter being sold at Dundee prices. State trading in raw jute ended in 1954 but continued with respect to jute goods, which would otherwise have undercut Dundee prices.[43] The jute industry argued that the decision to continue protection brought the UK into line with every other jute-processing country in the world, but in the event the amount of protection was reduced in 1957 and 1959. A Board of Trade report in 1959 on 'The Future of the Jute Industry' claimed that the industry had done very little to prepare itself for reduced protection, and the Scottish Office did not demur. As one official there remarked, jute businessmen, having found themselves 'in a fairly snug position', had been determined to 'resist the winds of change'.[44] In the 1960s the city of jute became increasingly dependent on inward investment by American firms producing watches or office equipment.

In the Highlands, population decline was reversed from the mid-1960s. The region was the recipient of three major investments: an experimental nuclear reactor at Dounreay in Caithness (built between 1955 and 1959); a pulp and paper mill constructed between 1963 and 1965 at Corpach, near Fort William; and an aluminium smelter constructed at Invergordon between 1969 and 1972. The Corpach mill was intended to provide a market for the products of Highland forestry, but from the outset faced stiff competition from Scandinavia. The establishment of the Highlands and Islands Development Board in 1965 brought about a marked increase in public expenditure aimed at stimulating economic activity. The most promising were those like knitwear and crafts that could be linked to the expansion of tourism and which encouraged people to move into the region.[45] Tourism benefited from increasing prosperity and leisure in the UK and abroad and from publicity organised by the Scottish and local tourist boards. In 1960 the Secretary of State for Scotland, Maclay, argued successfully for an increased road programme to cope with tourist traffic in the Highlands

---

43. 'Proposed Measures to Protect UK Jute Industry', Ministry of Materials files, 1953 and 1954, in Board of Trade papers, series 64, files 5104 and 5105 (BT 64/5104 and BT 64/5105), TNA: PRO.
44. 'The Future of the Jute Industry', 10 March 1959, Records of the Scottish Economic Planning Department, series 4, file 1545 (SEP 4/1545), and comment, 29 April 1960, on minutes of meeting with jute industry, SEP 4/1656, NAS.
45. Sir Kenneth Alexander, 'The Highlands and Islands Development Board', in Saville (ed.), *Economic Development*, pp. 214–32.

(at that date some important Highland trunk roads were still single track with passing places).[46]

Regional policy can be criticised for focusing too exclusively on industry and for neglecting employment opportunities in services. Nevertheless, much had been done to transform Scotland between the late 1940s and 1973. The urban environment had been transformed by the clearance of slums, and if many council housing estates on the fringes of cities were built too quickly and with insufficient social infrastructure and employment opportunities, new towns, on the whole, were more successful. East Kilbride (designated 1947), Glenrothes (1948) and Cumbernauld (1956) proved to be economic growth points, and encouraged the beginning of two more, Livingston (1962) and Irvine (1966). From the point of view of future economic growth, perhaps the best inheritance left by government policy in the 'golden age' was a transport infrastructure suited to the late twentieth century. In the mid-1960s three major bridges were built over the estuaries of the Forth, Tay and Clyde (at Erskine) and a beginning was made to the construction of a motorway system in Scotland.

EC MEMBERSHIP, OIL AND DE-INDUSTRIALISATION, 1973–92

The UK entered the EC in January 1973, giving Scottish industry better access to western European markets and, as Ewen Cameron notes in Chapter 7, bringing Scottish farmers within the Common Agricultural Policy. Entry to the EC also involved difficult discussions on the Common Fisheries Policy (CFP) of 1970, which required that EC fishermen be given equal access to all fishing grounds, although with exceptions for three-mile coastal zones to be reserved for local fishermen. As Sir Con O'Neill, a Foreign Office official who played a leading role in the negotiations with the original EC members, later remarked: 'the question of fisheries was economic peanuts, but political dynamite'. The only concession won prior to entry to the EC was a ten-year transition period during which existing twelve-mile fishery rights would be retained for the Shetlands, Orkney and the whole of the Scottish north and east coasts, and also six-mile limits on the west coast, enclosing the Minches. Sir David Hannay, another member of the Foreign Office negotiating team, believed that the British government did not pull its

---

46. 'The Road Programme', memorandum by the Secretary of State for Scotland, 18 March 1960, CAB 134/1687, TNA: PRO.

weight on fisheries policy, with damaging consequences arising from overfishing as a result of increasingly effective techniques.[47] On the other hand, when the agreement on coastal zones was revised in 1983 to give protected twelve-mile limits around the coasts of all member states, Scotland was given one of the most extensive areas of inshore fishing in the EC. A Royal Society of Edinburgh inquiry into the Scottish fishing industry has concluded that, while the CFP has failed to achieve adequate conservation of certain key fish stocks, the problem has occurred in spite of Scotland's large share of the quota in the North Sea. Direct Scottish employment in catching, fish-farming and processing amounted in 1999 to 19,800, just under 1 per cent of total employment; if indirect effects are taken into account, the total employment dependent on these industries was 48,000, roughly half the direct and indirect employment from North Sea oil at its peak.[48]

Entry to the EC coincided with developments in the international environment that brought to an end the 'golden age' of stable prices, uninterrupted economic growth and high employment. The flow of dollars from the United States, in the form of overseas investment, aid and military expenditure, which had done so much for international liquidity since the war, became inflationary by the early 1970s, particularly on account of deficit financing of the Vietnam War. The Bretton Woods system of stable exchange rates, which had imposed monetary discipline in the 'golden age', collapsed in 1973. Then, at the end of 1973, the Organisation of Petroleum Exporting Countries (OPEC) engineered a rise in the price of oil. Oil had been the source of about half of the energy consumption of western countries in 1973, and the adjustment to a quadrupling of prices between 1972 and 1974 led to investment plans being held back until adjustments to new conditions could be made. In Britain GDP, which had risen in every year since 1946, fell in 1974 and 1975. Stagflation was associated with increases in retail prices of 17 per cent between 1973 and 1974, and 26.6 per cent between 1974 and 1975, and inflation displaced unemployment as the principal problem of government. A further hike in oil prices in 1979, and counter-inflation policies that included high interest rates and a high exchange rate for sterling, led to another fall in GDP down to 1981. There was a sharp increase in unemployment, with the Scottish figures

---

47. Sir David Hannay (ed.), *Britain's Entry into the European Community: Report on the Negotiations of 1970–1972 by Sir Con O'Neill* (London: Whitehall History Publishing in association with Frank Cass, 2000), esp. pp. xiv–xv, 245.
48. Royal Society of Edinburgh, *Inquiry into the Future of the Scottish Fishing Industry* (March 2004), esp. pp. 1–3, 6–10, 12.

almost doubling from 5.7 per cent in 1979 to 11.3 per cent in 1982, with a continued rise thereafter until 1986 (see Figure 9.3). The Treasury's ill-advised monetary policies led to a boom in the late 1980s followed by a slump associated with an overvalued exchange rate for sterling. Scottish industry had to confront fiercer competition from foreign rivals that found they had surplus capacity in an international economy that was growing significantly more slowly than between 1951 and 1973.

The 1970s saw major changes in the conduct of regional policy. As unemployment rose throughout the UK in the mid-1970s, industrial development certificates were readily available for new investment in any region, and the system was abolished in 1982. The REP subsidy was stopped in 1977. On the other hand, the Industry Act of 1972 had established a new system of regional development grants for investment by manufacturing industry in buildings and fixed plant and machinery. Responsibility for this new system of selective financial assistance was given to the regional offices of the Department of Trade and Industry (DTI), supported by local advisory boards. In Scotland responsibility was transferred from the DTI to the Scottish Office in 1974. The recently established Scottish Economic Planning Department sponsored the creation of the Scottish Development Agency (SDA) in 1975. The Department itself continued to administer grants and low-interest loans to industry, since these had to be in line with government policy in other regions of the UK. However, the SDA was empowered to provide investment finance either by way of equity or by lending on broadly commercial terms.[49] The SDA's remit extended beyond industrial development to urban renewal. In 1976 the Glasgow Eastern Area Renewal (GEAR) project was started, on the initiative of the then Secretary of State for Scotland, Bruce Millan. It was the first attempt in Britain to co-ordinate economic and social development and over a ten-year period had some success in slowing down the decline of an area blighted by derelict industrial sites and some very rundown housing.[50]

Any assessment of regional policy has to take account of the very difficult economic circumstances of the late 1970s and the early 1980s. Shipbuilding, already in decline, had to be saved from collapse by nationalisation in 1977, but this did not prevent massive job losses in the 1980s. The prestige investments of the 'golden age' also fared badly. The car factory at Linwood was saved from closure in the mid-1970s by

49. McCrone, 'Role of government', in Saville (ed.), *Economic Development*, pp. 206–9.
50. Gavin McCrone, 'Urban renewal: the Scottish experience', *Urban Studies*, 28 (1991), pp. 919–38.

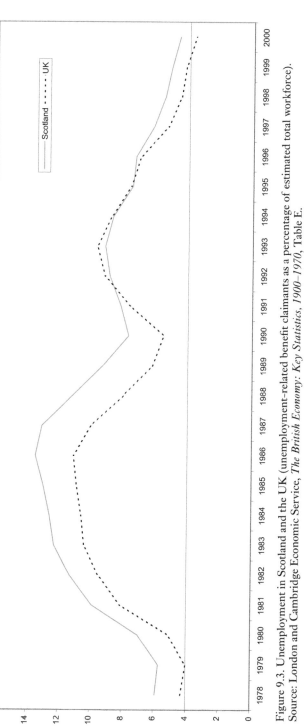

Figure 9.3. Unemployment in Scotland and the UK (unemployment-related benefit claimants as a percentage of estimated total workforce). Source: London and Cambridge Economic Service, *The British Economy: Key Statistics, 1900–1970*, Table E.

a government rescue package for Chrysler UK, which had acquired control of Rootes in the 1960s. Nevertheless, the factory finally closed in 1981. The commercial vehicle plant at Bathgate followed in 1986. In the Highlands, the pulp mill at Corpach and the aluminium smelter at Invergordon both closed in 1981. Only direct government intervention saved Ravenscraig from closure by the British Steel Corporation in 1982, and the end finally came in 1993. Not all of the developments of the 1960s failed, however. In that decade American firms, attracted by investment grants and cheap, skilled labour, had set up branch factories to produce electronic equipment in central Scotland. By 1970 total employment in the industry had increased tenfold in ten years to 30,000. The firms' presence in 'Silicon Glen' encouraged further inward investment, by Japanese as well as American firms, in the 1980s. Gross output increased fourfold in that decade and by 1990 the industry accounted for 42 per cent of Scottish exports. Concern was expressed about the limited diffusion of technology to indigenous firms, but multinational investment provided employment to replace that lost in traditional industries.[51]

The rise in the price of oil in 1973 came at a crucial time for the development of the Scottish oil industry. In 1971 the Forties field was found to be suitable for commercial exploitation, and exploration by international oil companies in the North Sea and off Shetland was intense from the autumn of 1972 onwards. Extraction of oil from these areas was expensive, but certainly economic at post-1973 prices. Construction yards for the building of giant oil rigs opened on the east coast, on the Clyde, and even at the remote site of Loch Kishorn in Wester Ross. Aberdeen became the administrative and supply centre for the North Sea oil industry, and substantial investment took place there, and at Peterhead and Montrose, and in Shetland. One complication was that much of this development took place in sparsely populated areas lacking the necessary infrastructure. The Scottish Office and Whitehall departments (the DTI for airports and the Department of the Environment for harbours) collaborated successfully with local authorities to transform this situation. For example, the Scottish Special Housing Association supplemented the efforts of local authorities, and a new road was built linking Aberdeen with the south. Oil-related employment rose to 38,000, and 55,000–65,000 if indirect effects are included, in 1976, with

51. Peter Payne, 'The economy', in T. M. Devine and R. J. Finlay (eds), *Scotland in the 20th Century* (Edinburgh: Edinburgh University Press, 1996), pp. 24–9; I. Turok, 'Inward investment and local linkages: how deeply embedded is "Silicon Glen"?', *Regional Studies*, 27 (1993), pp. 401–17.

a further increase to 58,000 and 80,000–90,000 respectively by the end of 1980.[52] On the other hand, as with electronics, doubts were expressed about the success of Scottish enterprise in exploiting the opportunity offered to develop an indigenous oil-related sector.[53] Moreover, Scotland, in common with the rest of the UK, may have experienced what has been called the 'Dutch disease', so called from the experience of the Netherlands, where the exploitation of natural gas in the 1960s was associated with high unemployment in traditional industries. The successful exploitation of oil tended to raise sterling's exchange rate after 1976, making it harder for traditional industries to maintain exports or compete with imports. Certainly the UK moved from being a net exporter of manufactured goods to being a net importer by 1983. The fortunes of the Grampian region, where 68.4 per cent of oil-related employment in Scotland was located by 1981, were not fully shared by west-central Scotland, where the corresponding figure was only 6.2 per cent.[54] Whereas Grampian's GDP per head was 120.5 per cent of the UK's in 1981, Strathclyde's was only 89.8 per cent; moreover the gap widened to 134.8 per cent and 88.3 per cent respectively by 1991.[55]

Despite the difficulties of industry (apart from oil-related activity), the gap between the Scottish GDP per head and the UK average was narrower in 1973–92 than in 1951–73. The Scottish figure rose from 94 per cent of the UK average in 1973 to 98 per cent in 1977, and although it slipped back from that level in 1979–81, and again in the late 1980s, it rose to almost 100 per cent in 1992. The loss of industrial jobs was only one side of the de-industrialisation coin. There was a remarkable increase in employment in financial and business services from 63,000 in 1971 to 204,000 in 1993. While not all of these jobs were well paid, it was surely not a coincidence that GDP per head in Lothian, with the financial centre of Edinburgh at its heart, was 110.5 per cent of the UK average in 1991.[56]

A POST-INDUSTRIAL ECONOMY, 1992–2000?

On 16 September 1992 the Chancellor of the Exchequer, Norman Lamont, was forced to suspend Britain's membership of the exchange-

---

52. McCrone, 'Role of government', in Saville (ed.), *Economic Development*, pp. 205–6.
53. Payne, 'Economy', pp. 29–33.
54. Iain McNicoll, 'North Sea oil and gas', in Keith Ingham and James Love (eds), *Understanding the Scottish Economy* (Oxford: Martin Robertson, 1983), pp. 227–34.
55. Lee, *Scotland and the United Kingdom*, p. 55.
56. Ibid., pp. 53, 55, 65.

rate mechanism of the European Monetary System and accept the inevitability of a large sterling depreciation. As in 1931, the floating of sterling was followed by economic recovery. Interest rates, unemployment and the rate of increase of retail prices all fell, as the UK economy pulled quickly out of recession and entered a period of stable growth. The last eight years of the century also saw a boom in the United States, fed by IT-induced productivity growth and related stock-market speculation. For the time being, at least, the international environment was broadly favourable to the Scottish economy. However, the renewed strength of sterling in 1999 once more handicapped exports and brought about a contraction in Scottish manufacturing from the beginning of 2000.

The recession of the early 1990s was unique in peacetime since 1919 in that Scottish unemployment was below the UK average (see Figure 9.3), and consequently Scottish GDP per capita rose relative to the UK average down to 1995, when it reached 101.9 per cent of that average.[57] Subsequent interpretation of Scotland's economic performance in the last five years of the century depends upon the method of measuring GDP. Contemporary official statistics, based on the relative weights, or importance, of industry and services in the economy in 1995, indicated poor growth performance compared with the UK as a whole. Even on that basis, Scottish GDP per capita in 2000, at 96.5 per cent of the UK average, was still relatively high compared with much of the twentieth century, and was exceeded in England and Wales only by London and the south-east.[58] In 2004, following new international conventions on the measurement of GDP, the Scottish Executive produced revised GDP data based on continuously updated, rather than fixed, weights. As a result of reducing weights on poorly performing industries, such as electronics, and increasing weights on rapidly growing sectors, such as banking and finance, Scotland's GDP per capita improved relative to other parts of the UK, so that it equalled the UK average in 2000.[59] On the other hand, GDP is a measure of total activity, not earnings. There are no figures for national income net of profits remitted to firms' headquarters in England or abroad. As the proportion of Scottish enterprises owned inside Scotland fell steadily from the 1950s, it is at least possible that the growth of income of Scots is not entirely accurately reflected in the growth of GDP.

---

57. UK excluding the continental shelf. See Scottish Executive, *Scottish Economic Statistics* (2003), p. 61.
58. National Statistics, *Regional Trends*, no. 38 (2004), p. 170.
59. I am indebted to David Bell for elucidating these statistical developments for me.

Be that as it may, prosperity was very unevenly distributed, with 852,000 people, or 16.6 per cent of the population living on or below the income-support poverty line in 1997.[60] Unemployment among individuals was falling from 1992, but recent research has shown that between 1992 and 2001 the number of workless Scottish households (defined as where at least one adult was of working age, but no adult was in paid employment) increased by 50 per cent from 241,000 to 364,000. The proportion of workless households in Scotland in 2001 was 3 per cent higher than in the rest of the UK, although unemployment was only just over 1 per cent higher. The Scottish problem was most heavily concentrated in Strathclyde, where in 2001 more than one in four households was workless, and 27 per cent of children were living in such households and therefore likely to experience poverty. At a time when unemployment was at historically low levels, many Scots depended on income support or incapacity benefit and lived in areas characterised by high crime rates, and poor health and educational outcomes.[61] Clearly the labour market was not working as effectively as it might be.

Economic policy focused on encouraging new firm formation and inward investment through the activities of Scottish Enterprise, which had replaced the SDA in April 1991. These efforts had some successes, with the creation of biotechnical, bioscience and other technology-based companies. However, Scottish Enterprise's target of equalling the average UK business birth rate by the end of the century was not achieved. Indeed, although the Scottish business birth rate rose marginally over the period 1994–9, there was a net loss of firms as other businesses closed.[62] Financial services contributed just below 7 per cent of Scotland's GDP in 1999, about the same as the electronics sector. Unlike the leading industrial sectors, financial services were largely controlled from within Scotland. Moreover Scotland was a big player internationally in financial services. Scotland's banking sector ranked sixth in Europe, as did Edinburgh and Glasgow combined as a fund management sector.[63] Scotland was not a post-industrial society in 2000, but little was left of the traditional Scottish economy of 1919, or 1960.

60   Scottish Poverty Information Unit, *Poverty in Scotland, 1999* (Glasgow: Glasgow Caledonian University, 1999), p. 22.
61.   David Bell and Gregor Jack, 'Worklessness and polarisation in Scottish households', *Scotecon*, University of Stirling (2002).
62.   Alexander Dow and Catherine Kirk, 'The numbers of Scottish businesses and economic policy', Fraser of Allander Institute, *Quarterly Economic Commentary*, vol. 25, no. 4 (2000), pp. 28–34.
63.   Brian Ashcroft, 'Accounting for impact of finances to [sic] economy', *The Scotsman*, business supplement, 24 October 2000, p. 5.

CONCLUSION

Management of the Scottish economy occurred at two levels: macroeconomic policy intended to provide a stable environment for the UK as a whole, and microeconomic policy aimed at specifically Scottish problems. Macroeconomic policy was not always helpful to Scottish industry, notably when sterling was overvalued. Even if the Treasury and the Bank of England had been wiser than they were, it would not always have been possible, using UK-wide taxes and interest rates, to deal simultaneously, for example, with inflationary pressures in the south of England and unemployment in Scotland. Likewise the Board of Trade had to take account of wider political issues than the fate of particular Scottish industries when deciding policy on tariffs. From the late 1930s regional policy came to be seen as a means of restoring balance to the economy by influencing where economic development took place. At first regional policy was on too small a scale to have much impact, and too much dominated by the criterion of levels of unemployment rather than the need to promote sound economic growth. However, from the 1960s regional policy was an effective means of managing economic change, both as regards areas with declining industries and (from the 1970s) as regards areas affected by the oil boom. Errors were made, notably in the siting of the new steel mill at Ravenscraig, but there were also successes, notably in the attraction of the electronics industry to central Scotland. At worst, regional policy moderated the impact of economic change on a society in which poverty was in any case too common an experience. At best, regional policy promoted change, not only though subsidies but also by the provision of infrastructure, notably housing, roads, and airports. The oil industry, 'Silicon Glen' and tourism all depended on Scotland's links with the wider world. Scotland, as a small open economy, could not be protected from economic change and policy had to be aimed at enabling the Scots to adapt to change. In this respect a lack of innovation, as measured by the birth rate of new businesses, remained a challenge for Scottish Enterprise as the century closed.

FURTHER READING

Campbell, R. H., *The Rise and Fall of Scottish Industry, 1707–1939* (Edinburgh: John Donald, 1980).

Gibson, John, *The Thistle and the Crown: A History of the Scottish Office* (Edinburgh: Her Majesty's Stationery Office, 1985).

Lee, C. H., *Scotland and the United Kingdom: The Economy and the Union in the Twentieth Century* (Manchester: Manchester University Press, 1995).

Levitt, Ian, *The Scottish Office: Depression and Reconstruction, 1919–1959* (Edinburgh: Pillans and Wilson for Scottish History Society, 1992).

McCrone, Gavin, *Scotland's Economic Progress, 1951–1960: A Study in Regional Accounting* (London: George Allen and Unwin, 1965).

McCrone, Gavin, *Regional Policy in Britain* (London: George Allen and Unwin, 1969).

Rosevear, Stephen, 'Balancing business and the regions: British distribution of industry policy and the Board of Trade, 1945–51', *Business History*, vol. 40, no. 1 (1998), pp. 77–99.

Saville, Richard (ed.), *The Economic Development of Modern Scotland, 1950–1980* (Edinburgh: John Donald, 1985).

Scott, Peter, 'British regional policy, 1945–51: a lost opportunity', *Twentieth Century British History*, vol. 8 (1997), pp. 358–82.

Slaven, Anthony, *The Development of the West of Scotland, 1750–1960* (London: Routledge and Kegan Paul, 1975).

In addition, the following guides to papers in the National Archives of the United Kingdom: Public Record Office, London, are useful:

Levitt, Ian, 'Scottish papers submitted to the Cabinet, 1917–45: a guide to records held by the Public Record Office and National Archives of Scotland', *Scottish Economic and Social History*, 19 (1999), pp. 18–54.

Levitt, Ian, 'Scottish papers submitted to the Cabinet, 1945–66: a guide to records held at the Public Record Office and National Archives of Scotland', *Scottish Economic and Social History*, 20 (2000), pp. 58–125.

Levitt, Ian, 'Scottish papers submitted to the Cabinet, 1966–70: a guide to records held at the Public Record Office (with addendum, 1964–66)', *Scottish Economic and Social History*, 22 (2002), pp. 1–22.

The Legacy of the Past and Future Prospects

G. C. Peden

By the late twentieth century Scottish GDP per capita was approximately the same as the UK average. Given Scotland's relative backwardness compared with England in 1700, the evolution of the Scottish economy since then may be regarded as a success story, although there have been periods of crisis and decline, especially in the 1920s and 1930s. It is tempting to ascribe that success to the Union of 1707, and certainly the Union has served Scotland well in terms of wider markets from the eighteenth century and in terms of regional policy and net public-sector transfer payments for much of the twentieth century. However, as Tom Devine showed in Chapter 1, the Scottish response to the opportunities offered by wider markets was vital, and in the nineteenth century the impact of the Union was relatively neutral as Scottish exports achieved market penetration on a world scale. It is worth noting, moreover, that a tendency for GDP per worker to catch up on the United States' level has been marked in all advanced industrial countries since the 1950s, as American best practice has been adopted,[1] so that convergence between Scotland and the UK average may be seen as part of a wider trend in response to market forces in a period when the international economy has been so organised as to encourage the transfer of technology, often through multinational companies. However, despite convergence with England's GDP per capita, and notwithstanding net public-sector transfer payments, prosperity in Scotland remains very unevenly divided.

At this point it may be helpful to revert to the divergent views of

---

1. See Charles Feinstein, 'Benefits of backwardness and costs of continuity', in Andrew Graham and Anthony Seldon (eds), *Government and Economies in the Postwar World: Economic Policies and Comparative Performance, 1945–85* (London: Routledge, 1990), pp. 284–93.

Campbell and Lenman on low wages (see Introduction, p. 2). Low costs, mainly wages, enabled Scotland to play a leading part in the first Industrial Revolution by developing its comparative advantage in coal, textiles, iron and steel, heavy engineering and shipbuilding in the nineteenth-century international economy (see especially Chapters 1 and 2 by Devine). However, Chapters 5 and 8 by Lee, in particular, but also Chapters 2 (Devine), 6 (Newlands) and 9 (Peden) point to income inequality being an important reason why Scotland took little part in the Second Industrial Revolution, based on electrical engineering and the combustion engine in the early twentieth century, and the mass production of consumer durables from the inter-war period. Scotland was a resource-rich country, first in coal and iron ore, and then, in the last quarter of the twentieth century, in oil. International comparisons of Scandinavian and Latin American countries suggest that the ability of countries to move successfully from the exploitation of natural resources to becoming part of the high-technology 'core' in world trade depends crucially on low inequality of wealth. Low inequality of wealth, as in Scandinavia, tends to encourage people to seek improvement through education, and to enable workers, managers and entrepreneurs to participate actively in the incremental learning processes that are characteristic of technologically progressive firms. In contrast, high inequality of wealth, as in Latin America, tends to lead to reliance on high-technology imports for small numbers of people, and a lack of development in the economy as a whole.[2] While Scottish industrial areas were never enclave economies, in the Latin American sense of being small sectors serving only international markets and lacking linkages with the rest of the country, Scotland's tendency to lag behind its Scandinavian neighbours in the Second Industrial Revolution may be a consequence of greater income inequality as well as path dependency following an early start to industrialisation.

Developments in microelectronics and biotechnology since the 1970s can be seen as constituting a third industrial revolution. It is too early to say how successfully this new technology has been embedded in the Scottish economy, but these new industries, combined with success in financial services, have given Scotland the chance to catch up on advanced economies. Not all Scots have participated in these successes, as the growth in regional inequalities in GDP per capita in the last quarter of the twentieth century show (see Chapter 6). Regional

2. Svante Lindarde and Andrew Tylecote, 'Resource-rich countries' success and failure in technological ascent, 1870–1970: the Nordic countries versus Argentina, Uruguay and Brazil', *Journal of European Economic History*, vol. 28, no. 1 (1999), pp. 77–112.

inequalities tend to reflect the patterns of the past. Some of the older industrial regions have still to escape the inheritance of the low-wage economy created during industrialisation. These same regions were those where unemployment was concentrated in the inter-war period and which required regional policy after the Second World War to bring about structural adjustment. Edinburgh, on the other hand, has dominated financial services since the eighteenth century (see Chapter 4) and has never required the assistance of regional policy. Aberdeen's prosperity as a centre for the oil industry is an exception to the rule of path dependency, and owes much to an active regional policy to facilitate development in hitherto sparsely populated areas in the city's hinterland (see Chapter 9). As in the rest of Great Britain, Scotland saw a remarkable proportion of the agricultural labour force redeployed into industry in the nineteenth century (Chapter 3) and the reduction of the size of the agricultural labour force has continued in the twentieth century (Chapter 7) to the point that agriculturalists must be outnumbered by urban workers in rural areas within commuting distance of the major cities. The Highlands have long been handicapped by topography, lack of good soil, a wet climate (in the west) and distance from markets; however, the growth of tourism since the 1960s holds out better prospects for the UK's most scenic region.

Experience of the second half of the twentieth century has shown that public policy can modify market forces to some extent. However, a small, open economy must always be dominated by market trends in the international economy, and historical experience suggests that the role of public policy is most likely to be effective when it is directed to enabling the Scottish economy to adapt to changing circumstances. The question is: will Scotland adapt to market trends by being a low-wage economy, as when it industrialised in the eighteenth and nineteenth centuries, or will it do so through highly productive labour, through skills appropriate to new technology, and through enterprise? The signs in 2004 are that the latter path is more likely. It is certainly more desirable. During industrialisation Scotland benefited from immigrants, both as workers and as managers of factories using what was then new technology. Scotland has been integrated with international financial markets since the 1840s and it is likely that much of the capital needed for future developments will come from international sources, principally via multinational firms. Scotland has benefited increasingly from inward investment and technology transfer since the eighteenth century and will continue to do so if it has a labour force, entrepreneurs and government capable of adapting to further change.

Index